Yellowstone

Yellowstone

The Creation and Selling of an

American Landscape,

1870–1903

Chris J. Magoc

The University of New Mexico Press : ALBUQUERQUE

MONTANA HISTORICAL SOCIETY PRESS : HELENA

Library of Congress Cataloging-in-Publication Data

Magoc, Chris J., 1960–
Yellowstone : the creation and selling of an American
landscape, 1870–1903 / Chris J. Magoc.—1st ed.
        p.   cm.
Includes bibliographical references (p.) and index.
ISBN 0-8263-2119-4 (alk. paper)
ISBN 0-8263-2120-8 (pbk. : alk. paper)
1. Yellowstone National Park—History. I. Title.
F722 .M23 1999
978.7'52—dc21   98-58035
                              CIP

Unless otherwise credited, all F. Jay Haynes photographs are
courtesy of the Montana Historical Society, Helena.

*For Mary Ellen
and for
Mom and Dad*

∾

Contents

List of Figures   ix
Preface   xi
Acknowledgments   xv

Chapter One   1
A "Pleasureing-Ground"

Chapter Two   21
The Selling of Wonderland

Chapter Three   53
1883: The Enterprise

Chapter Four   78
The Eatable Parts

Chapter Five   107
The March of Civil Improvement

Chapter Six   138
Indians, Animals, and Yellowstone Defenders

Chapter Seven   168
From Wonderland to Ecosystem

Notes   193
Works Cited   235
Index   255

Figures

❧

1. Map of Yellowstone Park   3
2. Northern Pacific Railroad advertisement, 1883   11
3. Northern Pacific Railway advertising brochure   25
4. Harvesting, Dalrymple Farm, Red River Valley,
Dakota Territory, 1877   27
5. Signal Hill near Central City, Dakota Territory, 1877   29
6. NPRR Marent Gulch Trestle, west of Missoula,
Montana Territory, 1883   30
7. Wickes, Montana Territory, 1886   31
8. Crow Indian Council at Last Spike, 1883   32
9. Buffalo Hunting, Montana Territory, 1882   33
10. Allen's Taxidermy Store, Mandan, N.Dak., 1894   34
11. NP Views Catalog, title page, 1884   38
12. Lackawanna Valley, 1855   40
13. *Life in the World's Wonderland*   41
14. Haynes studio with elkhorn fence, 1898   45
15. Giant Geyser in the Upper Geyser Basin, 1899   46
16. Bicyclists group on Minerva Terrace, 1896   47
17. Trout, Yellowstone Lake, 1897   47
18. Gibbon Falls, 1882   48
19. Falls of the Gibbon River, 1888   49
20. Upper Geyser Basin   50
21. In Yellowstone Park   51
22. Bismarck Bridge over the Missouri River, 1883   59
23. During the oration at Last Spike Pavillion, 1883   60
24. "Desecration of Our National Parks."   66
25. The presidential party at the Upper Geyser Basin, August 1883   71
26. Haynes' map of the Upper Geyser Basin, 1894   82

27. Liberty Cap and Capitol   85
28. The 'Formation'   87
29. Mammoth Hot Springs Terrace   88
30. Bath Pools, Mammoth Springs, 1882   89
31. Norris Geyser Basin   91
32. Old Faithful Geyser   94
33. Hot Spring Cone   100
34. Inspiration Point, 1881   101
35. Lower Falls   103
36. Great Falls from Red Rock, 1887   105
37. Yancey's in winter, 1887   111
38. National Hotel, 1884   113
39. Mammoth Hot Springs, 1895   114
40. Lake Hotel and Old Faithful Inn   117
41. Old Faithful Inn rotunda, balcony   119
42. Map of the grounds of Mammoth Hot Springs   134
43. Fort Yellowstone, Mammoth Hot Springs   136
44. Yellowstone Valley and Crazy Mountains, 1903   143
45. Wonderland, 1903.   144
46. Sketches of Wonderland   156
47. The End, 1883.   156
48. The Butcher's Work   160
49. "Buffalo in Enclosure, Nearly as Tame as Domestic Animals"   162
50. Theodore Roosevelt Arch   166
51. Greater Yellowstone Ecosystem Map, 1990   172
52. Targhee Forest/Yellowstone Park border, 1990   176
53. New World Mining District, Cooke City, Montana   177
54. Buffalo Jam, 1990   187

Preface

Yellowstone. Few American place names ring more hallowed than this, the first national park in the world. Witness the summer of 1988 when millions of people around the world watched horrific televised images of a fiery holocaust of timber laying siege to the park's world famous Grand Canyon, spouting geysers, and rustic hotels. Morbidly fascinated by a good sublime disaster, my eyes were drawn to Yellowstone that summer as well. And, like millions of other outraged taxpayers, I could not help thinking that the quickly formed media consensus about the fire was correct: American resolve and technology should have been able to stop this. Residents and business persons in the region had every right to be angry with incompetent government bureaucrats. Yellowstone would never be—as, one was to assume, it had always been—"the same."

Yet often in this postmodern culture of veneer, behind the visually driven media coverage lay the more complicating matters of history and culture. As a budding historian of the environment and a tourist myself, I could only hope that this was the case here—that the fire would prove to be less an ecological tragedy for Yellowstone than a public relations fiasco for its managers. This was not, after all, the first piece of American forest to go up in flames; would it not recover like the burned-over Allegheny foothill near my childhood home, albeit more slowly? Didn't an old ecology professor of mine say something in class one day about western lodgepole pine cones *needing* to burn in order to regenerate? But ecology mattered little in the face of the once-revered, now cremated, image of Yellowstone and its park rangers.

During the national wake held for Yellowstone that fall, I became troubled by these matters of nature and culture. What was it that initially inspired sacred designation and vigilant protection of this archetypically cherished landscape? More unsettling, how was one to reconcile the park's esteemed place of reverence in our national iconography (and the sincere outcry over the fire) with our widespread resignation toward larger environmental degradation? Nature-loving Americans weep over a forest fire surrounding Old

Faithful and fear not (or know not—it matters not to the tree) the more dam-
aging clear-cutting of the same timber just over the boundary of Yellowstone
Park. We welcome the malling over of our own neighborhood forest and
then patronize its nature store. *That* was the paradox that would not let go:
the genetic roots of the national nature-loving aesthetic—crystallized, so it
is often told, in the establishment of Yellowstone National Park—and its
blissful coexistence with rapacious natural resource development. It seemed
possible that the story of the first national park might reveal something of
the contradictory impulses of Americans toward the natural world.

That possibility invited me into Yellowstone's early history and now provides the framework for this interdisciplinary study. Its ponderous breadth
suggests correctly that the geographic scope of the book extends well beyond
the boundaries of the park. I contend here that although ostensibly "set
apart" from the surrounding region, Yellowstone was from the beginning,
and remains, both inextricably joined to the economic and cultural forces of
American civilization and biologically attached to the earth outside its
boundaries. I arrived at this premise by virtue of the Northern Pacific Railroad and its appropriation of Yellowstone's *Wonderland* sobriquet—a name
thereafter affixed to the extractive and scenic resources of the railroad's vast
domain. One of the chief contributions of this book, in fact, may be the
examination of Yellowstone Park's formative years in that larger context.

In the center of this broad horizon lies the grand and ghastly geothermal
landscape of Yellowstone. My interest here was never to provide a comprehensive history of park management and administration. That has been well
covered, most notably by Aubrey L. Haines, Richard A. Bartlett, and Lee H.
Whittlesley.[1] I delve into such matters to the extent that they help reveal my
essential purpose, which is to better understand the deeper American myths
and late-Victorian values held by all of the forces and figures contesting for
the future of the park and the larger extractive domain of Wonderland: the
tastemakers who suffused Yellowstone with meaning, the stewards who provided direction to its management, and the financiers and boosters of economic development throughout the region. In the end there are two central
issues under scrutiny: the ostensibly benign commodification of wilderness
for touristic consumption, and the limitations of arbitrary political and cultural boundaries in protecting regional ecosystems and the wider natural
world. Fundamentally, this work is fixed on the paradoxical human
impulse—taken to peculiar extremes in America—to both exalt and profane
nature.

I should be clear regarding the expression of American myth, for it is pivotal to this study's premise and its upshot. Here at the intersection of nature

and culture, myth denotes not an untruth, but rather a fundamental, enduringly large ideal born of both events and desires that strongly influences a people's actions on the land. In the nineteenth-century American West, as the primary myths of virgin land and Manifest Destiny were assumed by the culture to be axiomatic, they provided the moral ground for economic and political decisions driven by a privileged few, but whose environmental and human impacts cannot be overstated.[2] What transpired in the greater region of Wonderland derived from both the force of an expanding market economy and the superstructure of metaphor and myth that had been well established in the trans-Mississippi West by the time of Yellowstone's official exploration in 1870. The dualistic, often confounding nexus of nature and culture within this ruling framework is the essential subject of the book.

Although particular events provide chronological logic to this study, its organizing principle is more thematic. My hope is that this concentration on the central elements of cultural and ecological change in and around Yellowstone National Park will leave a fuller and more connective portrait of place than I could have attained with a blow-by-blow account. Aside from the momentous year of 1883, each chapter details through character and incident the various intellectual and material dimensions of the Wonderland transformation. Ideas and desires found physical expression in significant forms: photographic imagery, the consummation of the Northern Pacific Railroad and all that that milestone entailed, the delineated guidebook tour, rustic roads and hotels, the slaughter and salvation of wildlife, and the incorporation of the museumized Native American into the tourist milieu. A concluding epilogue revisits many of these issues a century later.

As I complete this ten-year exploration of Yellowstone National Park, I am dogged by irony. For the past several years, I have been involved with the development of the Rivers of Steel Heritage Area in the greater Pittsburgh region. Rivers of Steel is one of several such federally designated regions of the country whose mission is to preserve, interpret, and promote "living cultural heritage." The objectives are noble indeed: to save and tell of overlooked regional history and to preserve cultural traditions, historic sites, and natural resources. What drives it politically however, is what drives most everything else in America—economic growth. And so as I took my final aim at the tastemakers and moneychangers of Yellowstone, in real life I struggled with the same issues: preserving cultural integrity while promoting it, selling history and nature without compromise. Alas, the contradictions that living brings.

Acknowledgments

This work would never have been written without the encouragement of Professor John S. Patterson of the American Studies program at Pennsylvania State University, Middletown. The rudimentary idea for a Yellowstone study was born nearly nine years ago as a short paper in Professor Patterson's introductory American Studies seminar. His intuitive confidence in its ultimate potential emboldened me to pursue a life in American Studies.

The individuals who service the Interlibrary Loan desk at the University of New Mexico played a large part in my research, obtaining dozens of rare books and articles pertaining to Yellowstone's early history. I am grateful as well to Tom Tankersley, Yellowstone Park historian, who graciously guided me through the Park Archives and Research Library during a Christmas 1991 visit. The comments and corrections which he and park archivist and Yellowstone historian Lee Whittlesley offered early on were crucial. Finally, archivists and librarians at the following institutions provided vital research assistance during site visits: the University of Wyoming at Laramie, Merrill G. Burlingame of the Special Collections Division of Montana State University in Bozeman, the Montana Historical Society in Helena, the Denver Public Library, and the Minnesota Historical Society. I also wish to thank the Greater Yellowstone Coalition in Bozeman, Montana, for its gracious assistance in procuring a number of the contemporary images from the Yellowstone region.

I particularly wish to acknowledge the special cooperation and support of my co-publisher, the Montana Historical Society. Their assistance in retrieving and reproducing stronger versions of many of the images, as well as the society's promotion and marketing of the work were vital contributions.

I am grateful to several individuals at the University of New Mexico who served on my dissertation committee and helped me to cultivate this manuscript from its early crude form. Professor Vera L. Norwood, chair of the University of New Mexico's American Studies program, labored as the chairperson of my committee and as chief editor of the dissertation. A distinguished environmental historian, she provided invaluable expertise. Anthropologist Marta Weigle imparted great insight into the nature of nineteenth-century tourism (and "nature tourism"), railroads, and the West. Thomas Barrow of the Department of Art History contributed much to my reading of the Haynes photography and political imagery of the northern Great Plains. I am especially appreciative of the tireless work, keen judgment, and good and patient spirit of my editor, Larry Durwood Ball of the University of New Mexico Press. His repeated reading and comments of earlier drafts sharpened the substance and style of this book immeasurably. After all of these contributions, however, I am alone responsible for any defects in content or otherwise that remain in the following pages.

Although Yellowstone's summer burn rekindled(!) my interest in the park, my love for the place springs ultimately from my parents, Stephen and Frances Magoc, who introduced my brother Ron and me to Wonderland some twenty-five years ago. They endowed me with a love of the American landscape, a sense of adventure, and a very personal sense of environmental stewardship. There is at last my wife, Mary Ellen, whose undying faith and sheer endurance—invariably at the expense of her own needs—inspired this work from beginning to end.

—CJM, April 1997
Brackenridge, Pennsylvania

Yellowstone

CHAPTER ONE

A "Pleasureing-Ground"

I hope, in happier mood and under more auspicious circumstances, to revisit scenes fraught for me with such thrilling interest. . . . [A]nd with enraptured fancy gaze upon the mingled glories and terrors of the great falls and marvellous canon, and to enjoy, in happy contrast with the trials they recall, their power to delight, elevate, and overwhelm the mind with wondrous and majestic beauty.

—*Truman C. Everts, 1871*[1]

[Yellowstone Lake] possesses adaptabilities for the highest display of artificial culture. . . . [A]nd not many years can elapse before the march of civil improvement will reclaim this delightful solitude, and garnish it with all the attractions of cultivated taste and refinement.

—*Nathaniel Pitt Langford, 1871*[2]

The geysers of Iceland, which have been objects of interest for the scientific men and travelers of the entire world, sink into insignificance in comparison with the hot springs of the Yellowstone and Firehole Basins. The withdrawal of this tract . . . will be regarded by the entire civilized world as a step of progress and honor to Congress and the nation.

—*Ferdinand Vandiveer Hayden, 1872*[3]

IN THE SUMMER OF 1870, General Henry Dana Washburn and Lieutenant Gustavus Cheyney Doane led the first official exploration of the mysterious plateau region surrounding the headwaters of the Yellowstone River in Wyoming Territory. Upon their return to civilization, members of the Washburn-Doane expedition confirmed and added more remarkable stories of a weird and wondrous landscape. A second mission followed in 1871, headed by Ferdinand Vandiveer Hayden of the U.S. Geological Survey. Within months of the explorers' return, the United States government set apart from the developing territories of Wyoming, Montana, and Idaho a vast tract of geothermally charged wilderness defined by law thereafter as a "public pleasureing-ground"[4] (fig. 1). Promoters began to call it "Wonderland."[5]

To comprehend the place Yellowstone came to be in the late nineteenth century, it is necessary to understand how the 1872 Park Act—an apparently bold stroke of environmental wisdom—could have transpired during an era of vigorous development and exploitation of the American West. How indeed did the U.S. Congress arrive so easily at what to many people seemed an absurd proposal to set aside a vast acreage of public land from practical, private use. This chapter examines that question by way of three men who participated in and wrote about the pivotal expeditions of 1870–1871 —Truman C. Everts, Nathaniel Pitt Langford, and Ferdinand Vandiveer Hayden. Certainly other individuals figure into the genesis of the national park. Yet the Yellowstone careers of these men serve to distill the defining cultural and economic impulses of park history that were inextricably linked from its beginning: preservation of the reserve and development of the region outside. The encounters of Everts, Langford and Hayden suggest much of how the Yellowstone country would be advertised, interpreted, managed and transformed thereafter.

Everts's experience was more than he had ever hoped for—an unwitting, death-defying misadventure in the Yellowstone wilderness. His tale both captured the antimodern romanticism of genteel Americans and testified to the wild and domesticating forces that have contended in Yellowstone ever since. Envisioning the value of a civilized Yellowstone, the Northern Pacific Railroad instigated the 1870 mission and ultimately the creation of the park. They brought this American institution to pass, not alone but through an association with a prominent Montanan, Nathaniel Pitt Langford. His story links the sublime spectacle of nature that defined Yellowstone for Americans with the political and economic forces that later managed and developed the region. If Everts and Langford spurred Yellowstone's incorporation into American culture, Ferdinand Hayden completed it by confirming with scientific authority the unspeakable wonder of Yellowstone's geothermal features. Head of the U.S. Geological Survey, Hayden continued the chain of

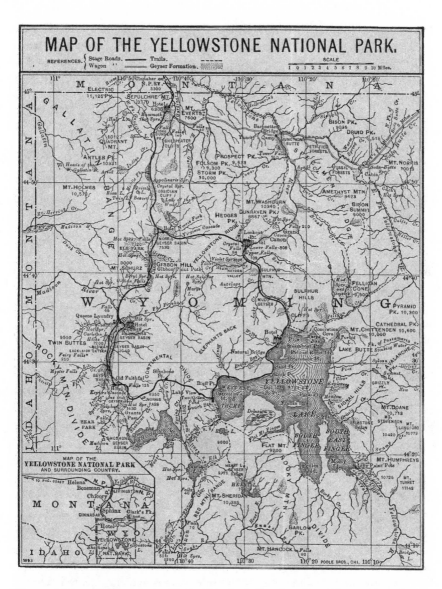

Fig. 1. Map of Yellowstone Park. Edwin J. Stanley, *Rambles in Wonderland* (Nashville: Methodist Episcopal Church, South, 1898). Author's Collection.

discovery and political machination that led to the park's creation. His eru-
dite stature and promotional posture reassured those who doubted the practical virtues of the national park bill. Yellowstone, Hayden declared, would
both spur national pride and accelerate the growth of the northwest.

Popular myth has obscured the fact that, even as American attitudes
toward nature were quietly shifting in 1872, the establishment of Yellowstone Park was driven ultimately by the hinged forces of nationalism and
good old-fashioned capitalism. Through these three central figures, Yellowstone's popular discovery appears less a progressive step toward modern
environmentalism than a profound expression of the dominant threads of
middle- and upper-class American life in the late-Victorian era. Those forces
indelibly shaped the definition and destiny of Wonderland.

The front page of the November 1871 issue of *Scribner's Monthly* featured
Truman Everts's harrowing account of his "Thirty-Seven Days of Peril" as
a member of the Washburn-Doane Expedition to the Yellowstone region. On
the eighteenth day of the journey, while the party was scouting the Yellowstone Lake area, Everts, a former tax assessor for the Montana Territory,
became lost. Unable to find his way back to camp, Truman Everts wandered
hopelessly in the wilderness. Surviving on thistle root and an occasional raw
bird or fish, Everts was found weeks later near Blacktail Deer Creek Plateau,
not far from the present north-central boundary of the park. When moun-
taineers "Yellowstone Jack" Baronett and George Pritchett discovered him,
Everts was in a catatonic state, reportedly weighing about fifty pounds. He
had no shoes, he had broken his spectacles, his clothing was tattered, and he
could scarcely stand on his raw and frostbitten feet.[6]

The mere publication of the story was incredible. Prior to the Washburn-
Doane Expedition, decades of previous reports of the bizarre natural features
found in the region of the upper Yellowstone River were largely dismissed
as flights of imagination. These accounts began with Native Americans who
were first to travel in the region. Many Indian tribes of the Great Basin region
believed that spirits living in water held tremendous power and could work
for or against an individual. Although some Indians may have feared Yellowstone's spouting, bubbling waters, many more were drawn to them as a
source of spiritual power and an aid to hunting success (an obscure band of
Arapahoes, known as Sheepeaters, actually lived there).[7] The Native American response prefigured the later reactions of many Christian tourists, who
would see both divinity and the devil in Yellowstone's geothermal wonders.

Nevertheless, the Yellowstone experience of Native Americans was not
only disbelieved but deliberately falsified long after the establishment of the

park. In his annual report of 1880, Park Superintendent Philetus Norris wrote that local tribes had "a superstitious awe concerning the rumbling and hissing sulphur fumes of the spouting geysers and other hot springs" and thus kept their distance from the region.[8] Although it became a guidebook staple, park historians have shown that Norris manufactured this argument, in part to allay anxieties about tourist safety after the infamous Nez Perce flight through Yellowstone in 1877 and a Bannock raid on a survey party the following year.[9] The fiction of cowering Indians conveniently complemented Norris's 1880 regulation that prohibited all Native Americans from entering the Park.[10]

In 1807 trapper-explorer John Colter became the first white man to see the Yellowstone region. For decades afterward, Jim Bridger and other mountain men regularly visited the area and returned with incredible "misty tales," as General Sheridan later called them, of a bizarre and fantastic landscape.[11]

One night after supper, a comrade who in his travels and explorations had gone as far south as the Zuni village, New Mexico, and had discovered the famous petrified forest of Arizona, inquired of Bridger:

> "Jim, were you ever down to Zuni?"
> "No, thar ain't any beaver down thar."
> "But Jim, there are some things in this world besides beaver. I was down there last winter and saw great trees with limbs and bark all turned into stone."
> "O," returned Jim, "that's peetrification. Come with me to the Yellowstone next summer, and I'll show you peetrified trees-a-growing, with peetrified birds on 'em a-singing peetrified songs."[12]

Although received as another one of Bridger's tall tales, he in fact described with typical flair the Petrified Forest, lying just southeast of the Lamar Valley, where fifty million years ago Yellowstone's volcanism caused silica-rich warm water to turn an entire forest to stone. Bridger's reports piqued the interest of Nathaniel Pitt Langford, whose efforts ultimately led to the establishment of Yellowstone Park.[13]

Nevertheless, later park guidebooks ignore or condescend to the Yellowstone experiences of previous residents and visitors, portraying Indians, trappers, and prospectors alike as ill-equipped to appreciate Yellowstone's remarkable natural features. Travel writer Peter Koch typically dismissed the latter as "mere utilitarians" and made clear who had laid proper claim to the region:

> This [Park] was reserved for the modern traveler, with his thirst for knowledge and his love of the beautiful. To him it has been fully revealed and may it forever remain sacred to his enjoyment.[14]

But the few written accounts of explorers prior to 1870 defy the notion of these men as uncultivated and suggest that Yellowstone's utilitarians were the first to view the region in romantic terms. While Koch would never have acknowledged it, romantic nature sensibilities extended far beyond the courtly class of later American tourists. Inherited from Europeans and Americanized by northeastern literati in the first decades of the nineteenth century, the new nature aesthetic looked first to picturesque scenes typified by well-crafted cemeteries and parks, and then to the more disturbing but compelling instances of the sublime—those rare locales that could provoke feelings of awe, pain, and gloom. From the visual power of Niagara Falls to the shrouded mystery of the forested Adirondacks, American travelers sought the ambivalent and curious combination of divine rapture and terror found in such places.[15]

In Yellowstone, both the sophisticated and the adventurous reveled in the scale, power, and sounds of the park's sublimity, invariably attempting to describe the ineffable. One of the first accounts was left by trapper Osborne Russell who, after entering the park's Lamar Valley in the summer of 1836, wrote:

> There is something in the wild romantic scenery of this valley
> which I cannot . . . describe; but the impressions made upon my mind
> while gazing from a high eminence on a surrounding landscape one
> evening as the sun was gently gliding behind the western mountain
> and casting its gigantic shadows across the vale were such as time
> can never efface from my memory but as I am neither Poet Painter
> or Romance writer I must content myself to be what I am a humble
> journalist and leave this Vale in Obscurity until visited by some
> more skillful admirer of the beauties of nature.[16]

Similarly, for prospector A. Bart Henderson, views of the hot springs and Lower Falls of the Yellowstone River in 1867 were "enough to cause anyone to shudder."[17] David E. Folsom's important 1869 account is both panegyric and prophetic: he is grateful for having seen such "beautiful places . . . that man had not desecrated," among them Yellowstone Lake, where, Folsom lamented, the "primeval solitude [would] be broken by the crowds of pleasure seekers which at no distant day will throng its shores."[18] The incredulous and reputation-conscious *Scribner's Monthly* and *New York Tribune* refused a descriptive manuscript offered by leaders of the Cook-Folsom Yellowstone Expedition.[19]

The following year, with an official military escort leading the Washburn expedition, *Scribner's* publishers changed their minds. Truman Everts's dramatic misadventure bore the stamp of truth. Equally important, the story expressed resonant cultural themes that appealed to the magazine's genteel and middle-class audience: the wayward explorer's wilderness ordeal presaged the *fin-de-siècle* core of late-nineteenth-century romanticism—specifically the nascent belief of cultivated Americans that an intense sensory experience with raw nature could retrieve a measure of character that had been absorbed by decadent civilized comfort.[20] Indeed, Everts's tale recalled an earlier primitivist prophet, Estwick Evans, the New Hampshire lawyer who voluntarily endured the winter of 1818 in the wilderness of the Old Northwest. Donning a buffalo robe and moccasins and accompanied by two dogs, Evans's celebrated four-thousand-mile journey bore witness to the incipient romantic philosophy in America. He spoke afterwards of the "advantages of solitude" and declared there to be "religion" in wildness.[21] A few years later, Thomas Cole and Nathaniel Hawthorne mused over the esthetic potential of losing oneself in the American wilderness as they strolled the wilds of the Catskill Mountains. The sensation of solitary, hopeless wandering, they suggested, could enhance the spiritual impact of the sublime.[22]

Deliberately roughing it was one thing; *getting lost* in an unearthly geothermal wilderness was quite another. As he recalled for *Scribner's,* with each passing day of wandering Truman Everts felt less the rapture than terror of Yellowstone. After recounting a litany of beauties he had seen on the third day, Everts was, by that time, "in no humor for ecstasy."[23] Struggling to the edge of the Grand Canyon of the Yellowstone River, he found the great falls of the Yellowstone roaring within three hundred yards, "and the awful canon yawned almost at my feet; but they had lost all charm for me. In fact, I regarded them as enemeies which had lured me to destruction, and felt a sudden satisfaction in morbid indifference."[24] This, of course, made the account and the place all the more captivating. By the time of Yellowstone's popular discovery, the appeal of terror had been codified as part of the sublime label.[25]

Moreover, in more comfortable hindsight, the wayward explorer doubted whether "distress and suffering can ever entirely obliterate all sense of grandeur and magnificence," and thus redeemed the Yellowstone landscape by recalling its capacity to interrupt occasionally the general pain and hopelessness of his journey. Standing on a precipice above the picturesque Yellowstone Lake, Everts reflected:

> All the vast country within this grand enclosure of mountains and lake, scarred and seamed with the grotesque ridges, rocky escarpments, undulating hillocks, and miniature lakes, and steaming with hot springs, produced by the volcanic forces of a former era, lay spread out before me like a vast panorama.[26]

Even a conflagration of Yellowstone forest, one of the worst terrors imagi-
nable, could summon a gloriously horrific response drawn from the nineteenth-century lexicon of the nature-romantic.[27] Everts passionately recalls
the night he fell asleep near his camp fire and awoke to the

> grandeur of the burning [which] surpasses description. An immense
> sheet of flame, following to their tops the lofty trees of an almost
> impenetrable forest, leaping from top to top, and sending thousands
> of forked tongues a hundred feet or more athwart the midnight dark-
> ness, lighting up with lurid gloom and glare the surrounding lake
> and mountains, fills the beholder with mingled feelings of awe and
> astonishment. I never saw anything so terribly beautiful.[28]

On the whole, the tale is less descriptive than "strictly personal."[29] Everts's
account is that of a Christian pilgrimage, complete with an evocation of its
traditional themes—danger and suffering, revelation of the "mysteries" of
a sacred place, and most importantly perhaps, deliverance. Everts recalls a
point of near surrender to overwhelming fatigue and the timely salvation of
a delusional, celestial message urging him on. Through the grace of "Provi-
dence," the ghostly image of an "old clerical friend" implored the explorer
to redirect his course and "put [his] trust in Heaven."[30] The encounter offers
redemption for both Everts and Yellowstone; his milieu now seems as
enchanting as it is threatening. Throughout the article, one hears evocations
of the American myth of providential deliverance rooted in the wilderness of
Puritan New England.[31] For the record, Everts received his deliverance less
graciously than Christian goodness or the *Scribner's* article would suggest:
he refused to pay the reward offered for his rescue, despite the fact that
General Washburn died months later of complications of tuberculosis stemming from the exhaustive search by his fellow explorers. Indeed, Everts was
found to be such an ingrate that Jack Baronett wished years later that "he
had let the son-of-a-gun roam."[32]

 Sacred, mysterious, forbidding. None of these meanings precluded Yellowstone's cultural enshrinement. On the contrary, in the East railroads and
promoters had long established the pattern of making nature's secluded and
harrowing places accessible.[33] The tantalizing lure of the sublime had its limits; not even the most daring romantic deliberately wanted to see Yellowstone as Everts did. Everts reassured his readers that the power, danger, and
vastness of the region would be tamed and concluded the tale of his unfor-
tunate odyssey with confident prescience:

> In the course of events the time is not far distant when the wonders
> of the Yellowstone will be made accessible to all lovers of sublimity,

grandeur, and novelty in natural scenery, and its majestic waters become the abode of civilization and refinement. [34]

Everts's call for the domestication of Yellowstone signified the imminent approach of tourist culture. Initially awestruck and overwhelmed by the emotive force of sublime western landscapes like Yellowstone, explorers of this era generally cast such places as mighty but in need of civilizing. Americans were traditionally uncomfortable with the idea of raw nature as a place of peril but paradoxically enthralled with the heightened experience to be found there. They looked forward with Everts to the time when the accoutrements of tourist travel would allow them to view Yellowstone's spectacular features without trepidation; its sublimity known more than feared. Thanks in part to the work of a fellow expeditionist, that time was coming.

In the summer of 1870, Jay Cooke faced the formidable task of promoting development of the land and resources lying along the projected route of the Northern Pacific Railroad. Cooke's job was to get the NPRR headed through the still little-known northern tier of the United States, from Lake Superior to the Pacific Coast—a distance of nearly eighteen hundred miles (fig. 2). The company's right-of-way extended across and between lands that were still more Native than EuroAmerican. Having gained wealth and prominence largely by financing the Union effort during the Civil War, Jay Cooke now wanted to sell one hundred million dollars in bonds to advance construction of the much-delayed railroad project. On June 4, Cooke welcomed to Ogontz, his suburban Philadelphia estate, Nathaniel Pitt Langford, a visitor whose interest in one part of the railroad's domain would ultimately make him the financier's perfect salesman.[35] Nathaniel Langford was a transplanted and well-educated easterner. By 1870 he had served as the "worshipful master" of the Montana Grand Lodge of Masons, a vigilante leader, and the internal revenue collector for the Montana Territory. The political warfare between President Andrew Johnson and the United States Senate, however, had denied him both the governorship of the territory and his position as tax collector, and he now looked to the railroad to secure his future. Langford's meeting with Cooke would do just that *and* fulfill his long-held desire to see the Yellowstone region. Langford returned to Helena on July 27 to see that the logistical arrangements for the nineteen-man mission, including the participation of General Henry D. Washburn, its leader and military escort, fell neatly into place.[36]

For more than four weeks, members of the Washburn expedition surveyed, sketched, and stood in awe of Yellowstone's remarkable features. They affixed names to many of them, including Old Faithful, destined to become the park's trademark geyser and leading attraction. Much to their surprise, the explorers' lone encounter with Native Americans occurred as they were spied cautiously by a small hunting party of Crow. Only the mishap of Truman Everts tainted the journey.[37]

Several members of the expedition recorded their observations nightly in diaries around the campfire. Regional newspapers, including the *Helena Herald* and the *Rocky Mountain News,* carried General Washburn's descriptive account, though the *News* titled it a "Montana Romance," adding the disclaimer that it "[drew] somewhat upon the powers of credulity."[38] Indeed, their descriptions demanded of readers faith, imagination and a fascination with the sublime. At the Yellowstone River's Grand Canyon, declared Nathaniel Langford, human "knees tremble and his countenance blanches with fear as he stands to gaze into the mighty solitude below."[39] The lure of the canyon, like its more famous namesake in Arizona, was its classically sublime contradiction of colorful architectural form, silence, and danger "in the extreme."[40] A visit there was not for the timid:

> The danger with which [the canyon] impresses you is harrowing in the extreme. You feel the absence of sound, the oppression of absolute silence. If you could only hear that gurgling river, . . . see a living tree in the depths beneath you, if a bird would fly past, if the wind would move any object in the awful chasm, to break for a moment the solemn silence that reigns there, it would relieve that tension of the nerves which the scene has excited, and you would rise from your prostrate condition and thank God that he had permitted you to gaze, unharmed, upon this majestic display of natural architecture.[41]

Appearing in *Scribner's* months before Everts's account, Langford's two-part "The Wonders of the Yellowstone" described the region's bizarre features in Victorian-lurid detail. Tapping the era's fascination with the exotic, Langford made Yellowstone's colorful peculiarity an immediate hit.[42] As Langford put it, the region was "unnaturally natural" in its conjunction of artificially appearing fountains and stylized geologic ruins. Holding a bewildering concentration of remarkable and eclectic features, Yellowstone aroused protean responses: at the canyon, all was "darkness and gloom . . . an empire of shadows and turmoil"; the same gorge's Lower Falls prompted "vivacity, gayety [sic], and delight." "One was the most unsocial, the other the most social scene in nature," Langford remarked. The seemingly unpredictable geysers, bubbling mud pots, and hot pools and springs produced

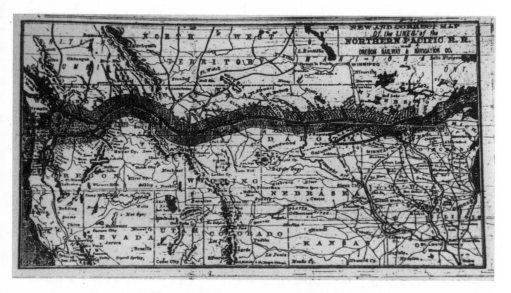

Fig. 2. Northern Pacific Railroad: The Only Rail Route to the Yellowstone National Park-advertisement in *The Northwest*, May 1883. Northern Pacific Railway Company Records. Courtesy Minnesota Historical Society, St. Paul.

confounding, occasionally ludicrous evocations of order and chaos, power and beauty, and unsavory, "diabolical" hellishness.[43]

Like Everts, Langford places a palliative call to civilize the place—to bring this "marvelous freak of the elements" into the "family of fashionable resorts."[44] By 1871, there was little question as to how that would be accomplished. As he wrote for *Scribner's*:

> By means of the Northern Pacific Railroad, which will doubtless be completed within the next three years, the traveler will be able to make the trip to Montana from the Atlantic seaboard in three days, and thousands of tourists will be attracted to both Montana and Wyoming in order to behold with their own eyes the wonders here described.[45]

It was a compelling vision, though a little premature. The Panic of 1873—triggered, more than coincidentally, by the Northern Pacific Railroad's financial collapse—helped push the completion date back another twelve years. But in 1871, Langford was bullish. He advocated a rail line traversing the Snake River Valley *and* the Yellowstone region in order to connect the north-

ern transcontinental line with the Union Pacific.[46] Another member of the
Washburn party, Samuel Thomas Hauser, had similar designs. A civil engineer turned frontier capitalist, Hauser later acquired a charter for the Northern Pacific Railroad's "Park Branch Line," to extend from its main route
across southern Montana through the Yellowstone Valley to Yellowstone
Park.[47]

Among the Washburn expeditionists whose observations were published,
Langford, because of his association with the railroad, had the greatest
impact. He presented Yellowstone not only to *Scribner's* readers but, more
importantly, to audiences on a grand speaking tour funded by the Northern Pacific. Langford's brother-in-law was Minnesota Governor William
Marshall, a developer of Northern Pacific lands, who would soon influence
the passage of the Yellowstone Park Act. With such personal and political
relationships, N.P. (later self-designated as "National Park") Langford was
perfectly positioned to become the park's first superintendent in 1872. At
that time a nonpaying, patronage position, the superintendency did enable
Langford to further the NPRR goal, one the Park Act itself initiated: the protection of Yellowstone from speculative commercial development—until the
railroad could reach its borders and acquire the tourist franchise.[48]

The annals of Yellowstone remember N. P. Langford best, neither for his
link with railroad interests nor his five-year administration of the park, but
for first propagating the fabled story of the conception of the national park
idea. More than three decades after the Washburn expedition, Langford
recalled that while camped near the confluence of the Firehole and Gibbon
Rivers on the last night of their 1870 journey, the party was musing about
the possibility of gaining individual control of desirable sites in the park for
a tourist franchise. In the midst of this discussion, Montanan Cornelius
Hedges countered that "the whole of it ought to be set apart as a great
National Park, and that each one of [the party] ought to make an effort to
have this accomplished." According to Langford, the suggestion "met with
an instantaneous and favorable response" from nearly all party members
who agreed to return to civilization and work earnestly toward that goal.[49]
Today, National Park Mountain shadows the site of that legendary discussion, marking this decisive moment in U.S. environmental history.

Thus was born the captivating and enduring myth that the world's first
national park was the creation of enlightened statesmen acting on the altru-
istic motives and transcendental inspiration of the 1870 explorers.[50] This
romantic tale has been the cornerstone of Yellowstone and national-park
popular culture for nearly a century and has only recently been challenged
in park historiography.[51] The epiphanous campfire conversation has endured,
despite the fact that no members of the party mentioned it after the expedi-

tion; Langford himself only brought it to light in 1905—by which time the national park idea had become a movement.[52]

The park-creation story is more complex, requiring not only the tale of our third explorer, but the nineteenth-century context of Americans' evolving attitudes toward nature. In 1870 Americans still stung from the century-old criticism leveled by pundits such as English clergyman Sydney Smith, who asked derisively in 1820: "Who reads an American book? or goes to an American play? or looks at an American picture or statue?"[53] Soon, however, writers like James Fenimore Cooper and the landscape painters of the Hudson River School found a large measure of American greatness in the nation's august, seemingly infinite wilderness.[54] Niagara Falls emerged as a place of great sublimity comparable to the grandeur and antiquity of European landscapes. But by mid-century, Niagara's growing commercialization proved to many observers that Americans were simply too crass and materialistic for a proper appreciation of the sublime.[55]

Moreover, notwithstanding the literary and artistic attention paid to this and other regions of the East, the statuary landscapes of the West mounted a greater challenge to European horizons. The monumentalism of California's Yosemite Valley and its nearby "Big Trees" moved the United States government in 1864 to grant small, carefully carved tracts to the state of California for public pleasure.[56] Americans audaciously put their trees up against the Parthenon. The Rocky Mountains both exceeded and compared to the fabled Swiss Alps. In Yellowstone, Nathaniel Langford noted the resemblance of geomorphic "spires, pinnacles, [and] towers" to the human landscape of classical antiquity found in Europe and the Middle East.[57] Appearing ancient, the region's landforms would be clothed with names and references to the Old World. And yet European culture, even as it continued to influence the naming and description of features in Yellowstone and elsewhere in the West, was tainted by fallen civilizations. The American West was colossal and "virgin," awaiting occupation.[58]

Important, too, are the early distinguished voices advocating the preservation of portions of receding American wilderness. For reasons of aesthetic gratification, and cultural and economic preservation, and even ecological survival, a chorus of environmental jeremiads arose from the 1820s forward. John James Audubon, William Cullen Bryant, Thomas Cole, Henry David Thoreau, and Susan Fenimore Cooper were among those who decried, as Cole put it, the "meagre utilitarianism" that seemed to define the American view of nature.[59] In 1841 Americans ignored more than resisted artist George Catlin's call for a vast "nation's Park, containing man and beast, in all the wild freshness of their nature's beauty." In 1851 Frederick Law Olmsted used nature as the instrument of both social control and aesthetic beauty in the design of New York City's Central Park. Thirteen years later, George Perkins Marsh published *Man and Nature,* a harsh critique of the impact of human (European and Middle Eastern) civilizations upon their environments, and a warning to Americans.[60] Slowly but perceptibly emerging from three centuries of unrestricted development and exploitation was the conclusion that the conquest of the nation's wild spaces was at hand and the recognition that nature—at least carefully chosen parts of it—should be preserved.

The preservation impulse was irrevocably linked, however, to an expanding, acquisitive society that, as at Niagara, converted the picturesque and the sublime into romantic, often salable objects of affection. The "elegant art" of landscape architecture, as Andrew Jackson Downing described it, expressed romantic ideals of an Arcadian paradise in an emerging suburban greenbelt of winding paths and tree-sheltered cottages.[61] Once located, the middle-class home itself suggested "an organic system":[62] plan-books recommended adorning the home with large plants, wallpapers of decorative natural motifs, and elaborately engraved woods; entrance halls were designed to be opened in summer; almanacs and albums featuring renowned American scenery lined the shelves and provided novel patterns for Staffordshire pottery and glassware; and manicured gardens and lawns came to define the ideal of domesticated nature.[63]

Thus by 1870, nature had not only helped widen the cultural distance between Americans and their European past, the nature-as-commodity impulse was surging. Whether manicured in gardens, reproduced on dinnerware, or conserved for future use, the capture of nature extended and reinforced both its cultural and commercial value.[64] Little wonder that the Northern Pacific Railroad and other interests envisioned dollar signs in Yellowstone. By the late nineteenth century, the enshrinement of Yellowstone and other western landscapes would ostensibly curb the aggressive impulse of resource exploitation, even as their commodification fed an increasing appetite for grand scenery. But if Americans could accept the idea of preserving special lands for public pleasure, it was still an unprecedented leap for the national government to set them aside, especially on such an immense scale. Bridging the gap between a fondness for nature and the establishment of Yellowstone National Park ultimately required—scientific authorization by the next important visitor to the Yellowstone region.

Sitting in Washington D.C.'s Lincoln Hall audience for N. P. Langford's first Yellowstone lecture that winter was Dr. Ferdinand Vandiveer Hayden, head of the United States Geological and Geographical Survey of the Territories. By virtue of his position and scientific world view, Hayden exemplified the increasing fascination in post–Civil War America with the classification and ordering of all things, not the least of which was the vast American West. For more than a decade, Hayden, a medical doctor by training, had been drawn to the momentous exploration and geological study of the western landscape. By the 1870s, he had become one of the leading scientific agents of Manifest Destiny.[65]

Nathaniel Langford's promotional blitz indicated a rising interest in the Yellowstone region, and Hayden saw an opportunity to seek congressional funding for an official government exploration. In addition to his intrinsic scientific curiosity, Hayden wanted to reinforce his own rising stature and the political position of the Survey office through a Yellowstone expedition. The railroad's interlocking network of supporters on Capitol Hill made likely Congressional support for such a journey. Hayden counted among his Washington associates two key supporters of the Northern Pacific Railroad and western exploration, Representative James G. Blaine, Speaker of the House, and Henry M. Dawes, the most influential congressman of the post–Civil War era. With friends like these, he could not have failed. Congress allotted the Survey office forty thousand dollars for a distinguished forty-man party of scientists and visual documentarians, including mineralogist Dr. Albert C. Peale of the celebrated Peale family, photographer William Henry Jackson, whose career would be propelled forward by the trip, and well-known landscape artist Thomas Moran, who joined the Survey under the paid auspices of the Northern Pacific Railroad.[66]

Hayden's entry into Yellowstone would mark another shift in the interpretation of the place—from natives, trappers, and wayward explorers, to a party of mostly Montanans organized by a railroad publicist, and now to a paid government expert. At the time, such figures were revered by the genteel for several reasons, as Hayden knew well:

> The scientific as well as the practical results of these explorations are
> of great importance to the material interests of the West. They have
> already enlisted the interest and sympathy of all classes of intelligent
> people from Maine to Florida.[67]

Yellowstone's legendary and inscrutable landscape begged for the scientific confirmation the Survey office would bring to it. The potential results seemed as vast as the wilderness itself: once verified, classified, and ranked, these geological wonders could serve the prosperity of the West, cultivate the aesthetic taste and scientific knowledge of urbane Americans, and culturally reinforce the new sense of nationhood in the postwar era.

The Hayden Survey report advanced these aspirations and, by pairing scientific analysis with emotional euphoria, functioned ultimately as a template for the volumes of popular Yellowstone travel literature that followed. Writing variously as scientist, poet and politician, Hayden's first priority was to make an unearthly landscape somehow comprehensible. Geysers begged to be named, ranked, and clocked. The Grand Canyon of the Yellowstone River, on the other hand, prompted the florid prose of the romantic. Like so many Americans who would follow him, Hayden's chronicle featured alluring references to classical forms of human culture that seemed to define the indefinable:

> But the objects of the deepest interest in this region are the falls and
> the Grand Canyon (of the Yellowstone). I will attempt to convey
> some idea by a description, but . . . no language can do justice to
> the wonderful grandeur and beauty below the Lower Falls; . . . from
> the summit the river appears like a thread of silver . . . the Gothic
> columns of every form standing out from the sides of the walls with
> greater variety and more striking colors than ever adorned a work
> of human art. [68]

In these allusions and lofty declarations lies the radical suggestion that here was something greater than humanity or civilization itself. Yet at the same time Hayden's purpose was to bring Yellowstone into the fold of the market economy. His narrative naturally assumed the incorporation of this landscape into an increasingly commodity-driven American culture. In Yellowstone's hot spring areas, the explorer promised, the visitor will find

> a striking variety of the most vivid colors. I can only compare them
> to our most brilliant aniline dyes. . . . There are also in the quiet
> springs and in the little streams that flow from the boiling springs,
> great quantities of a fibrous, silky substance, apparently vegetable,
> which vibrates at the slightest movement of the water, and has the
> appearance of the finest quality of cashmere wool.[69]

Hayden aspired to render Yellowstone "as free from technical language as possible consistent with scientific accuracy."[70] And he succeeded, identifying and valuing the landscape by reference to treasures of middle- and upper-class American life. Hayden's Yellowstone truly was a mercurial Wonderland of beguiling attractions.

Much of the report chronicles the expeditioners' scientific activities: confirming the discoveries of previous explorers, recording the temperatures of hot springs, and producing visual and cartographic documentation of newly discovered features. In perhaps the most telling act of imminent national claim to the landscape, the party named more than sixty of Yellowstone's natural features.[71]

For Hayden, the labeling and measurement of nature posed no conflict with a rapturous celebration of its sublimity. "The whole party," he wrote for *Scribner's,* "were filled with enthusiasm to catch a glimpse of the wonderful visions of which we had heard so much."[72] One of the later guidebooks of the region recalls the esteemed doctor as being at a loss to "compose himself in the presence of a geyser in eruption, but losing recollection of the material world for the time, rubs his hands, shouts, and dances around the object in a paroxysm of gleeful excitement."[73]

Hayden's complex role as scientist, tourist, and agent of development ushered in Yellowstone's future. His hope that the survey would produce "immediate practical results" came to fruition when the explorer returned East to compile his report and found on his desk a recommended inclusion for that document. Written on the stationery of "Jay Cooke and Co., Bankers, Financial Agents, Northern Pacific Railroad Company," was a letter signed by A. B. Nettleton, office manager for Jay Cooke:

Dear Doctor:

Judge Kelley has made a suggestion which strikes me as being an excellent one, viz.: Let Congress pass a bill reserving the Great Geyser Basin as a public park forever—just as it has reserved that far inferior wonder the Yosemite valley and big trees. If you approve this would such a recommendation be appropriate in your official report?[74]

Judge William D. "Pig Iron" Kelly was a Philadelphia jurist and a powerful long-time investor in the Northern Pacific.[75] Shortly after the letter from Judge Kelly, in December 1871, Montana Congressional Delegate William H. Clagett introduced a bill in the House to create Yellowstone National Park; similar legislation was brought forward in the U.S. Senate by Samuel Clarke Pomeroy of Kansas.

The brief legislative debate over Yellowstone in the winter of 1871–1872 reveals contemporary American attitudes toward nature. Articulating what became the prerequisite argument for the preservation of virtually every state and national park well into the twentieth century, Vermont Senator George Edmunds submitted that the region was "worthless" for utilitarian purposes and that its true value lay in making it a park:

[Yellowstone] is so far elevated above the sea that it cannot be used for private occupation at all but is probably one of the most wonderful regions . . . which the globe exhibits anywhere, and therefore we are doing no harm to the material interests of the people in endeavoring to preserve it.[76]

Proponents deployed Hayden's scientific classification of the region's geologic and material properties to defy arguments that its potential mineral or agricultural development made the land too valuable to be withdrawn from the public domain. Hayden's 1872 report unequivocally asserted that because of the region's volcanic origins, it was not "susceptible of cultivation," nor was it likely "that any mines or minerals of value will ever be found there."[77] Senator Cornelius Cole of California countered that the area might be settled and "improved" in the future, but Senator Lyman Trumbull of Illinois promised that the law could always be repealed later "if it is in anybody's way."[78] Trumbull's defense proved prophetic a decade later when park protectionists had to labor against railroad and mining interests who reopened the debate over the region's scenic-versus-extractive value.

The "worthlessness" argument had already been applied to the granting of Yosemite Valley and four square miles of Redwoods to California. There, only the most monumental parcels were set aside, and these had in the same way been proven useless to conventional development. Yellowstone's preservation would likely have been similarly restricted if not for Professor Hayden's suggestion that more hydrothermal wonders yet undiscovered probably lay elsewhere in the region.[79] Scientific authority compelled the drawing of park boundaries at the far-flung dimension of 3,472 square miles.

Langford's romantic story of the park's creation has obscured both the 1872 debate over the land's greatest economic value and the letter from Judge Kelly. For here is a myth that reveals both the American propensity to deny history and an ambivalent, complex relationship with nature. Americans advanced the idea of the first national park as a locus of the religious conversion of our attitudes toward nature. They could do so not by recognizing the economic opportunism and scientific reasoning in Yellowstone's inception, but by enshrining Langford's campfire epiphany. The comforting mindset that grew up around the Langford tale conveys the park as a "worldwide symbol, a flaming evangelist" for "remembrance" and environmental preservation, as one park historian proclaims.[80] From 1872 forward, Americans have blissfully and legislatively divided the realms of nature and economy, even as we incorporate one into the other. At bottom the creation of Yellowstone Park lies squarely within the culture of capitalism and the all-embracing vision of the West put forth by Hayden and the railroad.[81]

Having been born of economic promise and sanctioned by science, passage of the bill to create Yellowstone Park rested finally on patriotism. Here was an "exhibition," as Langford baldly put it, of exotic and truly national attractions.[82] Hayden could scarcely contain his enthusiasm:

> We pass with rapid transition from one remarkable vision to another, each unique of its kind and surpassing all others in the known world. The intelligent American will one day point on the map to this remarkable district with the conscious pride that it has not its parallel on the face of the globe.[83]

With the sublimity of its Grand Canyon and Yellowstone Falls, the unearthly hydrothermal forces, and the architectural effect of volcanic "ruins," Yellowstone seemed the divine fulfillment of America's cultural void. Moreover, as the railroad knew well, cultivated Americans whose consumption styles were increasingly fixed on nature, the exotic, and performance, would find the region irresistibly inviting.

Buttressed by the language of cultural nationalism, compelling romantic imagery, and a cadre of railroad friends and regional boosters, both houses of Congress swiftly passed the Yellowstone Park Act. In the Capitol rotunda, a prominent Yellowstone display featuring Hayden's geological specimens, Jackson's photographs, and Moran's sketches and magnificent panoramic painting of the Grand Canyon heightened the sense of curiosity and national pride as Congressmen prepared to vote. Evoking the memory of Niagara's boorish and poorly planned commercial development (and reflecting the interests of the railroad), Hayden's final argument was that, if the land was not set aside, small-time speculators and squatters might capitalize on Yellowstone's "beautiful decorations."[84] On March 1, 1872, President Ulysses S. Grant signed into law a bill setting Yellowstone "apart as a public park or pleasureing-ground for the benefit and enjoyment of the people."[85]

Universally positive reaction greeted the bill's passage. Sounding first and foremost the compelling theme of cultural nationalism, the *Nevada Territorial Enterprise* editorialized:

> It is pleasant to see Congressmen turn aside from their sterner duties and vote . . . for a measure looking to the adornment of the Republic. This will be the grandest park in the world—the grand, instructive museum of the grandest Government on Earth.[86]

An adornment, an "exhibition unlike any other upon the globe," Langford glowed; a "colossal sort of junketing place," opined *Scribner's*. Walter Trumbull, former assistant to Truman Everts who lobbied hard for the bill, predicted that once the railroad was completed, "probably no portion of America will be more popular as a watering-place or summer resort."[87] Anything but an alien wilderness, the Yellowstone region was now, above all, *an American place*—owned, occupied and undergoing acculturation. Looking back in 1898, John L. Stoddard's popular lecture distilled Yellowstone's exploration and "creation" as a divine act bearing supernatural responsibility:

> [The region was secluded] as though the Infinite Himself would not allow mankind to rashly enter its sublime enclosure. In this respect our Government has wisely imitated the Creator. . . . It has received it as a gift from God, and, as His trustee, holds it for the welfare of humanity. We, then, as citizens of the United States, are its possessors and its guardians.[88]

Truman Everts encountered and lived to tell about Yellowstone's terrible and divine sublimity, and N. P. Langford and Ferdinand Hayden became brokers for the popular interpretation, ownership, and future development and management of the greater Yellowstone region. All three explorers imparted to Yellowstone's future the great contradiction of America's germinating modernity—a force propelled forward by the twin engines of corporate capitalism and scientific rationalism, and softened by an antimodern desire for natural wonder and raw experience. Yellowstone's discovery resonated with a national audience intrigued with color and spectacle, power and the exotic. Entertainment, we now call it. Indeed, if such a place hadn't existed, spectacle-driven, nature-loving Americans of the twentieth century would have invented it. But Yellowstone Park was for real, thanks to the formidable power of the railroad, which could alone deliver a genteel citizenry to Wonderland.

CHAPTER TWO

The Selling of Wonderland

I had a vision of the future of this great country, The Iron Horse had jumped the North Missouria and was rushing up the bountiful valley of the yellow-stone [sic], carrying with it all its civilization and change. Instead of the Teepees of the wild red men, There were thousands of beautiful homes. In the bottom lands waived the rich grain giving bread to Millions. The hillsides were covered with stock supplying the world its meat. And still thundered on the Iron Horse up over the Rocky Mountains. . . . And I thanked God that right in the heart of all this noise and wrestless [sic] life of millions a wise Government had forever set apart that marvelous region as a National Park, where 'mid the encircling snow clad mountains water falls and canons grand; Bathing pools and spouting fountains of that Mighty Wonderland' the worn, the sick, and jaded could even find rest, and refreshment, and opportunity to study the Master's hand in nature.

—*Colgate Hoyt, 1878*[1]

My pictures are going all over the country; they are even going all over the world, and what I am doing is to show people that this is no desert, but a rich wonderland for tourists to marvel at, and for settlers to make their living in.

—*Frank Jay Haynes, 1879*[2]

LIKE MOST NATIONAL ICONS, Yellowstone Park is an American paradox, born of oddly and unconsciously contending impulses. Most conspicuously, perhaps, is that Yellowstone's creators set it *apart* from the civilization that inevitably shaped its future. Second, although Americans in the twentieth century would identify Yellowstone with the virtues of wilderness preservation, they established the park to claim the economic potential and national pride they saw in its natural curiosities. And as the reserve became a preeminent symbol of the touristic American West, Indians—another symbol of that heritage—were banished from its environs because they were bad for business.

Therein lies the heart of the matter: as an *American* paradox, Yellowstone's apparent contradictions dissolve under the heady glow and wide embrace of the capitalism from whence it came. In the northwest region of the late nineteenth century, the railroad, acting as both symbol and force of the market economy, arrived to trumpet and develop the region's natural resources, not the least of which was Yellowstone itself. After a self-inflicted financial crisis, several key events propelled the Northern Pacific Railroad westward and sparked a massive advertising campaign centered on the resources of a broadly redefined *Wonderland*. More than an enchanting appellation for the park, *Wonderland* now subsumed all: from the mid-1870s forward, advertisers combined the rhetoric of progress and the magic of photography to present a cornucopia of fertile land and industrial and touristic wonders from Lake Superior to the Pacific Coast. The railroad deployed Yellowstone as the imperial symbol and packaging for all of nature—scenic, arable and extractable—throughout the Northwest. With the intoxicating spirit of a modern advertising campaign, *Wonderland* melded the natural with the technological sublime, the wisdom of preserving nature with the energy of capitalism. In the 1870s, Yellowstone became a truly American place: culturally sanctified and economically incorporated.

Landscape photographer Frank J. Haynes operated at the center of the region's transformation. With an artist's eye and a sharp business acumen, Haynes personified the energy of the Wonderland era. His career is an Algeresque success story driven by ambition and ultimately the prevailing view of nature as convertible resource. Haynes's twenty-three thousand photographs pay homage first to the scale and movement of industrial capitalism into the Northwest. His Yellowstone Park and other scenic views illustrate the romantic infatuation of genteel Americans with nature and the exotic. Like the grandiloquent descriptions they accompanied, Haynes's images at once accelerated a westering industrial economy and increased the desire for, as Colgate Hoyt put it, that "marvellous region" of Yellowstone. The photographer and his patron sold to an acquisitive culture a view of the natural world that was at once bifurcating and all-embracing. With compelling imagery and raving boosterism, the sale of Wonderland reflected, fused, and resonated with the contrary impulses of Americans toward nature.

Although President Lincoln signed the charter for the Northern Pacific Railroad in 1864, the Northern Pacific struggled until Jay Cooke assumed management of the enterprise later that decade.[3] The financier exploited the press masterfully. Cooke invited newspaper publishers to his estate, delivered to them cases of wine from his private orchards, and offered a permanent exhibition of Northwest products in a room of his banking house.[4] The clever use of Langford and the Washburn expedition to Yellowstone typified Cooke's manipulation of the growing corporate-government alliance that he himself had helped establish during the Civil War. By 1873, Jay Cooke had advanced the Northern Pacific Railroad to Bismarck, the capital of the Dakota Territory—so named for the German monarch Cooke believed might help bring in much-needed foreign capital to the company. The money never arrived, and Cooke's over-borrowing against the still-unknown fortunes promised by the railroad triggered not only the financial collapse of Cooke's banking house, but a panic and depression throughout the U.S. economy. At this point the Northern Pacific stalled and became known as the line "From Nowhere Through No-Man's Land, to No Place."[5] It remained a public scourge far beyond the date of its completion a decade later.[6]

Following the Panic of 1873, however, the railroad engineered two significant developments to revive its fortunes and advance it toward Yellowstone Park and the Pacific Coast. First, it proposed the redemption of company bonds, then worth one-tenth their original value, in exchange for some of its extensive land holdings in the Red River Valley on the border of Minnesota and the Dakota Territory. Within a short time, the Northern Pacific had unloaded almost five hundred thousand acres to fewer than two dozen bondholders, many of them former or current railroad officials. The group then developed the region as a large commercial wheat-growing enterprise aptly named "Bonanza Farming." Railroad and regional boosters touted Dalrymple's Bonanza Farm as a mechanized Arcadia:

> [F]arming [here is divested] of most of its drudgery. . . . The homes
> in the valley are unsurpassed by farmers' homes in Ohio or New
> York. . . . The houses are neat, ornamental structures, with gardens

and groves about them. Trees grow well and nearly every small
farmer, especially, has his tree park.[7]

The reality belied this chimerical image: Characterized by large capital
investments, specialized production, and a paramilitary style of worker management, this was not about yeoman farming. The Bonanza operation epit-
omized the growing industrialization of the agrarian West that crushed many
independent farmers with fixed high prices, heavy debt from forced mecha-
nization, and inflated rates of transport and storage.[8]

So went the incorporation of the Northwest.[9] With the largest land grant
ever tendered by the U.S. government, the Northern Pacific commanded the
course of the region's development. The Northern Pacific held title to forty-
seven million acres lying in odd-numbered sections along the route—twenty
and forty miles wide respectively within the states and territories traversed
by the line (see shaded area of fig. 2). Beyond the right-of-way lay a ten-mile
indemnity area to which the railroad held purchase rights. Through its
checkerboard empire, the Northern Pacific reigned over up to 100 miles of
land on both sides of the tracks. It established subsidiary companies to control the best timber, mineral, and eventually, tourist resources of Wonderland.[10]

The popular utopian face of bonanza farming typified the larger image
transformation of the West. The geological surveys led the dismantling of a
pre-existing and prevailing view of the region between the Mississippi River
and the Pacific Coast as a savage-laden Great American Desert. Ferdinand
Hayden relished his role in the popular redefinition of the West, one in which
American genius and industry would convert arid and supposedly barren
landscapes into productive, mono-cropped gardens on a scale never seen
before. Sloganized as "Rain Follows the Plow," the message spoke to the
unceasing faith of Americans in both nature and their civilization.[11] Ameri-
canization of the West emphasized uniformity over diversity that in turn
required control of culture, ideology and environment.[12]

The subsequent avalanche of railroad advertising, travel books, articles,
and photographs reinforced Hayden's scientific counter-revelation that the
region's northern tier was laden with a myriad of resources. In the early
1880s, Henry Villard, president of the Northern Pacific Railroad, posted
hundreds of local recruiting agents throughout northern Europe to distrib-
ute hundreds of thousands of maps, posters, circulars, and pamphlets printed
in various languages. By 1883, the Northwest had become "the best advertised country in the world," and eventually the Northern Pacific name
became inextricably linked to the image of Yellowstone Park (fig. 3). [13] The

Wonderland lure was spacious and irresistible: "The Pleasure Seeker, The Sportsman, [and] The Invalid," as well as the more industrious sorts, would find recreation and profit in Wonderland—a sobriquet the railroad appropriated from Yellowstone Park in the 1870s to embrace the entire Northwest region.[14] Lands from Minnesota to Oregon, the company prophesied, would welcome "2,000,000 FAMILIES—10,000,000 SOULS," all to become "prosperous and many will acquire fortunes in a short period." Here was an Edenic paradise: "milder winters, earlier springs . . . unparalleled" soil fertility, and the lowest mortality rates in the world.[15] During an era of intense labor-capital conflict, Wonderland's "safety valve" appeal had the ring of urgency:

Fig. 3. Northern Pacific Railway advertising brochure, 1902. Courtesy Montana State University Library, Bozeman.

[There is a] great feeling of unrest and distrust pervading the whole
country. In places anarchism and socialism almost rampant, and
strikes and all manner of lesser evils following in their train. . . .
All through the [Northwest] region above mentioned are thousands
of acres waiting for these unhappy denizens of the city to come and
till them.[16]

As elsewhere in the West, railroads combined such swollen, politically
charged language with the prolific imagery of landscape photographers—
"operators," as they were called. Pictures were worth—and usually accompanied—thousands of words in promoting regional development. Through
several failed ventures in his native Michigan and in Wisconsin, young
Frank Jay Haynes learned an aggressive style of self-promotion and the
rudimentary skills of photography.[17] By 1875 he was serving an apprentice-
ship with photographic "Doctor" William H. Lockwood in Ripon, Wisconsin, where Haynes fully developed his technical knowledge, conducted
river tours, and took group portraits on Lockwood's boat. More significantly, Haynes learned to "take views" of the surrounding countryside.[18] The
Lockwoods, however, did not approve of the romantic affair that had developed between Haynes and Lily Snyder, one of Mrs. Lockwood's sisters. In
the summer of 1876, Lockwood informed Haynes that the renowned New
York City publishing firm, E. and H. T. Anthony, was looking for promotional photographs of the territory to be crossed by the newly resurrected
Northern Pacific Railroad. At the same time, Haynes's sister and wealthy
brother-in-law urged him to move to Moorehead, Minnesota—the terminus
of the railroad at the time and the ideal location from which to operate.
Haynes left that fall for Moorehead.[19]

   Initially the photographer was less than impressed with the rather desolate
northern plains; it was "so far from Anywhere," he complained to Lily.[20]
Still, he focused his camera on the nearby Bonanza Farms (fig. 4) and began
attracting considerable attention as the area's premier photographer:

   Any who are interested in this truly delightful region would do well
   . . . to mail [Haynes] an order that they might be able to see some of
   the "boss" farms that reproduce the wheat so much sought after. Mr.
   Haynes is an artist of ability and has already acquired a reputation
   which his work deserves.[21]

Haynes's Bonanza Farm views celebrate a managed and mechanized American Eden. Their popularity suggests a growing acceptance, at least among
nonfarming Americans, that the Jeffersonian republic of independent small

Fig. 4. Harvesting, Dalrymple Farm, Red River Valley, Dakota Territory, 1877. Haynes Collection, H-96. All Haynes Collection images courtesy Montana Historical Society, Helena.

farmers had begun a long, turbulent passage into myth. Emerging in the Red River Valley was the modern paradigm of large-scale efficiency.[22]

In October 1876, Haynes signed a contract with the railroad for additional Bonanza Farm views, soon expanding the arrangement to include "stereos of all important points from Duluth to Bismarck, 450 miles."[23] A Northern Pacific official instructed him to "show up our Country to the best advantage."[24] Haynes renegotiated his contract, allowing the railroad 12 prints from each negative for $1.50 each, while the photographer retained for his own collection all negatives, which he was free to reproduce.[25] It was a princely deal. Haynes co-owned the corporate view of the region yet maintained a good measure of aesthetic and financial independence.

The images brightened Haynes's prospects and his attitude toward the Northwest. That fall he wrote to Lily, "You may think I have changed my opinion of this country, but the more I see of it, the more I like it."[26] The photographer's published catalog of "Northern Pacific Stereoscopic Views," coupled with an exhibition of his work at the 1877 Minnesota State Fair, led the Northern Pacific to sponsor a photographic excursion to the suddenly booming Black Hills.

The Sioux Indians had held the Black Hills sacred as the *paha sapa*.

Although the 1868 Laramie Treaty guaranteed its protection from white intrusion, in the early 1870s gold prospectors and white settlers flooded the region. This led the Northern Pacific Railroad to instigate, in 1874, a Black Hills military expedition that helped insure the company's resurgence. Government explorers, led by General George Armstrong Custer, were to confirm reports of the region's mineral and agricultural promise. The railroad, however, eyed a sanctioned enlargement of the buffer zone between natives and settlers to reduce the size of the adjoining Sioux reservation and make its own disposable lands more valuable. Local boosters hoped the expedition would secure white control and a branch rail line into the region.[27]

Although the 1874 mission led to increased hostilities with the Sioux and ultimately Custer's demise at the Little Big Horn, the popular press interpreted the Black Hills takeover as a righteous and democratic adventure. Pundits painted Sioux control of the region as a sinister "monopoly" inhibiting national progress.[28] *The Lakeside Library*'s special edition featured "The Black Hills and American Wonderland," in which H. N. Maguire details the "history" of the Black Hills, complete with reports of "fearful atrocities committed by the Indians," and profuse illustrations of the national park.[29] Yellowstone geysers appear as the exotic, just desserts of the Black Hills invasion and Custer's defeat.

Traveling to the mining camps of the region, F. Jay Haynes produced what became the biggest selling views in his inventory. He photographed the bustling commercial and industrial activity of mining towns such as Deadwood, Crook City, and Lead. "Signal City, Dakota Territory" (fig. 5) is a telling image: Haynes lies amid his spread of photographic equipment with a Black Hills mining town and its surrounding denuded mountainsides serving as a backdrop to the scene. The view speaks metaphorically of Haynes's larger serendipitous and seemingly innocuous role as the eye of dramatic environmental and cultural change in the Northwest. Just one year following the disaster at Little Big Horn, eastern interest in the region could not have been greater. Haynes reported to Lily that he had "printed some 6 or 7 hundred Black Hills views, [and] the demand is for all I can print."[30] He declared that there were "Millions in [the business of photography]."[31] While companies extracted resources, the photographer mined the public fascination with events in the West.[32]

The Black Hills makeover signifies the increasingly specious role of image in creating America's tourist landscape. According to the Haynes photos and the accompanying literary boosterism, the history of the region begins with the end of Sioux control, Custer's martyrdom, and the establishment of the mining industry. Haynes's photographs and narratives, like Maguire's, pro-

Fig. 5. Signal Hill near Central City, Dakota Territory, 1877. Haynes Collection, H-132.

claim a righteously bloody new El Dorado and a complementary picturesque Yellowstone Park. And whether gracing the walls of Victorian parlors or placed in promotional circulars, the views encouraged interest in and acquisition of the Black Hills.

Like his patron, Haynes continued to multiply the opportunities laid before him. In 1879, shortly after moving his studio to Fargo, Dakota Territory, he journeyed to the St. Paul offices of the Northern Pacific where he

Fig. 6. Northern Pacific Railroad Marent Gulch Trestle, west of Missoula, Montana Territory, 1883. Haynes Collection, H-1068.

met Charles S. Fee, private secretary to the company's general manager. The two struck a relationship that would last two decades and serve the photographer well. Fee soon interceded with railroad officials to have Haynes appointed "official photographer" of the company. As General Passenger and Ticket Agent in the 1880s, Fee increased the number and variety of promotional materials used by the company and ordered greater numbers of Haynes's views. In 1885 he arranged for the photographer to buy one of the company's cars for less than half its value and have it retrofitted as a traveling gallery, studio, and living quarters.[33]

As the instrumental force behind Wonderland, naturally the railroad figured prominently into Haynes's inventory. From the late 1870s until the railroad was completed in 1883, he documented every step of construction as the Northern Pacific cut a swath of wilderness from the Dakotas to Puget Sound. The Rocky Mountains, particularly, presented great challenges to engineers and grand opportunities for Haynes to demonstrate the railroad's invincible power. In "Marent Gulch Trestle, 1883" (fig. 6), Haynes poses a standing locomotive with a group of workers 220 feet above the valley floor.

Fig. 7. Wickes, Montana Territory, 1886. Haynes Collection, H-1746.

Such images automatically conferred national significance on the Northern Pacific and reassured any nervous investors. Bridge and trestle photographs superimpose the preeminent technological symbol of an advancing civilization upon a receding wilderness. Neither Haynes nor his contemporaries ever moved earth, yet the camera itself was central to the transmogrification of the western landscape. If photographs speak proverbially "for themselves," these shots of vanquished rivers, valleys, and mountains tell of conquest in progress.

Indeed, Haynes, following the archetypal work of William Henry Jackson, presented the railroad as both conqueror of nature and procreative force of order.[34] Boomtown views displayed what appeared to be contented laborers, feeding the safety-valve myth of the West as a place where industrial capitalism, like democracy itself, would be redeemed by the wilderness. The promise belied the fact that by the 1880s, mining in the region had mostly reverted from small-time independent prospecting into the large-scale enterprise visible in scenes such as the commanding view of Wickes, Montana (fig. 7).[35] Labor-capital conflict would soon engulf Montanans.

For nearly three centuries, Native Americans and wild animals symbolized an ever-receding American wilderness; like the dense forest, they were forces to be overcome. In the Northwest, Haynes's lens framed their demise. Such

Fig. 8. Crow Indian Council at Last Spike, 1883. Haynes Collection, H-996.

imagery offered to an urban audience both assurance of civilization on the march and the romantic lure of adventure. At the Northern Pacific's 1883 Gold Spike celebration, for example, Haynes captured a group of Crows traditionally seated on the ground and well-surrounded by their hosts (fig. 8). These mementos proved popular with a public increasingly nostalgic for a defeated, exotic, and "vanishing" American Indian.[36]

In the greater Yellowstone region, Indian lands and numbers were indeed diminishing. Between 1825 and 1868, the federal government three times recognized and reduced in size the Crow Indian reservation. Through the 1868 agreement the Crows received a guarantee to the Yellowstone Valley east and south of the Yellowstone river to the present day Montana-Wyoming border; the eastern boundary reached the divide of the Bighorn and Tongue River drainages. Pressures for further cessions mounted: gold discoveries in the Clark's Fork region northeast of Yellowstone Park brought prospectors and speculators; the imminent approach of the railroad increased Anglo ranching activity on Crow lands; extermination of the buffalo elsewhere on the northern plains brought other tribes into the area, inciting conflict with the normally amicable Crow people.[37] By 1880, the year Indians were banished from Yellowstone Park, travel writers could point to the Yellowstone Valley north of the Park as a glorious embodiment of civi-

Fig. 9. Buffalo Hunting, Montana Territory, 1882. Haynes Collection, H-722.

lization's mastery over savagery: "the whole process of social growth [was unfolding] itself . . . like the successive revelations of a panorama," according to one travel book writer.[38] Tourists could now eye Native Americans from a passing train or in mass-produced imagery as quaint and exotic objects safely removed from nature into the tourist milieu.

Certain species of wildlife met the same fate. Haynes captured "Buffalo Hunting, Montana" (fig. 9) at the height of the last northern plains bison slaughters in the early 1880s. The victim in repose dominates the foreground of the image, his trackers command its middle space, while other bison in the distance await a similar end. Urbane viewers would see both the pathos

Fig. 10. Allen's Taxidermy Store, Mandan, N.Dak., 1894. Haynes Collection, H-3090.

of the receding West and a dramatic invitation to experience the thrill of a frontier venture. In addition, photographs of the "taxidermist's art" illustrate the taming of the wilderness while appealing to a growing class of gentlemen hunters. "Allen's Taxidermy Store" (fig. 10) offers a garish, museumized display of the wildlife sportsmen could expect to find on the northern Great Plains. Taxidermy, according to the *Livingston Enterprise,* was "almost if not quite as interesting as seeing the animals alive, and in many instances more pleasant."[39] One step further removed from the real thing, recorded images of taxidermic displays afforded vicarious possession of these vanishing relics of American wilderness. And within the creed of progress, once stuffed and mounted on walls (or captured on film), the animals were free to pass into history.

With an interest in making Yellowstone the marketing centerpiece of Wonderland, Charles Fee introduced F. Jay Haynes to the park in 1881. After taking views of the Grand Canyon, falls, and geysers that summer, Haynes wrote enthusiastically to Lily, "Better tell the *Argus* [the Fargo newspaper] that the latest news from Haynes the photographer is that he is getting several Hundreds [sic] of excellent views of the Yellowstone Park."[40] Haynes's relationship with Yellowstone would eventually transcend his association with the railroad and, through his son Jack, would continue throughout the park's first century.[41] By the end of his career, the photographer's Yellowstone views constituted the majority of his collection, and the Haynes name was virtually synonymous with the park. The railroad ordered more of his park images than from any other category of Haynes's vast inventory.[42]

Shortly after his first visit, Haynes applied to the Department of the Interior to become Yellowstone's "official photographer." He received this glowing and telling endorsement from officials of the U.S. Land Office and the railroad:

> The views published by [Haynes] have had an immense circulation,
> attracted considerable attention to the [Northwest] country, and
> become no small factor in the settlement thereof. We believe that the
> appointment we request for Mr. Haynes would vastly increase his
> usefulness in that direction . . . . [43]

The testimonial counters the "worthlessness lands" theory of the national park's inception; official Wonderland knew well that Yellowstone and its imagery held enormous value to the general economic development of the Northwest. It was as if the scenic and the extractive were two sides of nature's currency, each born of the everything-is-dollarable American impulse. From the beginning, leading citizens of Montana envisioned the park's creation as they did the coming of the railroad—as a vehicle for economic progress. According to the *Helena Daily Herald* on the eve of the bill's signing in 1872:

> The importance to Montana of the Congressional enactment [of the
> Yellowstone Park Act] cannot be too highly estimated. It will redound
> to the untold good of this Territory, inasmuch as a measure of this
> character is well calculated to direct the world's attention to . . . such
> resources of mines and agriculture as we can boast, spread every-
> where about us.[44]

Wonderland promotional materials fused seamlessly the natural and technological sublime features of the region. Initiated in 1878, the Northern Pacific's *Wonderland* series rendered the definitive parlor view of the Northwest. The guidebook's covers featured Native American and nature imagery. Inside, the railroad proffered in sanguine composition exotic natives and scenic marvels, Bonanza Farms and Pittsburghesque industrialization. A dizzying and familiar mix it was. Once fully inflated, *Wonderland* embraced all of Montana's gold-mining operations, now "the head of the gold-producing regions of the world"; facing that description, quite naturally, are engraved illustrations of Yellowstone's Old Faithful and Grand Canyon. The guide touted Butte's Anaconda Mine as "the greatest copper property in America," adding that it also "[makes] the most smoke"; Yellowstone's picturesque Gibbon Falls graces the next page.[45] For some readers, such juxtaposition served to equate human wonders with those of Yellowstone. For others, the park brought natural balance or redemption to the intrusion; for most perhaps, the images prompted a greater celebration of the march of industrial progress. Certainly exotic, grand scenery bespoke an aesthetic sensibility that appealed to a refined audience who could deftly divide the sacred from the profane.

Through the Yellowstone forest was heard the roar of civilization. At the head of Soda Butte Creek lay the Clark's Fork mining camp—renamed Cooke City in 1882 after a visit to the area by the son of the railroad financier. According to the nearby *Yellowstone Journal,* mountains providing "magnificent views" of the Yellowstone region also contained "rich deposits of both gold and silver."[46] The paper's panoramic illustration of Yellowstone gushed not only of cash-producing mountains but also of "parks, [with] their grassy carpets be-decked with flowers, mountain brooks forded by beaver dams . . . snow fields, forests and rocklands"; all, the paper bellowed, "blended into one grand scene."[47]

Occasionally the travel books included a description of the region given by Crow Indian chief Arapooish to a fur trader in the early part of the nineteenth century:

> The Crow country is a good country. The Great Spirit has put it exactly in the right place . . . It has snowy mountains and sunny plains; all kinds of climates, and good things for every season. When the summer heats scorch the prairies, you can draw up under the mountains, where the air is sweet and cool, the grass fresh, and the bright streams come tumbling out of the snow banks. There you can hunt the elk, the deer and the antelope, when their skins are fit for dressing; there you will find plenty of white bear and mountain sheep.
>
> In the autumn, when your horses are fat and strong from the mountain pastures, you can go down into the plains and hunt buffalo, or trap beaver on the streams. . . . The Crow country is exactly in the right place. Everything good is to be found there. There is no country like the Crow Country.[48]

This passage by Arapooish, describing the northeast part of the greater Yellowstone region that was the original Crow homeland, invariably served as a preamble to declarations of impending conquest by Euro-American civilization. I. Winslow Ayer, in his 1880 volume from which the quote is drawn, followed Arapooish with this dire prophecy:

> And Arapooish was about right. His country is a good one, and unless the Crows learn to make a better use of it than at present, they must soon yield it to those who will appreciate it for something besides its game. It is almost the last untrodden wilderness left in the United States; but even that is being invaded by advancing civilization.[49]

The Crows never learned. By the late 1880s the Crow reservation had been repeatedly reduced in size by the coming of the railroad and white settlers,[50] and the natives sufficiently contained to allow their incorporation into Wonderland (chapter 6). In the Yellowstone Valley extending west of the Cooke City mines, the Northern Pacific could boast of "farm after farm in the highest state of cultivation."[51] Yellowstone Park guidebooks described the renamed "Paradise Valley" in Arcadian terms. Summoning the horrors of "white scalps" and "Indian marauders," John Hyde's 1888 edition assured travelers that "the prosperity of the ranchmen of Paradise Valley" was now secure.[52]

Like the guidebooks and the Northern Pacific's Wonderland campaign, Haynes's inventory of *Northern Pacific Views* worked at once to obfuscate history and celebrate the region's multifarious natural wealth. His catalog descriptions served up the familiar mingling of industrial capitalism with natural scenery. Moreover, they reflected the symbiotic relationship between artist and patron and their commanding view of the region:

NORTHERN PACIFIC VIEWS

> This fine collection of Stereoscopic views embraces Scenes of all interesting points on the line of the Northern Pacific Railroad, from Lake Superior to the Yellowstone Park, along the Custer route to the Black Hills, and up the Missouri River to Fort Benton and the Falls. Each View . . . is an actual representation of the Improvements and Business Pursuits, Commerce, Agriculture, and Mining, Indian and Military Life on the Frontier, mingled with a varied assortment of picturesque scenery characteristic of the new Northwest. . . . No better idea of this region can be obtained than through Northern Pacific Views.[53]

The covers of *Northern Pacific Views* catalogs (fig. 11) obliquely but deliberately suggest a benign relationship between machine and nature, the ambiguity of the Northern Pacific epithet suggesting guardianship as much as
access. Besides betraying a fatherly relationship, the confident placement of
park and railroad renders a public-spirited company of cultivated taste.
Behind such imagery, Haynes's corporate employer marshaled and monop-
olized much of the extractive development of a vast region north of the
reserve. By 1882, through its subsidiary Park Improvement Company, the
Northern Pacific was orchestrating their much-delayed privatized control of
Yellowstone itself.

The pages of *Northern Pacific Views* glowed on: Black Hills views featured
"placer and quartz mining" along with "attractive scenery, etc." Views of

Fig. 11. NP Views Catalog
Title Page, 1884. Montana
Historical Society Archives,
Helena.

Helena, Montana, offered a "rich mineral district . . . and scenery [which] is grand."[54] The catalogs enumerated pages of prices in various sizes for dozens of Haynes views, rendering Yellowstone features as commodities equally worthy to the forests and minerals of Montana. Again, the cheery composite of nature and machine offers both picturesque cover and subliminal compensation for the offenses associated with the railroad generally during the Gilded Age. Certainly, Haynes and the Northern Pacific were not first or last in exploiting photographic imagery to both promote and veil a bifurcated course of development in the West.[55]

Moreover, neither Haynes nor the Northern Pacific Railroad created the paradox between Americans' love of nature and their landscape-transforming technology. Any contradictions dissolved early; most Americans saw none.[56] Champions of an agrarian republic, Thomas Jefferson and Tench Coxe came to reconcile the coming of a more mechanistic society, albeit not without ambivalence. Even Ralph Waldo Emerson and Henry David Thoreau, who, while proclaiming the virtues of the unspoiled American landscape, found irresistible the energy and ingenuity of nineteenth-century technology symbolized by the railroad.[57] Thoreau's experiment at Walden Pond had raised the uneasy dilemma of civilization's encroachment on nature, but finally postponed a choice between the two worlds.[58] George Inness's 1855 painting for the Lackawanna Railroad Company, *Lackawanna Valley* (fig. 12), had neatly (more than the railroad had hoped) reconciled the force of the machine with the American pastoral. No less a seer than Walt Whitman envisioned the railroad as enabling Americans to live in nature once again, returning the nation to its innocent past.[59] But as Whitman was fully aware—"do I contradict myself?"—there is no going back. Our idealism breeds delusion, modernity a need to escape. From the nation's founding, Americans have made of wilderness the middle landscape and romantic retreat we desire most. Each lies somewhere between a "virgin" nature that never was and the civilization we fear. The train seems nearer to Concord all the time.

When environmental innocence still prevailed, however, the industrial-natural motif was axiomatic. Speaking of the Red Mountain region of Montana, William Thayer boasts of it as "one of the most important undeveloped mining regions in the United States . . . [containing] vast deposits of gold, silver, lead, and tin." And, of course, "the scenery is surpassingly grand."[60] The title page of Theodore Gerrish's *Life in the World's Wonderland* (fig. 13) encompasses the complete package of themes associated with the region: repository of valuable resources, dramatic stage for the subjugation of the

Fig. 12. Lackawanna Valley. George Inness, 1855. Courtesy National Gallery of Art.

Indian and the heroism of Custer, gateway to the mythical Northwest Passage, and setting for the "unrivalled" scenery of Yellowstone Park. In 1880, Thomson P. McElrath's *The Yellowstone Valley* proclaims the supreme position now held by the tourist:

> On the lakes, and the railroad, and the rivers, every reasonable comfort is at the traveller's command, while he finds himself constantly brought into contact with sublime stretches of magnificent scenery, interspersed here and there with almost equally grand illustrations of man's mastery over the soil. . . . [The tourist] feels himself for the time being as true a nomad as any aboriginal sovereign of the wilderness. Time and action are subordinate to his will, and Mother Earth lavishes her choicest delicacies upon him to sustain his independence. . . . Returning to civilization, he speedily finds himself in the center of the busy scene that always prevails in regions where man is enabled to strike a daily cash balance with the earth by transmuting the sweat of his brow into gold.[61]

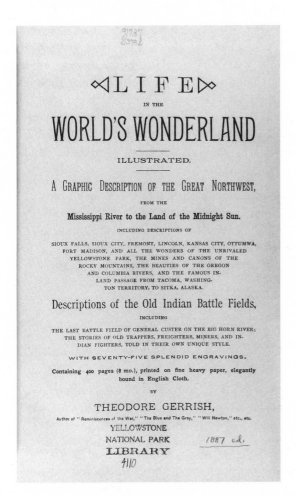

Fig. 13. *Life in the World's Wonderland.* Theodore Gerrish, title page, 1891. Courtesy Yellowstone National Park Archives and Research Library.

McElrath holds the sightseer firmly in command. Indeed, more than spectator, the traveler may temporarily become the Other: a "true" "aboriginal sovereign" of the West—the elimination of which was a principal objective of Americans throughout the century. This psychic masquerade reaffirms the imperial position of the modernizing tourist who always returns from the exotic milieu. Moreover, in the expansive and rugged Western wilderness, scattered mining sites and cleared forests counterpoise signs of human ingenuity and American progress. With sideshows featuring booming industrial activity and quaint, contained natives, the railroad as an instrument and metaphor for entrance into nature is complete. Separated from nature physically, and elevated above it culturally, the viewer controls the universe of Wonderland.

The intoxicating rhetoric of progress was certainly no place for regret. Still, the ravaging scars left by hydraulic mining were too much for at least one travel writer. Mining companies generally introduced hydraulicking into an area already exhausted of its richer deposits. The process involved shooting water through a hose at the cut of a mineral deposit to wash away earth covering gold-bearing rock.[62] L. P. Brockett, author of *Our Western Empire*— an otherwise unabashed celebration of cultural and environmental imperialism—provides a vivid description of hydraulic mining, as well as an elegiac lament of its effects upon the new Eden:

> [T]he regions where it is practised may be, before the miner's advent, like the garden of the Lord for beauty; but after his work is completed, they bear no resemblance to anything . . .. It is impossible to conceive of anything more desolate, more utterly forbidding, than a region which has been subjected to this . . . the whole vista is one of extreme desolation and ruin.[63]

Similarly, observers such as Hamlin Garland were less sanguine than the Northern Pacific's Land Department about developments such as Bonanza Farming. Garland mourned the loss of the yeoman farmer and its ecological impact:

> Pastures were where strawberries grew, and fields of barley rippled where the wild oats once waved. . . . All else of the prairie had vanished as if it had been dreamed. The pigeons, the plovers, the chickens, the vultures, the cranes, the wolves—all gone—all gone.[64]

These were isolated laments. For the vast majority of tourists and investors, the scenic and extractable resources of the northwest seemed boundless; hydraulic mining and Bonanza Farming, bright harbingers of civilization.

Selling Wonderland meant not only conveying the message that technology and industrial development had arrived throughout the region; it meant that Yellowstone itself—the premier natural attraction—would have to be tamed and made suitable for tourist traffic. In short, *improved*. After nearly three centuries of inexorable practice, Americans assumed the virtues of making wild space productive.[65] During *the incorporation of America*,[66] "improvement" usually denoted unrestrained exploitation of natural resources. From coast to coast, scores of "improvement companies" extracted oil and coal, cut down forests, drained swamps, and straightened rivers. Scenic landscapes were not above betterment. Companies east and west promoted unobstructed views of mountains, lakes, and rivers—all increasingly studded with luxury hotels.

Questions in Yellowstone, then, centered only on how the landscape would be made accessible and who would perform the task. As early as 1872, a number of observers and pundits made clear their concern that the park not become "Niagarized." The overcommercialization and privatized control of Niagara had been a national cultural embarrassment. In the original park debate, Illinois Senator Lyman Trumbull, whose son had served in the Washburn expedition, argued that "some person may go there and plant himself right across the only path that leads to [its] wonders, and charge every man that passes along the gorge of these mountains a fee of a dollar or five dollars."[67] A decade later, *The Yellowstone Journal,* generally bullish on regional development, warned:

> The danger from "improvements" is quite as serious as any threatened by the wantonness or thoughtlessness of visitors. The most sublime scenery, when scarified by a brutal engineer, may lose all its impressiveness, and the obtrusive ugliness of some misplaced hotel can disfigure the noblest landscape.[68]

The paper had good reason to fear. By the mid-1870s, the Interior Department was receiving lease applications from every brand of huckster. These included appeals to construct saloons, sawmills, a limekiln, an enclosed menagerie, a "race course and observation grounds," and a "landscape gardening plan for the park."[69] During the first five years of the park's existence, all such lease requests were referred to Nathaniel Pitt Langford, the first park superintendent. Langford turned down nearly all applicants, allowing only a few local residents to run pre-existing boarding houses and guide services. He routinely denied the more grandiose schemes, an action likely taken at the behest of his former employer, the Northern Pacific Railroad, with whom he maintained a close association.[70] The railroad certainly had the political wherewithal to make itself the preferred recipient of a concession franchise once it reached the park.

Congress vested control of the park with the Department of the Interior. A repository of patronage and conflicting interest, the Interior Department was known as "The Great Miscellany" for its collection of various unwanted government responsibilities.[71] The multitude of divergent and often contending matters subsumed by Interior included promoting mineral and timber development and protecting the national park; it bore all the myriad contending interests of a *Wonderland* guide. Charged with the dual mission of protecting Yellowstone's "curiosities" and providing tourist accommodations for the park, the secretary of the interior had no clear policy or resources for either. Not until 1878 did Congress even provide funds for park administration. As the unpaid first superintendent, Langford did not reside in the park and only once submitted a report on his activities.

Langford's successor, Philetus Norris, received a modest salary and made his priority the construction of a system of roads connecting the park's prominent features. In his five-year tenure (1877–1882), Norris denied nearly all lease requests, although in 1881 the Interior Department granted privileges for primitive accommodations to be established at Mammoth Hot Springs and the Upper Geyser Basin.[72] In the same year, Secretary Carl Schurz denied a request for hotel privileges at the park's major tourist attractions, citing the dangers of monopolistic control.[73] However, the assassination of James Garfield and the succession of Chester A. Arthur to the presidency in 1881 brought change to the Department of the Interior and to Yellowstone administration. Just six months into office, Secretary Samuel Kirkwood was replaced by Arthur's nominee, Henry M. Teller, who was favorably disposed to the interests of the Northern Pacific and to corporate development of the West in general.[74]

Although Norris had done a creditable job of administering the reserve, his opposition in late 1881 to a rumored private takeover of the park by Northern Pacific interests sealed his fate. As he began warning his superiors at the Interior Department about the prospect of Yellowstone's privatized capture, powerful supporters of the railroad discredited Norris as an eccentric egotist, and he was soon supplanted by a patronage appointee, Patrick Conger, brother of U.S. Senator Omar D. Conger, a long-time champion of the Northern Pacific. Yellowstone lease applications at this point were referred to Washington for approval. All of these moves set the stage for the Yellowstone Park Improvement Company—an aggressive enterprise connected to the railroad and with friends at Interior—to take control of park concessions (its story is at the center of the next chapter).[75]

Despite his gift of a set of premier views to Secretary Kirkwood, the Interior Department denied F. Jay Haynes's request to become the official Yellowstone photographer. In 1884 the department did grant Haynes a lease for plots of four acres each at Mammoth Hot Springs and the Upper Geyser Basin. At Mammoth, Haynes erected a Victorian-style studio-residence, which he adorned with a grand elk-horn fence (fig. 14). More significant for Haynes, in 1883 the Yellowstone Park Improvement Company named him its "official photographer [and] superintendent of art."

Although the sublime remained the key to Yellowstone's symbolic hold on the American imagination, Haynes's charge was to prettify and make inviting a rather uninviting landscape. William Henry Jackson's photographic

Fig. 14. Haynes Studio with Elkhorn Fence, Yellowstone National Park, 1898. Haynes Collection, H-3762.

work for the Hayden Survey had reinforced the awesome geomorphic affect that made the region worthy of park status. A decade later, however, Haynes's commercial patron wanted the region presented clearly as the domain of the tourist. Jackson's geyser images, for example, employed humans primarily for scale and veracity, while Haynes often captured groups of sightseers encircling the same features and intrepidly awaiting an eruption (fig. 15). Occasionally the view was playful. "Bicyclists on Minerva Terrace" (fig. 16) tempers what Melville might have called "the awful whiteness"[76] of Mammoth Hot Springs. Haynes softens the sublime and imposing look of the terrace with a group of (interestingly, Buffalo) soldiers propped with the most popular middle-class vehicle of the 1890s. In the same spirit, "Trout, Yellowstone Lake" depicts an irresistible genteel sportsmen's paradise (fig. 17).

Yellowstone has always been a place of power more than grandeur; much more weird than pretty. The familiar aesthetic of the picturesque proved elusive amid a strangely unnatural Yellowstone landscape. Established by the Hudson River School landscape painters, the picturesque dictated a subtly

Fig. 15. Giant Geyser in the Upper Geyser Basin, 1899. Haynes Collection, H-3942.

humanized and perfectly cropped landscape. Whether a painter, landscape designer, or photographer, the architect of the scene looked for lush greenery, winding pathways and other pleasing characteristics to complete the scene.[77] Creating such views in Yellowstone usually required artistic license. Taken on his second visit to Yellowstone, "Gibbon Falls, 1882" (fig. 18) is perhaps Haynes's most reproduced park image. Publishers copied it endlessly, but finding the human presence underplayed, other artists moved the sportsman front and center. No longer part of the picture, he has instead become the picture (fig. 19).

Fig. 16. Bicyclists group on Minerva Terrace, Yellowstone National Park, 1896. Haynes Collection, H-3614.

Fig. 17. Trout, Yellowstone Lake, 1897. Haynes Collection, H-3175.

Fig. 18. Gibbon Falls, Yellowstone National Park,
1882. Haynes Collection, H-778.

   New processes and advertising techniques further softened an alien landscape. Colorization of Yellowstone's features transformed what in black and
white had appeared stark and forbidding. Also, railroad literature and travel
books employed the montage technique popular in the era. Geysers, springs,
and canyons were cut, pasted and assembled in seemingly endless combina-
tions—automatically changing the original interpretation of the artist and
diminishing the scale and power of the subject. Although surrounded by gaz-
ing tourists, "The Giant" (fig. 15) still evokes the monumentalism of one of
the park's most potent geysers. When a similar Haynes view of the Giant is
reduced, pruned, and reassembled in a montage of the Upper Geyser Basin,
the sense of scale and power is reduced (fig. 20). Hotel imagery, too, enhanced

Fig. 19. Falls of the Gibbon River, 1888, Yellowstone National Park. Hyde, *Official Guide*, 17.
Courtesy Yellowstone National Park Archives.

the sense of improvement. "In Yellowstone Park" (fig. 21) presents a rather
savage look at Yellowstone Lake's eerie Paint Pots, coupled with the deso-
lation of Minerva Terrace at Mammoth; the imposition of the stately Fountain Hotel, however, tempers these sublime images, reminding the prospective tourist that civilization had indeed come to Yellowstone. To reinforce
Yellowstone's defining sublimity, the Northern Pacific hung hundreds of
mammoth (20-by–24-inch) Yellowstone images in depots and ticket offices.[78]

By the early 1880s, Yellowstone had become a symbol of good taste, the
themes of its commodification established. Aesthete Americans entertained
friends with stereographs and mammoth images of Old Faithful and the
Grand Canyon. They signified the exoticism of genteel Victorian taste.[79]

Fig. 20. Upper Geyser Basin. Haynes montage, in Wheeler,
6,000 Miles through Wonderland. Courtesy Yellowstone
National Park Archives.

Inevitably, as Yellowstone took on the designs of tourist culture, the sublime
qualities early travelers affixed to the place began to dissolve into cliché.
Reproduced everywhere from *Harper's Weekly* to ubiquitous travel and
guidebooks, Haynes's increasingly conventional views delivered to an urban
audience scenes they would expect to see verbatim upon touring the park.
Photographs at once inflated and reduced a forbidding wilderness to stilted,
iconographic imagery.

Fig. 21. In Yellowstone Park. Courtesy Yellowstone
National Park Archives.

The selling of Wonderland reveals the late-nineteenth-century origins of
a national absurdity of compelling, self-ruling logic: the deliberate and simultaneous exaltation and exploitation of nature. Americans were determined
to have Arcadia and eat it, too. Scenic images and florid descriptions elevated
Yellowstone to culturally hallowed—and therefore desirable and salable—
ground. The balance of views promoted unrestrained economic development
of lands surrounding the park. The Wonderland campaign commodified

Yellowstone and ultimately, by delivering Americans to their park, advanced
its preservation. With sales techniques commonplace a century later, the
same pages covered with romanticized Yellowstone imagery fueled the
engines of development; nature as camouflage. Indeed one might view the
Wonderland campaign as an antecedent of the "Tap the Rockies"[80] environmental popular culture of the 1990s.

Frank Haynes traveled the Northern Pacific line throughout the summer
of 1883 when the inherent tension between preservation and development
surfaced inside Yellowstone Park. In what proved to be an amazing, amusing encounter of opposing interests and ideas contending for Yellowstone's
future, the photographer worked as the objective and literal eye of a storm
that would last more than a decade.

CHAPTER THREE

1883: The Enterprise

As soon as visitors can reach the confines of this basin, with its gloomy
canons and rivers plunging into their depths, its boiling springs and mud vol-
canoes and spouting geysers, without leaving their parlor cars, the region will
be thronged. . . . But of course great caution should be exercised in granting
exclusive privileges. . . . The preservation of this wonderland as it is, in all its
original grandeur, should be the prime condition extracted from any or all
who are granted privileges from the government.

—*Yellowstone Journal, 1882*[1]

EIGHTEEN EIGHTY-THREE was a particularly energetic year in the development of the West. Standardized time zones brought greater order to railroad
travel and a vast wilderness; the Atchison, Topeka & Santa Fe Railway
began carrying freight and tourists to the West Coast; the last of the great
bison slaughters took place on the northern plains that fall, leaving cattle the
dominant consumers of the region's grasslands.[2] In the Yellowstone region,
three celebrated excursions of well-heeled travelers focused the nation's
attention there as never before and brought to a climax Wonderland's
decade-long encounter of nature and civilization. One of those resonant historical moments, Yellowstone's grand summer of 1883 distills the energy and
enigma of late-nineteenth-century Americans working to develop and preserve their national park.

The seminal excursion of the three, the "Gold Spike" extravaganza of
company president Henry Villard, marked the completion of the Northern
Pacific Railroad. It consummated the mythical promise of the Northwest and
dissolved the remaining distance between Americans and Yellowstone
National Park. Moreover, execution of the line fully incorporated the vast
Yellowstone-packaged territory from Minnesota to Oregon into the nation's
market economy. Beginning in September 1883, the Northern Pacific trans-
ported raw materials, finished goods and genteel tourists to and from the
American Wonderland.

The Northern Pacific celebration indirectly spawned the summer's other
two journeys. With Yellowstone's development assured, Wall Street financier
"Uncle" Rufus Hatch led a trainload of potential investors west on behalf of
the railroad's Yellowstone Park Improvement Company.[3] A novelist writing this story would have invented such a character. With cinematic, Gilded
Age flair, Rufus Hatch wined and dined a group of wealthy Europeans and
Americans. Banking on the dollarable potential of the park, he spent himself
silly that summer and left Yellowstone at war with members of the third
excursion. Known as "President Arthur's Yellowstone Expedition," the trip
was organized by General Philip Sheridan and Missouri Senator George
Graham Vest, leaders of an incipient movement aimed at stemming the privatized control of the park. Together with sportsman-conservationist George
Bird Grinnell, they formed the vanguard of a campaign to strengthen public management of the park.

The 1883 excursions offer both a denouement to the commercial impulse
of the Wonderland campaign and a prelude to the complex struggle of
preservationists on behalf of Yellowstone and other national parks. Carrying with them the baggage of late-nineteenth-century American culture, park
advocates were leading figures of a society that had made the rapid devel-

opment of nature its primary national business throughout the nineteenth century. Preservationists championed the effort to preserve and manage this squared-off remnant of wilderness even as they transformed its "attractions"—sublime scenery, Native Americans, and select species of wildlife—into tourist objects. Like the park itself, the Yellowstone Crusade[4] launched in the summer of 1883 was as far reaching as it was bound by a burgeoning civilization.

In the spring of 1883, Henry Villard reigned as one of the titans of Wall Street. Having assumed command of the Northern Pacific Railroad in 1881, Villard pushed construction of the line forward and by 1883 its completion was at hand.[5] But trouble loomed: that spring Villard personally surveyed the line's progress and discovered cost overruns totaling $14 million. Reports of the debt drove down the value of the company's stock and made Villard's creditors nervous. The press rumored that his opponents were out "to cripple Mr. Villard and his magnificent enterprises."[6] Villard dismissed the trouble and believed the spectacle of an extravagant "Gold Spike" celebration would restore the confidence of Wall Street and signify the "dawn of halcyon days" for the company and himself.[7] Recognizing the international significance of the event, the company evoked the fabled Northwest Passage in its invitation:

> The Northern Pacific Railroad . . . will not only open new and vast
> fields of commerce and industry . . . but also an expeditious and
> attractive route for travel and trade across the American Continent,
> and to Asia and Australia.[8]

Three hundred American and European dignitaries could not resist. Among the notables were political theorist Max Weber, dozens of prominent politicians, artists, and scientists from Great Britain and Villard's native Germany. Former president Ulysses S. Grant signed on to the excursion, along with ex-Secretary of the Interior Carl Schurz and several members of President Arthur's cabinet. (Vacationing in Yellowstone Park, the president excused himself.) Other Americans included Joseph Pulitzer and Joseph Medill, ten U.S. senators, twenty-six congressmen, nine governors, nine army generals, and dozens of local officials and railroad executives.[9] The distinguished party traveled in style. Each of the six Gold Spike trains consisted of two baggage cars, a dining car, and a suite of sleeping cars all outfitted with parlors, smoking rooms, bathrooms, and observation-coupes. Englishman Lord Charles Russell enjoyed this "Sybaritic life" on rails, for it "enabled the rich to create the clearest possible inequality in the customs of ordinary travel."

Though Lord Russell's inegalitarianism appears quite un-American, for the Gilded Age, it was quite right. The sumptuous travel of both the Villard and Hatch affairs that summer magnifies the generally elite nature of early Western tourism.[10]

This spectacle of class and conquest captured the nation's attention for several weeks. Beyond the automatic interest of a second transcontinental rail line, the endless fascination of mortal Americans with the opulent lifestyles of the rich and famous produced voluminous press coverage. The inquisitive tourists were themselves "stared at like so many animals in a zoo."[11] Setting the tone for other publications, the *New York Times* and the *Chicago Tribune* printed the entire guest list and followed every step of the excursion.[12] Western towns like Livingston, Montana, were particularly giddy. The "draft of this regiment of nobility," gushed the *Livingston Enterprise,* was "an achievement more remarkable than the completion of the Northern Pacific, which it came to attend."[13] Their exaltation included a comparison to the ineffable wonders of nearby Yellowstone:

> In a party such as this all are great and it is particularly hard to describe a thing without a comparison. The wealth of such men is so fabulous, their birth so noble and their greatness so great, our pen must pause—; as it is with writers upon our much lauded "Wonderland" so with us—; we are incapable of the task.[14]

Towns large and small hailed the trains with elaborate receptions. The burgeoning twin cities of Minneapolis–St. Paul vied for most grandiose. A parade in St. Paul featured 724 wagons and 4,300 marchers; the Minneapolis event stretched twenty miles and required seven hours for a full review. Both cities proffered exhibits of their industrial and agricultural goods—a seemingly endless progression of blankets, cotton bales, and flour mills. Minneapolis paraded wagons of Sioux Indians, "one with a statue of Father Hennepin proclaiming that while he discovered Minneapolis in 1680, Henry Villard discovered it in 1880."[15] Villard reveled in the lofty declarations and concluded a St. Paul address by linking the Passage to India theme with Yellowstone, its scenic gateway:

> Hereafter it will be easier for explorers and pleasure seekers by way of the Yellowstone park to visit the ancient countries of Japan, China and India than to go by way of the Atlantic Ocean, Mediterranean sea and Suez canal.[16]

Residents of Livingston, Montana, prepared for the train's arrival with the fervor of a messianic coming. Livingston had every reason to celebrate. The company platted the town and named it after a Northern Pacific official. Livingston would become an important maintenance center and the junction for the Park Branch line extending sixty miles south to Yellowstone Park. Its population had boomed from fifty persons in December 1882 to more than three thousand as the Villard train approached that summer.[17] Residents prepared a "beautifully brilliant spectacle" that would not disappoint.

> Over the main track, at a point opposite the eastern extremity of the platform, is erected an evergreen arch upon which is laid a canvas bearing the legend "Livingston the Gateway to Wonderland." . . .
> The end of the depot building is ornamented in varied and uniformly beautiful style. The central ornament is a very large and splendidly mounted elk's head, while heads of deer, mountain sheep, and buffalo are displayed above and around it. On one side is an evergreen circle within which is painted "Livingston the Denver of the Northwest" . . . Along the front of the depot appears another fine array of specimens of the taxidermist's art with a mountain lion projecting out over the platform as the most conspicuous figure. Two large frames against the wall surround "1883" and "H.V." done in evergreen. . . . The exterior of the building is decked with evergreens, flags and colored streamers in the greatest profusion, and Chinese lanterns hang from every available support adding another element of beauty and brilliancy. Beside these every window in the depot is ablaze with rows of burning candles, a headlight throws its glare over the platform and bonfires are blazing in the plaza in front of Park Street.[18]

This ostentatious display speaks loudly not only of Livingston's great ambitions, but of an age of American excess during which the "greatest profusion" of everything was just enough. Chinese lanterns reflect both the time-honored Northwest Passage theme and contemporary interest in things oriental. Wild garnish dominates. Evergreen trimmings and taxidermic "art" invite the traveler into the natural milieu from which they have been severed. In the same spirit, two of the private cars fitted up for the Villard excursion bore the names "Yellowstone" and "Adirondack"—two preeminent symbols of American nature affixed to the principal vehicle of its development.[19]

West of Livingston, Villard, with help from Interior Secretary Teller, treated his excursionists to what one passenger declared "the most interesting, exciting scene" of the journey.[20] At a place called Gray Cliff, some two thousand Crow Indians encamped and performed tribal dances through the night for the amusement of the passing trains. Passenger reviews ranged from utter racial disdain to the typically touristic: Nicholas Mohr remarked that "it looked something like a circus or a fair. The Indians are a truly fantastic race, gifted with a lively sense of color and certainly not without other fine artistic sensibilities."[21] The exhibition underscores the emerging role of Native Americans as exotic spectacle in Wonderland tourist culture. For British spectator Lord Russell, the display fortified his sense of white upper-class supremacy:

> [T]he scene was assuredly of a striking kind—the beauty of the place, the glory of the setting sun, the bright colouring, the fantastic move-ments and the commanding figures of the Indians side by side with the men of the White race—all combined to form a picture such as will probably never again be seen. Here were the representatives of an old dynasty which was almost dead, and, close by, in the luxuri-ous steam equipage (a compendium of the material civilisation of nineteen centuries) the successful invader, the ruthless, aggressive, all-conquering White man.[22]

The spirit and purpose of the Gold Spike excursion demanded the language and imagery of conquest (fig. 22).

On the morning of September 8, the trains rolled into Gold Creek, Mon-tana, for the linking of Northern Pacific rails.[23] According to one reporter, a "queer crowd" of some three to five thousand persons came to witness the ceremonies. Many of the common folk arrived on foot or horseback and waited five hours for the rites to begin. The Montana proletariat were less than amused as the Villard guests indulged in the gourmet victuals of the din-ing car while they took their only sustenance from the dog soup prepared by Crow Indians at sunset. To add further insult, the speakers' platform faced away from the crowd and toward Villard's traveling dignitaries. The masses spent most of the day milling around the copiously evergreen-festooned pavillion (fig. 23) and heard few of the speeches delivered that day.[24]

That may have been a blessing. Apparently less than exhilarating, accounts of "the creation, the discovery of the new world, the tea party in the Boston harbor, [and] the rise and fall of the Dutch republic" had the crowd "won-dering what in the world they had come for anyway." Secretary of State William Evarts expressed the familiar and delusive hope that the railroad would "assuage inequalities of nature and disparities of fortune among our own people, and spread peace, plenty, and prosperity to other nations."[25] At last came Crow Chief Iron Bull, who offered these somber remarks:

Fig. 22. Bismarck Bridge over the Missouri River. The Northwest 1 (February 1883), 1. Northern Pacific Railway Company Records, secretary's file. Courtesy Minnesota Historical Society.

This is the last of it—this is the last thing for me to do. I am glad to see you here, and hope my people of the Crow nation are glad to see you, too. There is a meaning in my part of the ceremony, and I understand it. The end of our lives is near at hand. The days of my people are almost numbered; already they are dropping off like the rays of sunlight in the western sky. Of our once powerful nation there are now few left—just a little handful, and we, too, will soon be gone.[26]

Following Iron Bull's eulogy, the driving of the Gold Spike began under a setting sun. Northern Pacific official H. C. Davis was handed not a gold spike, but the same rusty nail he had driven thirteen years before to launch the road's construction. Members of the Villard family took their turns before President Grant delivered the final blow. Later that year, the company completed its Yellowstone Park Branch line to the town of Cinnabar, Montana, just nine miles from the park boundary.[27]

Fig. 23. During the oration at Last Spike Pavillion, 1883. Haynes Collection, 1883, H-992.

The momentous Gold Spike event abetted the chimerical notion of nature's inexhaustibility. As the *Helena Daily Herald* put it, "just as the country is viewing with alarm the waste and shrinkage of our northern forests, there comes up a reassuring voice from the North Pacific coast, 'here is plenty, come and get all you want.'"[28] So much, in fact, that there was room for a vast geothermal public park. Enduring into our own time, the myth of abundance[29] allowed late-nineteenth-century Americans to cultivate and mingle blithely their nature sensibilities with the insuperable force of economic development. The fusion of commercial and romantic impulses created artificially natural remnants, celebrated the myth of progress, and obfuscated the darker realities of environmental change.

For some travelers to Yellowstone, change could not come soon enough. On his return from the Pacific Coast, Henry Villard escorted a number of his guests on a park tour. Nicolaus Mohr was among them. In a later memoir, Mohr curiously wrote very little of the park's natural features, dwelling instead on what he found to be austere conditions in the extreme:

The name "National Park" could lead one to believe that the landscape surrounding the volcanic wonders has been artificially con-

structed to give it the look of a park. Nothing could be further from
the truth. Except for a very few primitive paths, a few dikes through
the gulleys, and some timber trestle bridges, not a thing has been
touched. . . . [Y]ou won't believe how much dust and dirt we have
swallowed, or how many bumps and bangs we have endured in the
buggies, or what dubious and dangerous paths we have crossed in
order to reach the Upper Geyser Basin and return.

Mohr's narrative is filled with endless grumbling about the artless state of
the park. In this way, it resembles a stack of other well-heeled tourists' similarly petulant reactions to Yellowstone. Well-manicured European parks and
their picturesque American facsimiles ill-prepared the genteel for the primitive conditions and ghastly landscape of Yellowstone. Mohr's advice to
tourists was "to wait a few years until the Improvement Company for the
park has had time to do more work on this project."[30]

How the Yellowstone Park Improvement Company got to work there is
a vintage tale of the Gilded Age. On September 1, 1882, Assistant Interior
Secretary Merritt Joslyn authorized what became known as the "Park
Grab." Closely aligned with railroad interests, Joslyn signed a contract bearing the names of Carroll T. Hobart, manager of the Northern Pacific Railroad's Park Branch line; Henry F. Douglas, a sutler at Fort Yates; and Uncle
Rufus Hatch, a renowned Wall Street financier. The quietly greased approval
of the application seemed to reverse the Interior Department's position on
park concessions. In early 1882 Secretary Teller had disallowed the extension of privileges for local entrepreneur George Marshall, who sought to
expand his hotel operations in the Upper Geyser Basin to other areas of the
park.[31]

Petitioners for the Improvement Company played on fears that unless a
"legitimate" enterprise with substantial financial backing were in control
of the park's improvement, Yellowstone would be vulnerable to second-rate
hucksterism. Secretary Teller argued that it was in the government's best
interest to keep the number of individuals allowed "to engage in the business enterprises in the Park" at a minimum. Such an exclusive operation
could help *protect* the park "with the least possible expense to the government."[32] Since 1872 park advocates had argued that the reserve would "pay
for itself" through the granting of leases to parties who would accommodate
the park for tourist travel; revenue generated from concessionaire privileges
alone, they believed, would make federal appropriations unnecessary.[33]

The company's original contract generously allotted 4,400 acres at the

park's most desirable sites, the rent for which was not to exceed two dollars per acre. The terms called for hotel facilities near the "center" of Old
Faithful, the Grand Canyon, and Yellowstone Lake, all of which afforded
the company and paying guests premier, restrictive access to the sights. Further, the agreement allowed the company "so much of the timber, coal and
other material within said park as may be required," fruit and vegetable
farms, yachts and sailboats on Yellowstone Lake, and stipulated that the
park's hot mineral waters could be channeled for use in bathhouses and
hotels. Finally, the contract specified exclusive company control of these
activities for a period of ten years.[34]

The company wasted no time. Before the ink on the contract was dry,
Hobart had two steam sawmills and one shingle mill sitting at the end of
the Northern Pacific line at Livingston awaiting transport to the park. By
December construction of a hotel at Mammoth Hot Springs was well under
way. Hobart fed his men on the venison of park wildlife. They denuded the
area surrounding Mammoth Hot Springs of timber, using it to construct a
hotel, warehouse, stable, and other structures for dairying and laundering.[35]

That same fall of 1882 brought U.S. Senator George Graham Vest of
Missouri to the Dakota Territory on an investigation of Indian matters. Stop-
ping to eat dinner in a crowded saloon, Vest sat alone in a corner, but
serendipitously found himself within earshot of a group of men bragging
about a shrewd business deal they had just swindled from the government.
His attention seized, Vest learned of the concessionaires' monopoly on
Yellowstone Park. Shocked by this revelation of robber baronism in the
nation's park, Vest, chairman of the Senate Committee on Territories,
resolved to end congressional neglect of the reserve. He returned East and
began working with General Philip Sheridan on legislative remedies for
Yellowstone's protection.[36]

The ensuing debate tested the 1872 judgment of Yellowstone's value. Congress passed Senator Vest's resolution calling for an investigation of the government's contract with the Yellowstone Park Improvement Company. But
it rejected subsequent legislation which, among other measures, would have
greatly enlarged the park. Miners working gold and silver deposits northeast
of the reserve argued that Sheridan's proposal to extend the reserve in their
direction would "leave [them] in a worse fix than if [the land] had been left
with the Indians."[37] Impugning the value of an unproductive parcel of public land, Kansas senator John J. Ingalls asserted that "the best thing the Government could do with the Yellowstone National Park is to survey it and sell
it as other public lands are sold." In a stinging rebuke, Vest denounced America's materialistic culture:

The great curse of this age and of the American people is its materialistic tendencies. Money, money, *l'argent, l'argent,* is the cry everywhere
until our people are held up already to the world as noted for nothing
except the acquisition of money at the expense of all esthetic taste and
of all love of nature and its great mysteries and wonders. I am not
ashamed to say that I shall vote to perpetuate this Park for the American people. I am not ashamed to say that I think its existence answers
a great purpose in our national life. . . . There should be to a nation
that will have a hundred million or a hundred and fifty million people
a park like this as a great breathing place for the national lungs.[38]

Vest anticipated eloquently the purpose of national parks in modern life.
Within decades, droves of harried middle-class Americans embraced the
spirit of his argument.

In the end, provisions to the Sundry Civil Appropriations bill for the 1884
fiscal year voided all Interior Department contracts, thereby nullifying the
"Park Grab." The measure secured a forty-thousand-dollar appropriation
for the superintendent and his assistants to administer the park. The act
stated that Yellowstone leases were to be no larger than ten acres and facilities could be placed no closer than one quarter-mile of any prominent park
feature. Thus the 4,400 acres initially signed over to Hobart and Hatch had
been reduced to ten, though they were still free to divide that acreage among
the park's most desirable sites. In addition, Secretary Teller issued regulations
prohibiting tourists and concessionaires from "killing, wounding or capturing" park animals (with the exception of notorious predators). The new rules
also outlawed fishing by means other than "hook and line."[39]

General Sheridan urged a final amendment allowing the secretary of the
interior to request troops from the secretary of war for the protection of the
park. Three years later, when Congress threatened to cut off funding for park
administration because of perceived incompetence, the clause proved critical to the park's survival (chapter 4). Never formally recognized as more than
"acting" superintendents, U.S. Cavalry officials managed the park from
1886 until the establishment of the National Park Service in 1916.[40]

Meanwhile, Superintendent Conger began protesting to Secretary Teller
the company's ranching operations and destruction of timber. He and his
men tried in vain to prevent those and more egregious violations: Hobart's
attempt to channel the mineral-laden waters of Mammoth Hot Springs to
the hotel bathhouse and the shooting of park game for the hotel menu. A
local rancher upheld Conger's complaints in a letter to Teller: "By God,
they're fixing that thing so that if you want to take a whiff of a park breeze,

you will have to pay for the privilege of turning your nose in that direction."[41] But the superintendent ruled without the force of law and with help
only from a "herd of irresponsible imbeciles," as one witness described his
assistants.[42] With no enforcement provisions in the 1883 regulations, Conger and his men served chiefly as laughing stock for the Improvement Company. His grievances with the company, recorded in letters to Teller, illustrate
who was in charge of Yellowstone in the winter of 1882–1883:

> Hobart has boasted in my hearing of his influence with you and he
> told one of my Assistants that you had promised him that I should
> not visit Washington this winter and he also said that the reason you
> would not write me was, that you was [sic] not going to have my
> letters paraded before Congress.[43]

Back East, Hatch tried desperately to rescue his now-constricted enterprise.
That spring he began planning a Villard-like excursion to show the park off
to prospective investors. Hatch predicted wildly that the publicity generated
by the two journeys would bring one hundred million dollars of foreign
capital into the region.[44] Lured perhaps by Hatch's promise to cover all
expenses, "his collection of celebrities [was] simply wonderful." As the *New
York World* glowed, "Barnum never succeeded in bringing together, even in
wax, so many illustrious personages."[45] His train consisted of one entire car
used for the storage of numerous "cases of champagne, claret . . . and other
things necessary for the [party's] luxurious existence"; a typically ornate dining car; four elegantly upholstered Pullman sleeping cars; a private car housing John C. Wyman, the party's orator; and a grand observation car from
which the guests took rifle shots at Wonderland wildlife. Service was first-
rate: Hatch's "bed boys" and other "darkies" impressed Londoner William
Hardman with their "rapidity and dexterity."[46]

The spectacle of Hatch's splendid cortege certainly did not go unnoticed
in Gardiner, Montana. Lying on the northern boundary of Yellowstone Park,
Gardiner was little more than a year old that summer and boasted twenty-
one saloons. "The town is fairly well-ordered," wrote the *Livingston Enterprise,* "but its inhabitants are probably not conspicuous for religious tendencies as two dance halls and four houses of ill fame flourish in their
midst."[47] Hatch's genteel party presented the rough-hewn Americans with
quite a sight: "One earl came with thirteen trunks; another had a retinue of
servants; and there were enough monocles, tight pants, and effete manners
to thoroughly amuse the natives." The *Livingston Enterprise* punned that
Hatch's "big bugs" were "hatched out from both sides of the Atlantic."[48]
Carnival atmosphere aside, the newspaper understood well the meaning of
the journey:

[Hatch] has contrived to bring together a party composed of representatives of the national elite of America, Great Britain, Germany
and France, and has brought them thus far upon an excursion to his
leasehold property, the Yellowstone park. Doubtless the members of
the party, as well as outsiders, understand the fact that their presence
here is the grandest advertising scheme ever inaugurated and carried
to a successful conclusion.[49]

The growing perception that summer was that the Improvement Company
had indeed come to *own* Yellowstone Park: Edward Pierrepont, one of the
well-heeled tourists vacationing there that summer, hoped for the continued "good management" of the reserve by Hatch and Hobart; what began
as the National Hotel at Mammoth Hot Springs by summer's end became
"Hatch's Hotel"; and the *Chicago Weekly News* declared that the "Rufus
Hatch Department" was locked in a three-way struggle for control of the
park with the Interior and War Departments.[50]

As holder of the "leasehold property," the Improvement Company had
pledged to have ready for the 1883 season suitable accommodations at reasonable prices. What visitors actually found was something else altogether.
The Mammoth Hot Springs Hotel, although open, remained crudely unfin-
ished throughout the summer. It was elegant compared to conditions at the
barracks-like tent hotels erected at some of the other park features. Norris
Geyser Basin boasted four beds per tent with two persons in a bed; the overflow slept on the floor. There were no chairs. Two guests shared towels and
washbasins and carried their own water from a nearby stream. One candle
in an empty whiskey bottle lighted each tent. "The pillows were the thinnest
ever seen in this free country, with not a sheet or pillow-case in the entire
'hotel,'" wrote William Hardman.[51]

All of this for five dollars a day. For an extra dollar, one could enjoy the
pleasure of a private tent. Three dollars and fifty cents per day would fetch
a horse. The team of Wakefield and Hoffman, under contract with the
Improvement Company, provided exclusive stage services at the unseemly
rate of ten dollars per day. Even the price of the Mammoth Hotel bootblack
drew complaints: after having his shined shoes returned to him, one guest
asked, "how much?" "Quarter," said the company's hireling. "Boy," said the
man, "the Secretary of Interior says 10 cents." "The secktary ain't runnin'
my part of this ranch," returned the boy. "Shell out yer quarter."[52]

By the end of the summer, newspapers turned from the sensation of Hatch's
excursion to the story of Yellowstone's monopolistic capture. From a damning cartoon in *Harper's Weekly* (fig. 24) to William Hardman's caustic commentary for the London press, public opinion of the enterprise soured:

Fig. 24. Desecration of Our National Parks. Cartoon by W. A. Rogers, *Harper's Weekly*, 20 January 1884. Courtesy Library of Congress.

> The free-born citizens of this Great Republic who "run" this estab-
> lishment are independent enough, too, to brook neither criticism nor
> complaint. With nothing to eat, and not a house or shed within
> twenty miles, you are at their mercy and they know it.

Hardman, for one, remained optimistic that prices and accommodations
would improve, "feeling that the energetic Americans will have many
improvements by next summer and every succeeding summer."[53]

One such aspiring Yankee was George Marshall. A pioneer mail carrier, in
1881 Marshall erected a crude inn at the forks of the Firehole River in the
Upper Geyser Basin and in 1883 remained the Improvement Company's lone
competitor. In spite of Hatch's efforts to have him expelled, the Interior
Department extended Marshall's lease. Margaret Cruikshank, a discrimi-
nating traveler in the Park that summer, deemed Marshall's Hotel intolera-

ble: "When only teamsters and hunters visited the Park I suppose he gave satisafaction. . . . But now that crowds throng here and [are] of a more fastidious sort Marshall won't do. Marshall must go," she declared.[54] Hatch could not have agreed more, particularly after Marshall charged him ninety-seven dollars to accommodate his party for one night. He announced the bill as Marshall's "death warrant," pledging to erect a tent hotel nearby to undercut his business.[55]

Marshall proved to be the least of Hatch's problems. Ultimately, it was the summer's third journey led by the preservationist coterie of Senator Vest and General Phil Sheridan that doomed the Hatch excursion. Sheridan, Civil War hero and celebrated Indian fighter, had ordered the military escort for the Washburn expedition and additional reconnaissance of the area in the 1870s.[56] He first toured Yellowstone in 1881 and returned in September 1882, incensed to "find the park rented out to private parties." Sheridan resolved to protect the reserve from its perceived principal threats—the slaughter of wildlife by market hunters, the vandalism of geysers by tourists, and the exploitative activities of the Improvement Company. He argued that "improvements in the park should be national, the control of it in the hands of an officer of the government." Presaging the later role of the cavalry, Sheridan pledged to protect the national park "if authorized to do so . . . by use of troops from Forts Washakie on the south, Custer on the East, and Ellis on the north."[57]

General Sheridan's concern for wildlife is ironic in view of his earlier leadership in the near-extermination of the North American bison. Recognizing that animal as the sustenance of the Plains Indians against whom he was engaged in warfare, in 1876 Sheridan advised the Texas legislature to, "send [skin hunters] powder and lead, if you will. . . . [Let] them kill, skin and sell until the buffaloes are exterminated."[58] Six years later, however, with the conquest of Indians a *fait accompli,* and with Yellowstone's role as a national reserve of disappearing species endangered, Sheridan came to their defense.

Attitudes had indeed changed since 1872 when Cody and Sheridan accompanied the Grand Duke Alexis of Russia on a sporting afternoon kill of over fifty bison on the northern plains.[59] With the slaughter of the last major bison herd in 1883, conservationists made the creature the cause *célèbre* of a decade-long campaign to better protect Yellowstone wildlife (chapter 6). Even legendary bison hunter Buffalo Bill Cody reported to the *New York Sun* that spring that the wanton slaughter of game "does not find favor in the West as it did a decade or so ago."[60] Various motives drew western frontiersmen and eastern gentry to the idea of conserving wildlife.[61] Writing in the spring of 1883, Governor Schuyler Crosby of Wyoming saw a bounteous future of surplus meat and sportsmen tourists:

> By absolutely protecting the several thousand square miles of the Park for even a few years, it is believed that it will become so strongly stocked, that the overflow in to the Northwestern Territories . . . will add greatly to the food resources of the settlers in the neighboring Territories, and invite true sportsmen from all parts of the world to visit our region and annually spend large sums among our people.[62]

Others like George Bird Grinnell brought a scientific perspective to the incipient protection movement. Grinnell's journey to Yellowstone began with a well-heeled childhood during which he joined his uncle Thomas in hunting and mounting wildlife "specimens." The Grinnells were close to the family of naturalist John Audubon, and George later attributed much of his interest in natural history to John's wife, "Grandma Audubon."[63] With an ornithology degree from Yale, Grinnell worked on the scientific reconnaissance of the northwest region. He served Custer on the 1874 Black Hills exploration, studying the lifeways of Plains Indians and collecting animal trophies for eastern museums. In 1875 General Sheridan invited Grinnell's participation in a military exploration of "Unceded Indian Lands" of the Northwest. On that trip he glimpsed the marvels of Yellowstone and poaching of its wildlife for the first time.[64]

In 1876 he fortuitously passed on General Custer's ill-fated journey to the Little Big Horn, instead focusing on his new job as natural history editor for *Forest and Stream* magazine. Eventually promoted to editor-in-chief, Grinnell steered the publication increasingly toward game and forest preservation issues.[65] Grinnell above all championed the romantic notion of Yellowstone as an inviolable natural monument to a more virtuous America:

> There is one spot left, a single rock about which this tide [of immigration] will break, and past which it will sweep, leaving it undefiled by the unsightly traces of civilization. Here in this Yellowstone Park the large game of the West may be preserved from extermination; here . . . it may be seen by generations yet unborn. It is for the Nation to say whether these splendid species shall be so preserved, in this their last refuge.[66]

Cheap immigrant labor, of course, had built the railroad that carried Grinnell's civilization west and established the park. The indirect role of scientists like himself in bringing bison to the brink of extermination was imperceptible to men like Grinnell. For the conservationist and his contemporaries, Yellowstone would remain invulnerable from the "unsightly" forces of industrialization and immigration, even as their own lives were inextricably entwined with them.

In late 1882 Grinnell targeted the Yellowstone Park Improvement Company in a series of damning editorials. He tracked the enterprise closely and reported its activities to his audience of genteel sportsmen. Grinnell recalled how officials of the company, "with tears in their eyes," decried the vandalism of geysers and made the case that they had come to "save the Park for America." They mentioned only

> incidentally that they wished in return . . . to have a monopoly of the hotel, stage and telegraph privileges in the Park, but they said this would be a small matter, and that they would scarcely pay expenses.

Then, Grinnell recounted, they had no choice but to

> charge for the guides and the horses which the tourists would require while in the Park, and were to have the sole right to all timber and available lands; and now we are told quite as a matter of course that this company is going into the cattle business, and that the Park, which has been set aside for the people, is to be turned into a big stock range for the benefit and behoof of the Yellowstone Park Improvement Company. Truly the modesty of these monopolists is startling, but not more so than the meekness with which the people endure this monstrous invasion of their rights.[67]

Like Grinnell, George Vest had avoided the crusades of his time until 1883. He had not even been to Yellowstone Park. The only suggestion of his later park advocacy occurred as a young lawyer when he showed a propensity for defending the underdog. In 1853 Vest, a southerner and states' rights advocate, found himself in Georgetown, Missouri, defending a black slave accused of the rape and murder of a white pregnant farmer's wife. He successfully cleared the man, but a hostile mob publicly burned the slave before he could be released. His own life now threatened, Vest remained in town to practice law and serve the region in a long political career. In 1870, in an oddly more celebrated case, Vest delivered an impassioned winning defense of an accused dog.[68]

George Vest's serendipitous saloon encounter with Hatch and company in the fall of 1882 drew him to take up Yellowstone's cause. That winter, he and Phil Sheridan realized that their legislative victory drastically trimming the Improvement Company's lease would only partially solve the park's problems. They soon conceived the idea of a presidential Yellowstone excursion to focus national attention on the park. They had little trouble persuading President Chester Alan Arthur to go along. Because of a flurry of congressional activity and a hectic social schedule, the winter of 1882–1883 had been especially hard on the president. A physician had diagnosed hypertensive heart disease brought on by high blood pressure and a related kidney ailment. Reporters described his appearance that spring as "far from well" and "savage and dangerous."[69]

President Arthur continued a hectic travel schedule throughout the spring of 1883—fishing in Florida, presiding at the opening of the Brooklyn Bridge, and journeying to the New Jersey shore. After stinging charges from Democrats that the junkets came at taxpayer expense, the White House denied that the Yellowstone expedition—the first by a U.S. president—would "cause any expense to the Government." Rather, this would be "an official exploration party, and the President is to accompany it as an invited guest." Proof seemed to lie in Grinnell's prediction of increased protection for the national park following the journey.[70] The president himself longed for the restorative power of a hardy western adventure:

> I have had enough of what is called society in winter in Washington.
> I want to get a hundred miles away from the nearest politician,
> where I can take a rest in my own way, and be relieved from the
> social and political pressure that is so hard to avoid. . . . As to the
> spice of danger there may be, that only adds to the interest of the
> journey. I shall rough it, just as the rest do, live and sleep in the open
> air, wear out my old hunting suit, and for the first time in my life,
> become a savage. Such a trip will be worth more to me in instruction
> and health than twenty seasons at Newport or Saratoga would be.[71]

Like Grinnell's hopes for the "last refuge," the president's desire to "become a savage" suggests the circular antimodern impulse of many of his contemporaries.[72] After bringing civilization to their fathers' more primitive America, the nation's dominant classes grew anxious and beleaguered with late-nineteenth-century urban life and infatuated with romantic remnants of primitive North America—Native Americans, big game and wilderness. With *fin-de-siécle* decadence creeping in, genteel Americans craved—and imagined—the virtue and vigor of a bygone era. "Roughing it" in places like Yellowstone Park offered such moralizing adventure. General Sheridan wrote to his friend George Vest, "On leaving Washington, we will bid adieu

Fig. 25. The Presidential Party at the Upper Geyser Basin, August 1883. Haynes Collection, H-1052.

to civilization. . . . On your return, my dear Senator, I am sure you will feel as if your longevity has been increased twenty years."[73]

One hundred and seventy-five pack animals carried the baggage of the party, which included the president, Senator Vest, General Sheridan, Secretary of War Robert Lincoln, Judge Daniel G. Rollins, General Anson Stager, Wyoming Territorial governor J. Schuyler Crosby, Major-Surgeon W. H. Forwood, guide Jack Baronett (Truman Everts's rescuer), and Colonel Michael V. Sheridan. Fearing their "pleasure [would] be destroyed," Sheridan and Arthur strictly forbid the press, although they did ask well-traveled Frank Haynes to photograph the excursion. The enterprising photographer incorporated a number of popular views from the presidential trip into his inventory (fig. 25). Colonel Sheridan, the general's son, sent daily dispatches to the Associated Press.[74]

The excursion stopped first at Fort Washakie, situated south of Yellowstone. There, Shoshone and Arapahoe chiefs held council with the president, sharing a pipe and presenting Arthur with a pony for his daughter.[75] As with the Villard party, Secretary Teller had helped Sheridan arrange for a performance of tribal dances and a mock battle. Sheridan declared the spectacle "decidedly unique and interesting."[76] And poignant, historically: the general had pursued the destruction of Native American civilization for two decades on the battlefield; reduced to touristic display, the struggle was now complete.

For weeks, Americans followed their president through the greater Yellowstone region. As the party traveled through the Wind River Mountains south of the park, Colonel Sheridan reported the president "lost in reverie. [He] has no time here to fish and hunt. He can only sit and ponder on the vastness of the scenery about him." On August 21, the colonel delivered this stirring report:

> We had climbed to the summit of a long hill about five miles from Camp Arthur, when there suddenly burst upon our view a scene as grand and majestic as was ever witnessed. Below us, covered with grass and flowers, was a lovely valley many miles in extent, through which was threading its way the river on whose banks we had just encamped. Along the whole westerly edge of this valley, with no intervening foothills to obstruct the view, towered the magnificent Teton Mountains, their snowy summits piercing the air 13,000 feet above the sea level and 8,000 feet above the spot on which we stood in reverent admiration. It was the universal sentiment of the party that that sight alone would have fully repaid all the toils and perils of the march.[77]

With the purple prose of romanticism, Colonel Sheridan reasserts the sense of wondrous discovery of the region's early explorers. Yellowstone's capacity to humble even the president of the United States further elevated its stature. As the *Chicago Tribune* declared, the "greatness of [Arthur's] position does not cast a shadow on the intense sublimity of nature's architecture around."[78] The drama of the journey continued when Major Forwood, scouting the area surrounding Yellowstone Lake, found the remains of "an extinct species of rhinoceros and two vertebrae of a large fossil saurian."[79] Delivered east for study and exhibition, the discovery reaffirmed the importance of Yellowstone as a repository of the nation's natural history.

The party spent a great number of hours hunting and fishing. This was a sporting group, members of the post–Civil War movement of upper-class men who governed themselves with the self-proclaimed moral superiority of the "Sportsmen's Code." Eschewing the base utilitarian motives of pot- and market-hunters, gentlemen of the era redefined hunting as recreational sport that would build strong character and recapture lost American virtues. The genteel hunter killed with style and grace, never for profit, and for sustenance only when roughing it.[80] In that spirit, members of the party "shot an elk of enormous size and weight," several antelope, and a "good supply of mountain grouse and wild ducks." As commander of the expedition, General Sheridan gave "peremptory orders that no more shall be killed than is absolutely necessary for the wants of the command." Upon entering "the sacred precincts of the park," he gave "strict orders that nothing shall be killed."[81]

Except fish, of course. According to Vest, the president came equipped with an "array of tackle enough to bewilder an entire fishing club."[82] In one afternoon he pulled thirty-five fish from Yellowstone Lake. Engaged in a friendly contest to see who could pull in the greater number, the party's angling altogether yielded several hundred pounds of fish. Columnist Eugene Field later published short stories inspired by the Arthur expedition, one describing the intentions of a Shoshone chief to move farther west to escape the expert fishing of U.S. presidents.[83]

On this mission to increase the security of the park, General Sheridan could not keep some of his own soldiers in check. An assistant superintendent reported that he had seen "couriers to the President's Party [who had] slayed all kinds of game they could find." One soldier tried hauling away a one-hundred-and-fifty-pound souvenir he had hacked off one of the geyser cones (he was accosted and punished). Even the immediate party violated regulations, leaving several smoldering campfires; one in the Upper Geyser Basin torched over twenty acres of forest.[84]

Throughout the journey, President Arthur maintained the appearance of a plebeian tourist, even inviting fellow pilgrims into his encampment. Rufus Hatch's English guests were appalled to find the American president barely distinguishable from some of the seedy western locals. Witnessing his return from a rough day-hike, they whispered pejoratively about Arthur's scruffy look, noting that "the skin hung in strips from his nose, which did not improve his appearance."[85]

Their revulsion continued when the president's party reached Mammoth Hot Springs. Rather than lodge in the relatively elegant confines of the National Hotel, the sojourners opted to rough it in an enclosed lot adjacent to the superintendent's residence. Snubbed but undaunted, Hatch sent a "quartet of English voices" out to serenade the president around his campfire and to invite him to a hotel reception. Arthur agreed, but with the Hatch party clothed in their finest apparel, the American head of state and his entourage "shocked" the English visitors with "the informality of the affair and the neglect of niceties of full dress." To cap the offense, a verbal dispute between the president and Colonel Sheridan abruptly ended the affair. Arthur retired to camp, leaving the hotel waiters to enjoy the spoils of the party—"two dozen quarts of excellent champagne and two boxes of cigars."[86] Without question, to be in and around Yellowstone that summer was to witness a classic encounter of British and American culture.

Returning from a journey he described as "better than anything I ever tried before," President Arthur stopped to pay respects to the Villard party laid over in St. Paul.[87] At a gala dinner celebration, the president added to the testimonials being showered upon the Northern Pacific and the scenic crown of its commercial empire:

> Coming to you from that wonderland of America, I have traveled a
> thousand miles by the Northern Pacific railroad. Nothing I have
> read, nothing I have ever heard, has equaled what I have seen, which
> convinces me of the importance of this great enterprise, and that it
> has not been over-estimated by its most sanguine friends. All honor,
> then, to the zeal and energy which has given to that enterprise such
> tremendous success.[88]

Speaking less of nature than of commerce, the president's effusive praise of "the enterprise" fuses the Northern Pacific to Yellowstone, proclaiming both as monuments on the landscape of American capitalism.

But before the dust settled that summer, the euphoria of the railroad's Yellowstone venture was on the wane. While still in the park, the preservation-minded presidential excursion caught strong wind of Hatch's activities. One dissatisfied tourist told Senator Vest that after having arranged for a Montana man to guide him through the park, Superintendent Conger informed him that, via the Improvement Company, Wakefield and Hoffman held exclusive transportation rights. The upset traveler took the notice to Vest, who "read it, handed it to President Arthur, and burst out, 'There, I told you that [they were] in collusion with this Park Improvement Company.'" Arthur reportedly laughed it off, but the order was immediately revoked in favor of the vexed tourist.[89] Hatch did not help his cause when he tried to provide a little comic western theater to the presidential party. Dressing himself as a cowboy and surprising Arthur in his camp, the financial wizard nearly got himself apprehended: unbeknownst to Hatch, a rumored kidnapping plot of the president involving a Texas desperado, sixty-five cowboys and renegade Indians, had the soldiers on alert and spoiled the fun.[90]

When a reporter informed Hatch that Vest, Sheridan, President Arthur and Secretary Teller held a summit meeting in the park to "[declare] war on Uncle Rufus," Hatch grew indignant: "Congress has no power to go behind our contract, nor can it dissolve the bargain. I could have saved all this trouble last winter by employing a certain Senator as attorney for $5,000 per year to grease the wheels." He went on to announce his desire for a railroad into Yellowstone Park.[91] The *Chicago Weekly News* summarized the agitated state of park affairs at summer's end:

> It is evident that the next Congress will have a desperate struggle over the Yellowstone Park. There are three departments now claiming to rule—the Interior, War, and Rufus Hatch Departments. The Secretary of the Interior has felt so weak comparatively that no instructions have been issued to Superintendent Conger, whose hands are completely tied up. . . . The Hatch Government assumes to boss the park . . . and a free-for-all fight rages between the three factions. . . . The public is crying out for angels and ministers of grace to defend them.[92]

With the imbroglio now something of a national fiasco, Special Agent Scott Smith of the General Land Office investigated the situation in Yellowstone in October 1883. He returned with a report berating both the operations of the Improvement Company and the administration of Superintendent Conger.[93] Heated correspondence then ensued among Teller, Conger, and Hobart. Teller accused Hobart of violating park rules and Conger of not enforcing them. In the end, it proved easier to replace Conger than to challenge the railroad power behind the Improvement Company. This might have been a positive step had Conger not been supplanted by a brazenly predatory (and short-lived) administrator, Robert Emmett Carpenter.[94]

Meanwhile, rumors that the Improvement Company was floundering filtered northward. A relationship that began with Montanan open arms degenerated quickly as local merchants demanded payment for materials used in the construction of the Mammoth Hotel. The company owed substantial sums to local and distant suppliers—more than $85,000 to St. Paul businessmen for the furniture, carpeting, and glassware now gracing the hotel.[95] Conger wrote of widespread "dissatisfaction and resentment" against the company. One local described the company as a band of "marauders, vandals, and sharks" out to "Niagarize" the "Wonderland of the World."[96]

Problems mounted throughout the winter. Hobart pressed Rufus Hatch for capital, but nothing materialized. Uncle Rufus charged the company's failure to Vest's congressional investigation, which "weakened public faith in the enterprise."[97] Things got ugly in February 1884 as forty unpaid artisans who built the Mammoth Hotel staged a sit-down strike. They insisted on possession of the hotel until they were paid.[98] Hatch's predictable response to these events was to file for bankruptcy, retorting facetiously:

I have no hesitation in saying that I would consider a proposition [for the purchase of the company] from Senator Vest, General Sheridan, any officer of the Northern Pacific Railroad, William Endicott, Jr. of Boston, or even an honest cowboy.[99]

Ultimately, in October 1885, the remains of the Improvement Company reverted to, not surprisingly, a group of officials from the Northern Pacific Railroad. The Northern Pacific now held seven hundred of one thousand shares of the renamed Yellowstone Park Association. This raucous episode in Yellowstone concessionaire history ended where it began—with the railroad in possession of the franchise.[100]

Eighteen eighty-three is a watershed in Yellowstone history, most obviously because the summer's publicity windfall led to a sharp increase in visitors—American and European.[101] To the delight of culturally self-conscious Americans, Yellowstone's showy summer brought reports like this from the *London Daily Telegraph*: "When the European stranger reaches the Mammoth Hot Springs of the Gardiner river he will be more than repaid for having traveled 5,000 miles from England to see them."[102] English artist Arthur Brown produced dozens of watercolor sketches in the park that summer and transformed them into a slide presentation for English audiences, complete with "specimens" collected during his tour. At home, the *Livingston Enterprise* predicted that after the season's "gratuitous advertising," future seasons in Yellowstone would find park hotels "as crowded as are those of Long Branch or Coney Island." A group of New York artists painted fifty panoramic views, measuring thirteen by eight feet, for use in a touring play about Yellowstone. And years later, visitors still referred to "Mr. Haynes' camera" which presented the president's "famous expedition of 1883" to the world.[103] American affection for Yellowstone Park truly commenced in 1883.

Less discernible then was the political impact of the Hatch and Arthur excursions. While the president himself took no decisive action regarding the park, Senator Vest, as George Grinnell editorialized, "did not travel with closed eyes and ears." He believed the trip strengthened the resolve of all those working for improved management and protection of Yellowstone Park.[104] Among that group was Lieutenant Daniel Kingman of the Army Corps of Engineers. Appointed in the spring of 1883 to engineer construction of Yellowstone's Grand Loop Road connecting major features, Kingman outlined the stakes of the impending struggle over Yellowstone's development:

Then, if there are numerous small, quiet hotels scattered here and there throughout the Park, where visitors can have plain and simple accommodations at moderate prices, the overworked and the sick, as well as the curious, will come here . . . But if it ever becomes the resort of fashion, if its forests are stripped to rear mammoth hotels, if the race-course, the drinking saloon and gambling table invade it, if its valleys are scarred by railroads, and its hills pierced by tunnels, if its purity and quiet are destroyed and broken by the noise and smoke of the locomotive . . . then it will cease to belong to the whole people, and will interest only those that it helps to enrich, and will be unworthy of the care and protection of the National Government.[105]

As Kingman's alarming picture suggests, the Hatch fiasco established the terms of debate over Yellowstone's future. After more than a decade when the railroad's commercial vision dominated, a more national, public view of the park began to emerge. Civilian defenders and park officials set out to define the rudimentary framework for modern national park management.

A harbinger of twentieth-century environmentalism, the protection crusade nonetheless incorporated the inherent contradictions of nature preservation in a modern industrialized society. Champions of the receding wilderness, park defenders also were leaders of that civilization. In 1883 these early conservation patriarchs initiated a successful attack on the monopolistic capture and exploitation of Yellowstone, which offended democratic sensibilities. At the same time they brought to the debate a set of romantic notions about wilderness that promoted the orderly control and visual consumption of Yellowstone. Wise stewards, crass villains, but mostly in between, Euro-Americans were now in charge of the national park. That summer's three journeys punctuated the imperial position they now enjoyed over nature, Native Americans, and the past.

A trainload of irony accompanied the celebrity stature and preservation impulse brought to Wonderland in 1883. The events in and around Yellowstone National Park that summer celebrated human mastery of the continent even as they promised a more dutiful preservation of the nation's pleasure ground. Commencement of the stewardship discourse began only after Wonderland had been incorporated into the market economy by way of the Northern Pacific Railroad's conquest of the greater extractive landscape. The superfluous publicity given Yellowstone in 1883 served at once to instigate the transferral of Yellowstone's development and management to government experts, and to advance the increasing commodification and consumption of its natural wonders.

CHAPTER FOUR

The Eatable Parts

But scenes of beauty and wonder, that would entrance the lovers of nature elsewhere, become tame and casual to the sated senses of the wanderer in Wonderland.

—Ashley Cole, 1884[1]

I do not understand myself what the necessity is for the Government entering into the show business in the Yellowstone National Park.

—Senator John J. Ingalls, 1883[2]

MORE THAN A CENTURY after its making, few Americans perceive Yellowstone Park as a living, precariously balanced ecosystem. How then do we see
it? What *is* nature here? Dominated by the iconic Old Faithful, current popular notions of Yellowstone originate with the early rendering of this landscape. While the political struggle over the park's development continued
in the 1880s, the delightfully vexing cultural challenge facing Yellowstone
authorities was to comprehend the incomprehensible for increasing numbers
of visitors. Over the next two decades, park boosters and officials continued
to measure, name, and endlessly describe Yellowstone's most powerful,
bizarre, and spectacular features. Yellowstone enthusiasts successfully accul-
turated an inscrutable wilderness. They fashioned a romantic mecca, a pro-
cession of "sublime spectacles."[3]

The programming of Yellowstone engendered a more inviting landscape
by animating the psychic and emotional impulses of Victorian Americans.
Governed by the ubiquitous guidebook, the Yellowstone aesthetic heightened the expectations of travelers and gave sanction, structure, and meaning
to what was essentially the accumulation of images.[4] Park pundits—led by
government officials, railroad boosters, and provincial Yellowstone enthusiasts—drew on the fundamental themes of their late-nineteenth-century
world to determine what was to be seen and how it was to be understood.
Equally important, why it should be seen: the labeling and explication of
Yellowstone Park made visiting there a moralizing experience for upper- and
middle-class Americans. Yellowstone *literateurs* suffused the national park
with the language of romanticism, classical antiquity, Christianity, and the
technologically sublime. Ironically, yet logically enough, the familiar terms
of an urban, upper- and middle-class acquisitive society rendered inspira-
tional and consummable the alien and primitive wilds of the Yellowstone
country they had "set apart."

A Fine Art

For both explorers and tourism boosters, achieving some measure of understanding and control of Yellowstone's strange and feral wilderness required
first the assignment of labels. Throughout the nineteenth century, place naming allowed Americans to stake imaginative claim to the forbidding West. In
Yellowstone, national purpose and the foreign, mercurial nature of the
hydrothermal environment made the act of nomenclature momentous and
perplexing.[5]

The 1870 Washburn party firmly established Yellowstone's initial infernal
motif. With some apprehension in marking and describing sites like Hell-

Broth Springs, Hell's Half Acre, and Devils Den, Nathaniel Langford
defended the theme by asserting how utterly alien the place was, "so full of
exhibitions which can suggest no other fancy."[6] Tourists found the names
tantalizing and terrifyingly apt. The satanic strain of park nomenclature
received full treatment in an 1892 poem by William Tod Helmuth (a.k.a.
Satan) titled, "Yellowstone National Park and How It was Named."

> So hie you my Charon to earth, far away,
> Fly over the globe without any delay,
> And find me a spot quite secluded and drear,
> Where I can drill holes from the centre in here.
> I must blast out more space, survey the spot well,
> For the project on hand is the enlargement of Hell.[7]

With the hellish motif, Yellowstone tourists could dare the gates of a sinfully
tempting and terrifying underworld and live to joke about it.

Geological surveyor Arnold Hague considered it "one of the hobbies of
[his] life to see a proper nomenclature established in Yellowstone." For
Hague, an aesthete government scientist, naming was no frivolous matter,
nor was it to be left to amateurs. Throughout the 1880s and 1890s he and
his geological survey crew supplanted numerous place names that had gained
popular local usage with titles he believed were more befitting of the national
park. He found particularly offensive the habit of affixing obscure, locally
derived personal names to features that had identifying, suggestive characteristics. And so Hart Lake—named for Hart Hunney, an old-time area
hunter—became Heart Lake because of its shape; Mount Stephens is now
Prospect Peak. Hague allowed Virginia Cascade, named for the wife of a
Yellowstone concessionaire, because of a coincidental move to name some
features of the nation's first national park for prominent states. Many of
those which Hague found "exceedingly objectionable" are now either lost
to time or stubbornly embedded in Yellowstone nomenclature.[8]

Likewise, G. L. Henderson believed "the proper presentation of the park
[to be] a fine art." Henderson, whose extensive Yellowstone career included
assistant superintendent, hotel builder, concessionaire lobbyist, and tour
operator, ascribed hundreds of place names to Yellowstone features.[9] The
work of Henderson, Hague, and previous name-givers pleased naturalist
John Muir, a distinguished park maven. In an 1898 article, Muir found
Yellowstone sobriquets "so telling and exhilarating that they set our pulses
dancing." The names, he said, "conjure up fine pictures" and "call you to
camp."[10] Some were very fine pictures indeed. Despite Hague's intentions,
geophysical description often deferred to touristic allure: flattering appella-

tions like Sapphire, Ruby, and Silver, as well as the dozens of names culled from Greek mythology, speak more of the sophisticated heritage of the namers and an acquisitive society than the actual properties of the landscape.

Officials also faced the challenge of literally affixing names to the features. In 1880 Superintendent Norris posted signboards next to a number of "natural and artificial points of interest." The geysers, however, defied him:

> It is found that posts placed near enough to prominent geysers to properly designate them, unless unusually well set, are liable to be washed away; also, that the lettering upon the boards in such localities . . . is, from chemical action or the direct effect of hot water and steam, liable to be completely obliterated.[11]

Notwithstanding such resistance, officials continued to name and mark Yellowstone. Titling assigned touristic merit to a feature, allowing visitors to "experience" Yellowstone by checking off predetermined objects of interest as the tourist coach rolled by.

The omniscient Yellowstone guidebook provided the checklist and certified an authentic tourist experience. Writing for *The Century Magazine* in 1903, Ray Stannard Baker noted with amusement the tourists "devouring their guide-books and checking off the sights as they whirl by, so that they will be sure not to miss anything or see anything twice."[12] From the mid-1870s onward, guidebook and travel book writers codified, organized, and amplified the Yellowstone aesthetic derived from early explorers. A flood of guiding words for the unknowing traveler constructed the tourist landscape, determining meaning and governing perception. Consequently, the possibility of personal discovery yielded to the inherent predictability of consumer packaging.[13] Consumption by guidebook consigned the privilege of encountering Wonderland from the intuition and soul of the individual to the expertise of the authority.

This, of course, was the goal. As park enthusiast A. B. Guptill put it in 1885, Yellowstone literateurs were to "roll away the barriers of inaccessibility and dispel the mists of information and skepticism which have hedged in and enshrouded" the region.[14] The wording of Wonderland, then, displaced wonder and mystery with a set of predetermined facts, beliefs, and heightened expectations implanted in the tourist's mind. By the 1890s, the "mists" had indeed lifted and a circuit of attractions appeared. Guidebooks mapped the location and names of the "principal geysers" of the Upper Basin (fig. 26). In Yellowstone, as elsewhere, the work of mapping subtly exerted dominion over nature and devitalized its wonders. A map asserts ownership and knowledge of place. We no longer recognize this fact, but limning it bare

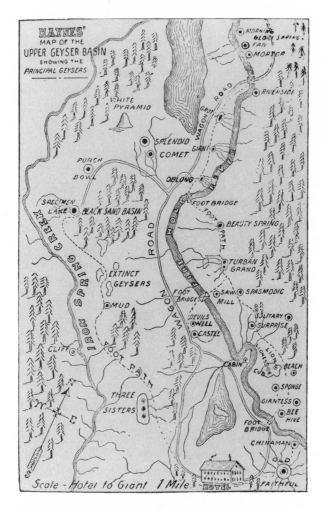

Fig. 26. Haynes' Map of the Upper Geyser Basin.
A. B. Guptill, with photographs by F. Jay Haynes,
All About Yellowstone Park. Courtesy Yellow-
stone National Park Archives.

with flat lines on paper attenuates the vital essence of nature. The cartographic projection of Yellowstone delineated perception of the landscape
even as it further authenticated its importance to civilization.

Manuals steered the pilgrim along the conventional tour of park attractions in a timely, regimented fashion. Indeed, the click-and-drive movement

of late-twentieth-century tourists seems rooted in the efficiency specifications of the Victorian era: "The next move on the program . . ." or, "It requires fully two hours to view. . . ."[15] Equally important, the "curiosities" were to be seen in not just any order, as John Hyde's 1888 manual made clear:

> While stop-over privileges . . . and opportunity [are] afforded for special excursions to such objects of interest as can not conveniently be embraced within the regular tour, there is nothing to be gained, but, on the contrary, much to be lost, by any material deviation from the route laid down in these pages. That route has many advantages, not the least of them consisting in the fact that the wonders of the Park are visited in such sequence that the interest, astonishment and delight of the traveler increase with each succeeding stage of the tour, until the crowning glory of the entire region is reached in the Grand Canon of the Yellowstone.

Virtually every guidebook prescribed this "natural order" of absorbing Yellowstone—starting from Mammoth Hot Springs and achieving the proper emotional "climax" at the Grand Canyon. The park itinerary served up the notable features as menu items to be consumed in order of visual delicacy. The railroad's five-day "couponer's" tour gave visitors ample time to see "fairly well the choice morsels to be found there." The Northern Pacific's *Wonderland* guide put it quite plainly:

> Where can I go—what can I see that is new to me—where can I have the most fun and pleasure . . . where can I see and learn the most in my vacation—or to concentrate it, as Armour concentrates the *eatable parts of a bullock* into a small vessel of "extract of beef." . . . [emphasis added][16]

As they devoured the sights, tourists also relied on the guidebook for scientific validation of an object's significance. Writers invariably listed the height of waterfalls, the estimated age and depth of springs, and the height and force of each "important" geyser. Measurement and science made familiar sense of Yellowstone, while oddly reinforcing the park's transcendent stature.[17] Yet numbers and hyperbole did not always match the reality, leaving believers disillusioned. Taking a tour in 1886, George Wingate took issue with the depth of the Middle Falls as it was listed in his otherwise "very accurate guide book. But whatever the measurement," resolved Wingate, "it is of appalling depth." Alice Wellington Rollins' guidebook had promised that the Obsidian Cliffs would "glisten in the sun like burnished silver." Upon inspection, Mrs. Rollins had to admit that "the cliffs are hardly a 'value' in the scenic effect." Some visitors recorded this fundamental concern of unful-filled expectations—an inevitable result of word-mediated, prepackaged nature. Lamenting the unrealized hopes of his Yellowstone visit, Francis M. Gibson attributed his disappointment to "having heard so much of its splen-dor and wonder" before actually visiting.[18]

Some travelers resisted the literary explication of Yellowstone and called for resistance to guidebook culture. Writing for *Recreation* magazine in 1901, Myra Emmons deemed imposition of scientific-touristic evidence "in vain" in the face of nature; "the Park furnishes all," she declared.[19] John Muir appealed to the traveler's transcendental impulse:

> A multitude of still, small voices may be heard directing you to look
> through all this transient, shifting show of things called "substantial"
> into the truly substantial, spiritual world whose forms flesh and
> wood, rock and water, air and sunshine, only veil and conceal, and
> to learn that here is heaven and the dwelling place of angels.[20]

Nature writer Ray Stannard Baker echoed the sentiment: "Undue emphasis may have been laid upon the odd, spectacular, bizarre—those things, dear to the heart of the American, which are the 'biggest,' the 'grandest,' the 'most wonderful,' the 'most beautiful' of their kind in the world." But, he urged, "the Park is far more than a natural hippodrome." The true "charm of the Park," argued Baker, was not in the curiosities, but in its "deep, untouched wilderness, the joy of the open road."[21] Like the presidential excursionists of 1883, followers of the era's "wilderness cult" took the advice seriously, camping off the well-worn paths of Wonderland's Grand Loop. Indeed, the call to surmount an increasingly circumscribed Yellowstone came as early as 1881, when a park guide named Sawtell, referring to a manual tourists car-ried with them that season, remarked: "If it were not for that there article in that there magazine, these yer springs would be considered a big thing; and I think the best way to do is, let the magazine go to thunder and enjoy the scenery!"[22]

Few visitors heard the plea, the trappings of interpretation being essential to the tourist "experience." Americans fed on Wonderland as it was offered: a parade of nature's sideshows at Mammoth Hot Springs, the geyser basins, Yellowstone Lake, and the Grand Canyon. There, sightseers found metaphor-ical representations of antiquity, industrialism, and Christian mythology. This thematic interpretation in turn prompted a dialectic of impressions sacred and profane, ludicrous and fearful, industrial and natural, bucolic and sublime.

Fig. 27. Liberty Cap and Capitol (left image). Courtesy Yellowstone National Park Archives.

Stairway of By-Gone Centuries

In his 1888 Yellowstone guide, *Wonderland Condensed,* G. L. Henderson directs the reader to sight number twenty-four, the Liberty Cap (fig. 27, center), standing imposingly at the foot of Mammoth Hot Springs. The author described the thirty-seven-foot-high cone of travertine deposit as "an ancient witness who could, if it would, reveal the sealed secrets of the past."[23] The protruding rock evoked the image of the ancient Phrygian Liberty Cap which graced early national coinage—symbol of both classical antiquity and Americana. Early park officials believed the Liberty Cap to be an "extinct" geyser in need of maintenance and repair. Worried that the monolith might fall over on some unsuspecting tourist, Philetus Norris braced it with timber supports, but the rock's enormous weight soon crushed them. Distressed but undeterred, the superintendent fancied another idea:

> [I]t therefore becomes a question of scientific as well as practical
> interest whether a sufficient quantity of water from the much more
> elevated Mammoth Hot Springs cannot be cheaply conveyed into the
> ancient supply-pipe of the cone, if, as seems probable, it is still open,
> or, if not, alongside of it, in order to throw an ornamental column of

water to any desired height. . . . [T]he terrace-building properties of
the water would soon encase this interesting cone with the inimitably
beautiful-bordered pools of the terrace formation, and also ultimately surround it with an effective and permanent support.[24]

Although Norris never executed the scheme, years later John Hyde's guidebook hoped that "the deposits of lime may gradually fill up the fractures and
cavities, and renew the youth" of Liberty Cap.[25] Yankee ingenuity ultimately
failed to "restore" what appeared dead and dysfunctional in the shadow of
the vibrant terraces of Mammoth Hot Springs above.

Writing for the *Magazine of Western History* in 1890, Francis Sessions
described the impressions of his party as they first approached the sight:

All at once we exclaimed, "Look at the Stair!" which appears in the
distance like grand frozen waterfall terraces, but it is only the white
formation from the Mammoth Hot Springs [apparently quoting his
guidebook] "exquisitely filligreed and richly covered terraces," and
we had a feeling of awe, as when we first visited Niagara falls.[26]

The awesome whiteness and cascading look of Mammoth naturally evoked
the image of America's best known sublime phenomenon. Some thought it a
"a frozen" or "petrified" Niagara."[27] Upon closer examination, the springs
piqued the scientific curiosity of visitors. Edward Pierrepont observed that
the

wonderful formations are in strange artistic shapes, made by mag-
nesia, soda, lime, sulphur, and probably silica, held in solution by
the hot water, which, flowing over, slowly hardens much as water
congeals when passing over a surface in an atmosphere below the
freezing point.[28]

For the writer of *Harper's Weekly*, aesthetics superseded chemistry: "at
least if you are not scientific, but imaginative, you will make up your mind
that you understand this process, and you will be content." He toured the
compelling artistry of the terrace pools, declaring that "the brush of the
painter has not yet succeeded in reproducing them." Visitors typically noted
that the sublimity and beauty of "the formation" could only be fully appre-
ciated by mounting it.[29] Images of promenading tourists (figs. 28, 29) invited
human presence.

Above all, Wonderland authorities tempered Mammoth's forbidding mien
by likening its geological formation to the course of Western civilization.
"Do you notice," asked G. L. Henderson in 1888, "how like our human

Fig. 28. The 'Formation.'
Rollins, "The Three
Tetons," 1887. Author's
Collection.

world is this terrace building world?" Its ancient origins evoked the millen-
nia of human history: "the stairway of by-gone centuries," Henderson proclaimed.[30] Accordingly, as tourists ascended the formation, they encountered
dozens of sights whose names derived from classical and Eastern mythology.
Intuitively elevating Mammoth to the status of European and oriental landscapes, the predominant Roman and Greek theme spawned such titles as
Diana Spring and the Hymen, Jupiter, and Minerva Terraces. At Minerva,
the more vulgar but essential predilection of desire yoked itself to discover-
ing the process of natural antiquity: known also as the "coating terraces,"
Minerva lured tourists and entrepreneurs to glaze various objects with its
flowing travertine, creating their own Yellowstone "specimens."[31]

While classical names humanized Mammoth Hot Springs, they also suggested transcendent timelessness. In *Wonderland Condensed,* Henderson
posited the unsettling question: "Will the United States exist when the Orange
Cone is done building?" The travertine cone began building, he noted,

Fig. 29. Mammoth Hot Springs Terrace, Yellowstone National Park.
George T. Ferris, ed., *Our Native Land*, 1891. Courtesy Montana State
University Library Special Collection, Bozeman.

"before the Divine Republic of Plato had been written." Mammoth's "Infant
Cones were at work," he declared, when Columbus set sail for the new
world; Liberty Cap "is older than Cleopatra's Needle, or the Pyramids, or
Solomon's Temple."[32] Such allusions elevated Mammoth to the stature of
Oriental culture, which fascinated Victorian Americans. But beneath Henderson's high-flown remarks lay the bolder notion that in Yellowstone's
colossal ancientness, nature had eclipsed the timeline of great human events.

Beyond souvenir making at Minerva, other Mammoth sites enhanced the
sense of Yellowstone as a mirthful, as well as meaningful, tourist locale. At
the Pulpit Terrace, visitors traditionally posed as a religious orator behind
the white terrace wall. Male tourists could take to the soothing mineral waters
of nearby Bath Lake (fig. 30), enjoying a "luxury which ancient Rome with
all her wealth and power could not afford her citizens." Until it was outlawed in the 1920s, tourists delighted in the healing properties and frolicking
pleasures of Bath, and later, Ladies Lake.[33] In the acculturation of Mammoth

Fig. 30. Bath Pools, Mammoth Springs. W. W. Wylie, *Great American Wonderland*, 1882. Courtesy Yellowstone National Park Archives.

Hot Springs, Yellowstone literateurs fused these diverse qualities—the sublime and the beautiful, the mythic and the merry—under the predominant theme of classical antiquity. Visitors to Mammoth found a baffling ensemble of wonders clothed in human terms but hinting at the infinity of nature.

The Terrible Side of Nature

Although Mammoth Hot Springs evoked the sublime archetype of Niagara, Wonderland's most singular appeal lay in its spouting geysers, which had no American analogue—at least in nature. Park mavens instead culled images from Christian mythology and their own industrial civilization to create order and meaning from Yellowstone's strange thermal features. Besides appearing foreign—appallingly so to many travelers—the geysered landscape proved somewhat precarious for sightseeing. L. P. Brockett's 1881 travel book offered a fantastic but fearsome locale:

Yet geyserdom is no paradise. . . . It seems more like a place of death
than life—your horse's feet are scalded in the hot streams—you must
be careful where you tread, lest the thin crust break beneath you,
and let you down into the boiling pools, and sudden death below.
The air is stenchful with the breath of noxious gases. Flowers do not
bloom; grass cannot spread its greenness; trees, if they come within
the circle of the geyser action, stand bleached, leafless, lifeless. It is
the terrible side of nature which you see.[34]

In 1883 George Thomas reported a visit to the Norris Geyser Basin (fig. 31)
as "never to be forgotten," while cautioning the prospective traveler of the
danger of "dropping into a hole and being scalded to death." Yellowstone
so appalled Londoner William Hardman that he could easily believe the Nor-
ris-born, guidebook canard that "the Indians avoided it as a place of evil
spirits." The *Brooklyn Daily Eagle* found it utterly uninviting, "a place that
one is willing to look at from a distance."[35] Clearly, touring geyserdom bore
little resemblance to a stroll through Central Park.

Yet foreboding depictions such as these further consecrated Yellowstone
as a place of modern, secular pilgrimage. Rather than deter visitors, the infernal associations and threatening nature of the geysers intrigued and helped
render the park worthy of separation. Since the ordeal of Truman Everts, the
travails of touring beguiled the adventurous to sacred ground. A few like
George Wingate declared the sight of steaming geysers truly Elysian:

These white and mysterious columns with their steady upward
movement appeared in the gray light of early dawn like an army of
spirits assembling; and gave one a most vivid idea of the Judgment
Day "when the trumpet shall sound and the dead shall be raised."[36]

Visitors more often saw hell. One of Rudyard Kipling's drivers found the prevailing analogy of perdition amusing, remarking, "seems a pity that they
should ha' come so far just to liken Norris Basin to Hell. . . . Guess Chicago,"
he mused, "would ha' served 'em, . . . just as good."[37] Americans variously
declared Yellowstone's geyser regions lurid, sacred, infernally profane, and
irresistibly compelling. Whether they thought it heaven or hell, the association of power and danger at the geysers hallowed Yellowstone as transcendent and, like some future fearsome ride at Coney Island or Disney World,
eminently touristic.

The freakish nature of the Gibbon Paint Pots (now Artists' Paintpots)
elicited an equally rich mix of impressions. "Here," said J. H. Dawes, "is a
steaming, bubbling mass of hot mud, of various dingy shades of color, the

Fig. 31. Norris Geyser Basin. Courtesy Yellowstone National Park Archives.

whole appearance much resembling that of a cauldron of boiling paint." Alice Wellington Rollins pitied their apparent inability to erupt: "sputter, sputter, sputter—gurgle, gurgle, gurgle—blob, blob, blob—and then for a moment, silence, is something so ludicrous that no one can stand beside it and not laugh aloud in sympathy." The Paint Pots effected farce, grotesquerie, amity, even beauty: Dawes found their colors "arranged with a precision so exact that it would delight the heart of the most methodical artist in Christendom. . . ." George Thomas had even heard that "the paint had been used and was good for paining [sic] houses."[38] There seemed to be both utilitarian promise and human artistry in the outlandish sight.

Similarly, the Midway Geyser Basin embraced contrary attractions provoking a polarity of responses. The horrific aspect of Excelsior, the park's most powerfully explosive geyser, had inspired the basin's most popular appellation—Hell's Half Acre. Fearing that, perhaps, the title was too ominous, Superintendent Norris affixed the name Midway in 1878.[39] Visitors invariably counterpoised the fearful connotations of the legendary Excelsior with the artful beauty of the Grand Prismatic Spring. As A. M. Mattoon put it, "separated by only a few feet there are two objects, the one superlatively uncanny, horrible and repulsive; while the other is exquisitely fascinating, beautiful and attractive."[40] Like the park on the whole, the Midway's capacity to elicit confounding reactions enhanced the view of the region as a commodious treasury of exotic phenomena.

With the largest concentration of thermal features in Yellowstone Park, the Upper Geyser Basin was the capital of geyserdom. According to Olin D. Wheeler, the locale boasted "not less than twenty . . . first class geysers."[41] Lying in the picturesque Firehole River valley, the basin's demeanor appeared less threatening than other geyser areas (fig. 20, upper image). John Hyde's guidebook instructed visitors to capture a panoramic view of the basin from an elevated mound near Old Faithful. From here,

> the entire band of geysers may be seen and heard as they give their concert with hot water trumpets in perfect diapason, each performer, at regular intervals, taking a solo part, and uttering his loudest tones in harmonic combination.[42]

This inviting musical similitude echoes the many narrators and visitors who referred to the geysers as "performers" on a natural stage. The Reverend Edwin Stanley saw the geysers "all out on parade, and all playing at once [in] a gorgeous display"; in 1901, a new wonder "opened" for public exhibition at the Upper Basin.[43] Advertising reinforced this view of the geysers as entertainers who played, often at their own impetuous whim, for human spectators. The geysers thus joined baseball, Barnum, and a host of other late-Victorian amusements of modernizing culture. For Americans to see the geysers as troupers was imaginatively to embrace them into their world as good, clean, anthropocentric fun.

Geysers not only performed, they labored. The geyser basins universally inspired visions of industrializing American cities. W. W. Wylie's 1882 guidebook likened the Upper Basin to "a great manufacturing city, except that instead of the vast columns of dirty smoke, there are here the white, delicate clouds of steam." A 1902 account of a Pittsburgh journalist thought the scene "curiously reminiscent of a Western Pennsylvania oilfield with busy engines drawing the oil from the bowels of the earth." One traveler saw the geysers "puffing like so many colossal engines." Norris Basin, wrote William Hardman, "is full of rumblings and murmurings" that sounded like the "noise of a busy establishment with much machinery hard at work."[44] For the urban genteel, the geysered landscape evoked the technological sublime of bustling eastern and European cities—without its attendant environmental degradation or class struggle. Here was a pristine fantasy of industrialization.

In geyserdom two of America's passions—nature and work—congealed. The fusion of the technological and natural sublime in the geyser basins and,

in a more palpable sense, on the broader landscape of the Northwest, satisfied a wider impulse in American culture: to be both "Nature's Nation"[45]
and an industrial power. Attraction to scenic–industrial landscapes—the
geyser basins appeared at once to be both—exemplified the paradox between
Americans' love of nature and their transformative, mechanistic civilization.[46] And by deploying industrial imagery, park connoisseurs ennobled the
work of geysers, suggesting modern purpose and elevating their power to
that of industrial civilization.

Scientific measurement naturally followed. Popularized in the 1890s, the
Bunsen Theory revealed the operation of the geyser basins' underground
"plumbing" system. The combination of modern science, the American pre-
occupation with statistics, and the impulse to control nature resulted in
geyser "timetables." A staple of any self-respecting Yellowstone guidebook,
they enumerated geysers by name, height, interval, and duration of eruption.[47] Along with performance schedules posted in the hotel lobbies, timetables exemplified the effort to domesticate these chaotic earthly forces for
pleasure. Some defied regulation: Francis Sessions believed the legendary
Excelsior geyser, for example, to be "too choice of its powers." Alluding to
Excelsior's eruption during the visit of President Chester A. Arthur in 1883,
Sessions complained that it "only played when generals or presidents come
to see it."[48]

No geyser performed to the expectations of anxious tourists like the
"delightfully accommodating" Old Faithful (fig. 32). For those disappointed
by "the capricious conduct of his kinfolk," Old Faithful proved to be the salvation of geyserdom. "The common run of geysers," wrote Henry M. Field,
"come at all hours, with or without warning . . . doing the most unexpected
things," and thus are "not to be depended on"; only Old Faithful "played
by the clock." "Dear Old Faithful," wrote Margaret Cruikshank, was so
"entirely all that we had anticipated and was so reliable . . . that we learned
to love him." Like many tourists since, one of her drivers condensed the
merit and meaning of Yellowstone Park into this singular attraction: "When
I invest my money in Geysers I'll take Old Faithful every time. Why if it
weren't for him, there'd be no Park, the whole thing would be a fraud."[49]

With its hourly play, Old Faithful became the emotive entree of Yellowstone, the point of mediation between a rational civilization and a capricious
wilderness. "With watch in hand," tourists anticipated the timely eruption
of Old Faithful with religious fervor. The sublimity of the scene, wrote William
Thayer, "[transcended] visions of the Moslem's paradise." Conscious of the
European landscapes of past travels, Theodore Gerrish equated the geyser
with the "Jung Frau, Lake George, and the Milan Cathedral." Visitors

Fig. 32. Old Faithful
Geyser. Hyde, *Official
Guide*, 66. Courtesy
Yellowstone National
Park Archives.

quickly and permanently established Old Faithful, the "reliable friend of the
tourist" as the park emblem.[50] Thus did the sentimental favorite of Yellowstone enter the iconography of the American landscape.

Although other spouters failed to meet the standards of Old Faithful, each
one absorbed a palpable human characteristic: the Castle "strongly [resem-
bled] the ruin of an ancient stronghold"; architecturally pleasing "fantastic
arches" drew visitors to the Grotto; the Economic Geyser favored them with
industrial efficiency, recycling every drop of its gushing waters.[51] Lavish
names like the Jewel, Turquoise Pool, and Silver Globe Spring lured tourists
to the geyser basins as well. Indeed, the Silver Globe prompted an urge, E. V.
Smalley wrote, to "realize solid wealth out of this phantasmal display of bul-

lion. . . . [and] stamp it with 'In God We Trust.'" A. M. Mattoon saw one eruption in moonlight and imagined a "fountain of pure liquid silver."[52]

Finally, although most observers described the geysers in gender-neutral terms, there were suggestive expressions of maleness: as in "[his] discharge . . . [and] clean shaft," and how "he gratified us." As overtly sensual as late Victorians got, Margaret Cruikshank's Yellowstone account crackles with an earthy personification of the geysers slaking the desires of tourists.[53] Other male park pundits like G. L. Henderson and Eugene Smalley wrapped the geysers in feminine sensuality, as in this depiction of the Evangeline:

> [Her] innner heart has depth and warmth and purity and power such
> as the poet ascribes to woman when most exalted by those human
> qualities that make her *the object of adoration* as sister, lover and
> mother of men and gods. . . . She seems to laugh as she tosses her
> jewels upward through the lavishness of one whose stores are inex-
> haustible [emphasis added].[54]

Smalley, a publicist for the Northern Pacific Railroad, likened the geyser craters of the Upper Basin to the "breasts of huge Amezons [sic]," in which one could see "indescribable beauty."[55] The feminine objectification of geysers was a natural metaphorical leap: after all, the billowing steel mills and smokestacks of the East that the geysers evoked were often rendered as "she" and bore women's names.[56] To extend the point, deeper patriarchal currents of Western civilization have for centuries viewed sublime natural and technological objects of power as feminine, and therefore in need of taming or control.[57] Casting the geysers in sensual and capricious terms fits that time-honored tradition.

With the geysers clothed in seductive names, florid descriptions, and prolific imagery, tourists voraciously consumed them. Georgina Synge boasted that her party "feasted on geysers all afternoon" in the Upper Basin. The Grand "fully satisfied" George Wingate's tour. Less fulfilling, however, was Margaret Cruikshank's day in the Upper Geyser Basin, which left her feeling cheated:

> So few geysers spouted while we were in the valley that I sensed the
> pictures in the guidebook (where from 20 to 30 are represented in
> full blaze) of prose exaggeration, but Ernest Clouph, who was with
> the party, who made the book, says he has seen between 50 and 60
> going at once. *Next time I'll stay until I am satisfied* [her emphasis].[58]

The traveler's visual hunger could only be satiated by matching experience to the commodified simulacra that lured them there. As the "Nation's Art Gallery," Wonderland beckoned tourists to appraise a colonnade of alluring pictures and artifacts.[59] But the museum motif suggested a hall of fixed, stilted images, not a mercurial, living environment.

When the geysers did not perform, tourists commonly tried to incite an eruption by throwing various objects into their craters. In 1883 William Hardman's party did their "best to provoke [the Monarch] by pitching great lumps of rock down his throat so as to destroy his equilibrium." Save for a "little grumbling," however, the Monarch resisted their proddings. Others laundered their clothing in the geysers. It "affords amusement to the tourist," offered Hardman wryly. Margaret Cruikshank remembered Old Faithful as the "good-natured monster" that laundered the uniforms of President Arthur's military escort in 1883. Cruikshank knew well, for she "did some washing there [her]self."[60] Profaning the geysers as appliances brought them closer still to the prosaic world of the tourist.

When word spread that laundry soap produced a volatile geyser reaction, sales boomed to a degree "all out of proportion to the standard of cleanliness" of park tourists. "Every impatient tourist," Arnold Hague noted, "wanted soap to feed his favorite geyser." Even he tried it "for the sake of photography" and scientific research. After assuming command of the park in 1886, the U.S. Cavalry "frowned upon" the practice.[61] Until then, geyser-soaping played on the notion of park features as performers—like feeding coins to a nickelodeon.

Tourist mischief also included routine specimen hacking and name carving on the formations. Superintendent Norris established the destructive precedent when he chiseled away a half-ton geyser cone specimen for exhibition at the Smithsonian Museum in Washington, D.C. At Old Faithful Rudyard Kipling spied sightseers who, after witnessing an eruption, proceeded to scrawl their names in the bottom of its surrounding pools, "Nature [fixing] the insult indelibly."[62] Owen Wister found the practice most unseemly:

> Why will people scrawl their silly names on the scenery? Why thus
> disclose to thousands who will read the evidence that you are a
> thoughtless ass? All very well if you wrote your name, address, and
> the date on the North Pole; but why do it in some wholly accessible
> spot where your presence represents no daring, no endurance, noth-
> ing but the necessary cash to go there?[63]

Gender- and class-based theories dominated public discussion of park vandalism. Acting Superintendent George Anderson noted "the propensities of women to gather 'specimens,' and of men to advertise their folly by writing their names on everything within their reach." Eugene Smalley warned of the vulnerability of park treasures to feminine assault:

> [I]n a museum of wonders and curiosities not guarded by coverings of thickest glass, and unprotected railings, and policemen, and the defensive force of the sense of others' ownership, "her" is out of place. In the Yellowstone National Park she is a brutal destroyer, a repulsive egotist, careless of other peoples' rights and happiness, pleased to murder the beautiful, happy in scarring God's finest work, delighted to scorn the grand and show indifference to the wonderful. . . . Essentially an American product, "her" is terribly abundant in our free country, and a conscienceless vandal wherever she goes.

Vandals, declared G. L. Henderson with the same conviction, were not of "the better class of visitors."[64] Clearly the matter transcended gender and class, and officials sought to impose greater discipline. Lost in sublime reverie at Mammoth in 1885, Theodore Gerrish encountered rude "indications of the old familiar civilization": bold signs with firm instructions, "'DO NOT WALK ON THE FORMATIONS'; 'GATHER NO SPECIMENS'; 'WRITE NO NAMES.'"[65]

Notwithstanding assertions to the contrary, vandalizing tourists were neither uncultivated nor indifferent to Yellowstone's wonders. The vain impulse to mark and retain material reminders of one's pilgrimage to a treasured cultural landscape was not without precedent. It followed instinctively the longstanding custom of relic collection at sacred sites, as well as the intellectual currents that gave this wilderness meaning. American culture having suffused and circumscribed the Yellowstone region, mischievous souvenir collectors reclaimed for themselves a piece of the sacralized, increasingly supervised "People's Park."[66] Without the customary protection given to an indoor museum, and with the sovereignty of personal discovery given over to the calculation and hype of guidebook culture, visitors marked their experience with audacious acts of individuality.

The conundrum of protecting Yellowstone surfaced again in the summer of 1885 when one less-than-guilty party of visitors was punished nonetheless, an incident which led to far-reaching change in the control and future of Yellowstone Park. In March 1884 a number of forces—persistent vandalism and poaching, the impotence of park regulations, and corruption and perceived incompetence of administrators—had brought an end to federal park laws and the imposition of Wyoming law in Yellowstone. At that point a cadre of rugged, unlettered frontiersmen enforced Wyoming rule, meting

out justice just as one might imagine. It did not aid their sense of fair play
that the act imposing Wyoming jurisprudence called for these officers of the
law to split the fines received from all offenders.[67]

   And so in August 1885, Constable Joe Keeney and Justice Hall unwittingly
apprehended a group of esteemed tourists for the "offense" of leaving luke-
warm coals at a camp site. The camping party, they soon learned, was led by
Joseph Medill, publisher of the *Chicago Tribune* and chair of the national
Republican party, and Judge Lewis Payson, a congressman from Illinois. The
"trial" that followed was a rude comedy of western justice, featuring, among
other things, Justice Hall seeking legal advice from Judge Payson and Medill
calling Hall a "damned old dogberry" (at which Hall summoned a diction-
ary to learn the exact meaning of the insult). Upon their return to civilization, Payson and Medill called for an end to Wyoming rule and the establishment of a "national tribunal" in Yellowstone.[68] At the same time, the U.S.
Congress was heading in the opposite direction, with many strongly arguing
that the park could someday be turned over entirely to Wyoming Territory.
In the end, the Wyoming legislature repealed its beleagured Yellowstone law,
and Congress, after heated debate, voted to end the troubled civilian administration of the park. The momentous upshot of the Payson-Medill campfire followed. With no funds and no other alternative, the secretary of the
interior exercised the most critical provision of Senator Vest's 1883 bill: he
brought the United States Cavalry riding to the rescue of Yellowstone
National Park. It would stay for thirty years.[69]

Searching for Arcadia

The national-park status conferred on the Yellowstone plateau set more than
one precedent. The first park in America to be so designated for a freakish,
even hideous appearance, it more likely evoked visions of a World's Fair than
Central Park. Yellowstone's unpleasant demeanor caused the most enthusi-
astic admirer to admit that the park was "not a 'pretty place.'" Ashley Cole
thought that "no one would take the trouble to visit it twice for general
scenery."[70] Equally unimpressed, J. H. Dawes reported to the Buffalo, New
York, Historical Society in 1891:

> The points where something of importance is to be seen are sepa-
> rated from each other by from ten to twenty miles of totally uninter-
> esting country. It has, of course, something of ordinary mountain
> scenery, but before one reaches the Park that has ceased to be a nov-
> elty. It has forests, but they are singularly dull and monotonous.

The "whole effect," added Dawes, was "dispiriting in the extreme."[71] Many visitors declared "park" a misnomer in Yellowstone. Picturesque archetypes of the East and the English countryside had ill-prepared visitors for this place. Bucolic, variegated compositions of meadow and tree proved elusive in Yellowstone. Here, the "face of virgin nature" was a burden between attractions. "The hills," Rudyard Kipling moaned, "are choked with timber that has never known an axe."[72]

Park narrators judged only a few well-framed arrangements at places like Gibbon Falls and Kepler Cascades to be "romantic beyond description."[73] Situated off the beaten path, Hayden Valley saw more bison than tourists. Yet as Olin D. Wheeler proclaimed, "no one who has a love for the good, the true, and the beautiful can look out upon this glowing exhibition of waving plain and not feel the spirit within stirred to something better for it."[74] Almon Gunnison found "infinite sunniness" in the view from atop Mount Washburn. "Arcadia," he wrote, "never had sweeter peace than this, with grass so green, and little streams so bright and musical," and, best of all, "no trace that ever human foot had found its loveliness."[75] Gunnison would never have guessed that Native Americans had beaten him to the spot by a few centuries. In these remote locales, romantics got the virgin history and moral virtues they expected from nature.

The majority of travelers drank in idyllic scenery at the ornamental Yellowstone Lake. "Stroll along the shore," urged Olin D. Wheeler, and the "esthetic part of our nature is ministered unto." The *Wonderland* booster pronounced it a "gem worth all we have come to see." Graceful swans and a "Petrified Indian" tree stump (fig. 27, left image)—presumably better than seeing the real thing—enhanced the aesthetic appeal. Tourists loved the custom of catching trout while standing on the famous Hot Spring Cone (fig. 33), turning and "dropping them into the hot water in the crater of the cone," thereby cooking them "without removal from the hook." As Nathaniel Langford predicted in 1871, Yellowstone Lake invited "adaptabilities for the highest display of artificial culture."[76] Another such accommodation was Captain E. C. Waters' *Zillah,* a "smooth-running, seaworthy little vessel" that added much to the "attractiveness of the lake as a resort," as Captain Anderson reported in 1891. The cruise afforded "marvelous views of forested shores and islets," along with a stop at Waters' "zoological garden" on Dot Island.[77] The *Zillah* deposited the Yellowstone pilgrim on the lake's north shore, satisfied of the picturesque and longing for the sublime spectacle that lay to the north.

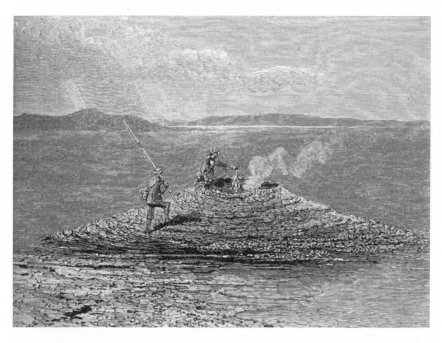

Fig. 33. Hot Spring Cone. Ferris, *Our Native Land*. Courtesy Yellowstone
National Park Archives.

The Art of God

At the Grand Canyon of the Yellowstone River, the rhetoric of consumption
endemic to Wonderland tourist culture came fully unhinged. Occasional references to the "grotesque" forms and "lurid" coloring of the canyon walls
recall visitor reactions to other areas of the park. Overwhelmingly, however,
travelers deemed this Yellowstone's Promised Land and gushed accordingly.
Nature writer Emerson Hough instructed tourists to "study it hour after
hour, to drink in with unabated zest the same view." *Harper's Weekly* called
travelers to "look and look and glut your eyes."[78] After the Grand Canyon,
declared Ashley Cole, "the sated senses" of the Wonderland tourist could
never again be satisfied. He declared the view from Inspiration Point (fig. 34)
"Majesty sublime: a memory for my dying hour!" as he peered into the gorge
below:

Fig. 34. Inspiration Point, 1881. Haynes Collection, H-675.

Before us stretched away the cañon, a great serpentine gorge, its peaks, turrets and domes, the faces of the mighty cliffs, the boulders below, all blazing with golden yellow and vermilion, mellowed with purple. Above, the blue sky; on the crest of the cliffs, a feathery line of green plumes from the pines; below these painted walls; . . . The scene looked as if some tropical sunset had burst in this fantastic chasm and splashed its walls and minarets with undying pigments of orange, crimson, violet and green.[79]

The railroad's *Wonderland* promised something for everyone in the canyon's democratic sublimity:

> The man of God will see . . . the power and glory of Jehovah, maker of worlds and ruler of the universe. The artist, the painter or sculptor . . . will think only of pigments and proportions in daring and heroic forms. The devotee of science will meditate upon the centuries necessary to have wrought such results, and strive to discover some principle or fact in geology. The lecturer . . . will think over what rhetorical periods and startling comparisons he may frame, that enraptured audiences may hang breathless upon his words. The common run of humanity, the *hoi polloi,* will see a vision—a picture that causes them to stand in awe and silence, and caring less as to the why and wherefore of what produced such amazing results, "shall see of the travail of their souls, and shall be satisfied."[80]

Such florid prose—and there was lots of it—fused the secular purpose of the modern tour with the sacred spirit of ancient pilgrimage. Tourists digested views with evangelical zeal. Embracing the majestic Upper and Lower Falls, (fig. 35) the Canyon evoked the more heavenly aspects of the sublime—magnificence, light, color, infinity. Indeed, Yellowstone Park's "resplendent, awful gorge . . . culminated the glory of the holy place," and for many, redeemed its overall odd and hellish landscape.[81] Pilgrims came to "worship" at this "art of God." "Bare your head, humble yourself," Olin D. Wheeler implored.[82] The trek to the canyon—and in a larger sense, to Wonderland—helped to answer late-Victorians' ever-widening search for deeper spiritual meaning and sacred activity, of which their own lives seemed increasingly devoid.[83]

The rhetoric of the sublime drove digestion of the Grand Canyon more than any other sight in the park. "Who can describe the indescribable?" asked Olin D. Wheeler; then he, like so many others, took up the challenge, pointing out the "four special points" from which visitors were to view the sight. After proclaiming descriptions of the scene to be "beyond the power of language," George Wingate spent pages attempting it nonetheless.[84] Feigned inexpressibility served invariably as the preamble to a shower of details. The robust prose of the ineffable permeates not only promotional narratives but private diaries like that of A. M. Mattoon:

> All who have ever seen this tremendous chasm, stand ready to certify that no pen can describe, no tongue can give any adequate idea of the mingled grandeur, magnificence, beauty and sublimity of that

Fig. 35. Lower Falls of the Yellowstone River, from Red Rock, 1899. Haynes Collection, H-3903.

scene. . . . Inadvertently [the tourist] stands with bated breath and silently drinks in the grandeur of the scene that will remain a life-long memory with him.[85]

Awestruck Americans embraced the canyon as a celestial sight that more than any other rendered Yellowstone worthy of national stature. The precipice also inspired the old familiar nationalism: visitors compared it favorably to Niagara and ranked its "architectural" beauty ahead of European antiquities.[86] And again they put forth the romantically ridiculous notion that wild nature—at least at this sight—transcended the world from which they had come. Once more Wonderland culture pushed forward the radical core of the sublime.

On his first-ever wintertime trek to the Grand Canyon, photographer
F. Jay Haynes dramatically reawakened the sense of terror and awe that
marked Truman Everts's sublime Yellowstone experience almost two decades
before. Setting out in deceptively mild weather in early January 1887,
Haynes accompanied the renowned Arctic explorer and Civil War veteran
Lieutenant Frederick Schwatka, who had contracted with the *New York
World* for a chronicle of the journey. But a few days into the journey, the
party encountered the blinding snow and bitter cold of one of the worst
Yellowstone winters on record. Schwatka suffered a hemorrhage of the lungs
and was forced to abandon the party. What started out as "Schwatka's
Yellowstone expedition" was now Haynes's.[87] Undaunted, the photographer
and a small group of men carried on. Summoning images of the wonderment
expressed by Yellowstone's earliest visitors, Haynes later described the eruption of geysers amid the icy covering of trees as a "glorious" and "unprecedented spectacle . . . never yet beheld by tourists."[88] The party proceeded
to the snow-covered Grand Canyon before beginning the return trip which
would take them to John Yancey's cabin in the northeast section of the park.
At the summit of Mount Washburn, however, the party struggled for two
days and nights in the midst of a raging blizzard and very nearly perished.
They finally reached Yancey's with Haynes' ninety exposures remarkably
intact.[89]

The *Harper's Weekly* story and the subsequent photographs (fig. 36) rein-
spirited Yellowstone with power and peril. Such a death-defying struggle to
"discover" an increasingly predictable landscape in its wildest and most
inviolate condition seemed heroic and fanned the fascination with raw
wilderness experience.[90] With Yellowstone now "captured" in winter, another
barrier had fallen; another dimension of its wildness measured.

By 1890 an avalanche of narrative and imagery reduced the sublime
mantra to cliché and convention. Sublimity ultimately encased the gorge in
the sentimental glaze of late-Victorian America. Captured as transcendent
spectacle, the Grand Canyon was processed increasingly as pure image. Most
Yellowstone narrators amplified the approved drill of earlier authorities—
sometimes literally. As W. W. Wylie recalled in 1882, "Professor Hayden
Says:—'But no language can do justice to the wonderful grandeur and beauty
of the Canon. . . . '" Words and images led travelers to the preferred position for "doing" the Canyon. The Guptill-Haynes guide of 1894 pointed out
the exact location from which its frontispiece illustration was shot. Margaret
Cruikshank's "very best stereographs" drew her to the precise spot from
which Frank Haynes had taken them. Apparently she could not get enough,
for as she said of the images, "Didn't I *devour* them when I got home?"

Fig. 36. Great Falls from Red Rock, 1887. Haynes Collection, H-1893.

Sometimes the hype self-consciously prepared tourists for disillusion. Herman Haupt's manual described the scene as "deeply impressive, so much so that," adding without a trace of irony, "even with the most exalted anticipation the tourist will be greatly disappointed."[91]

Nay, *especially* with such exaltation. Like rote prayers before a statue, the cant of the ineffable fastened both transcendent meaning and insatiable expectations to the tourist's Grand Canyon. Integral to the comprehension and marketing of Wonderland, the celestial aura of the gorge primed visitors for a sensory gluttony of images. Beyond emblazoned pictures of heaven, pilgrims took from the park crescendo one more thing: reinforcement of the romantic premise that everything in nature and under heaven—outside the realm of the sublime that the canyon symbolized—was clearly something less.

In addition to the gratification of the Wonderland tour, tourists eventually consumed Yellowstone through the customary assortment of souvenirs. As early as 1890, the Haynes catalog of *Northern Pacific Views* offered the following beyond the photographer's stock of park views: postcards, souvenir playing cards, lantern slides, and "charms, gems, and circles."[92] With the mystic made plain and the sacred profane, Wonderland had advanced toward the ultimate stage of nature consumption. Tourists could now carry home with them facsimiles of a moralizing national landscape that served also as tokens of taste and class.

Kansas Senator John J. Ingalls had recognized it all as "show business." Transformed as a parade of romantic objects inspiring power, fear, beauty, and desire, Yellowstone whetted the Euro-American taste for nature as a virtuous commodity. Steered by an efficient inventory of preferred sights and preconceived responses, an audience of well-groomed nature sensibilities and consumption habits devoured Wonderland. The tourist vanguard of the late nineteenth century tempered chaos by presenting a natural theater of sublime and freakish attractions. They grooved a path between nature and culture and willed the inevitable upshot: Yellowstone became easier to know and increasingly difficult to discover.

CHAPTER FIVE

The March of Civil Improvement

[Yellowstone Lake] is dotted with islands of great beauty, as yet unvisited by man, but which at no remote period will be adorned with villas and the ornaments of civilized life . . . Not many years can elapse before the march of civil improvement will reclaim this delightful solitude, and garnish it with all the attractions of cultivated taste and refinement.

—*Nathaniel Pitt Langford, Journal of the 1870 Washburn Expedition*[1]

We reach the Fire-Hole [Lower Geyser] Basin . . . Here should be located good hotels and outfitting-posts . . . to the Upper Geyser Basin an additional eight miles, where a hotel should be located. From here to Yellowstone Lake via the Natural Bridge, fifteen miles. Following the shores of the lake twelve miles, along which good hotel accommodations should be found . . . to the Lower Falls, one mile, in the vicinity of which hotel accommodations should be found.

Following the Grand Canyon and on to Tower Falls . . . and back by Mt. Washburn to Mammoth Hot Springs, a distance, as traveled from the Lower Falls, of eighty miles, along which distance hotel accommodations should be found at least every twenty miles. At the Mammoth Hot Springs should be good hotel and outfitting accommodations . . . and on to Norris Geyser Basin, twelve miles, where should be located hotel accommodations.

—*Charles F. Driscoll, American Architect and Building News, 1883*[2]

Throughout this portion of the park the road is a fine one, furnishing at every turn captivating views.

—*Olin D. Wheeler, Wonderland, 1893*[3]

ECHOING THE PROPHECY OF N. P. Langford, architect Charles F. Driscoll
outlined his roomy vision for the improvement of Yellowstone National Park
during the eventful summer of 1883. With the Yellowstone Park Improvement Company fiasco in mind, Driscoll went on to vehemently reprove the
prospect of a "monopoly privilege" on tourist accommodations in Yellowstone. American democratic sensibilities had found unseemly the company's
abuse of the concessionaire privilege. Yet the assumption that Wonderland
would be connected and enhanced with an extensive system of roads and
hotels was itself never in question. Indeed, the certainty of the park's development had dictated administrative policy in its first decade: From the notion
that concessionaire rental fees would pay for park improvements to Secretary Teller's suggestion that franchise operators would protect the reserve,
presumptions of the virtues of private enterprise guided the thinking of park
stewards well into the 1880s.

Mismanagement of the Improvement Company only reaffirmed the
Department of the Interior's conviction that the railroad—not their misfit
subordinates—had to take hold of the park's development.[4] By 1888, the
Livingston Enterprise, reviewing the increased involvement of the railroad
in park affairs, noted "that the authorities look upon this solution of the
problem with relief . . . for that seems to be the only way by which tourists
could be certain of finding good accommodations, and government be sure
of securing adequate facilities for sight-seers."[5] It made perfect sense. If, after
all, the agrarian and mineral resources of the West were best developed by
the holy alliance of growing corporate-government power, why not romantic scenery?[6] In Yellowstone, as elsewhere in the increasingly syndicated western economy, business joined itself to a grand national mission. The combination of railroad capital, federal authority, and refined romantic aesthetic
would overwhelm the few crude and independent lodges that squatted in the
face of the park's incorporation. From 1885 through the turn of the century,
these larger forces suffused Yellowstone's built environment with both Victorian spectacle and the emerging fashionable rusticity of the modern era.
From a crude and alien wilderness they formed a cultivated people's park.

The physical domestication of Yellowstone was a three-pronged affair executed by railroad interests and the United States government and monitored
by the watchful eye of conservation-minded sportsmen elite. Architects
enlisted by the railroad furnished the park with rustic accommodations,
while the national government applied engineering expertise and financial
resources to improve roads connecting the attractions. For their part, preservationist forces designated themselves arbiters of genteel, republican taste,
most famously by establishing limits to the railroad's arrogation of the park.

Incurable romantics, they waged a tenacious, decade-long struggle against a proposed private rail line across the park's northern tier. Like most epic engagements however, the triumph of preserving Yellowstone's sanctity bore its share of irony and self-delusion.

Charles Driscoll's commodious vision would have placed a minimum of ten substantial hotel complexes in Yellowstone Park. Although never fully realized, his fantasy reflects the prevailing view that the nation's park merited accommodations more fastidious and more numerous than the provincial, scattered facilities of the park's first decade. Yellowstone's early locally bred hostelries had established minimal yet colorful boarding standards the railroad certainly had to exceed.

In 1871 Bozeman residents James C. McCartney, Matthew McGuirk, and Harry Horr constructed in the shadow of Mammoth Hot Springs several lodges for the accommodation of travelers. Ferdinand Hayden, whose party helped christen these first park motels that summer, described one as "very primitive, consisting . . . of 12 square feet of floor-room." In 1874, English traveler Lord Dunraven commended them only as "the last outpost of civilization—that is, the last place where whiskey is sold."[7] Immediately after the inception of the park, the three entrepreneurs applied for leases to secure their claims. Authorities denied their requests and showed them the park door.[8] Horr and McGuirk eventually relinquished their settlements, but McCartney proved to be immovable. In spite of an 1872 U.S. Supreme Court case denying the rights of squatters in Yosemite, McCartney firmly believed that possession prior to the birth of Yellowstone Park was nine-tenths of permanent settlement. McCartney prevailed, enduring into the late–1880s when he relocated his enterprise five miles north. There, still without a park lease, he continued to feed, house, and offer over-priced refreshment to tourists.[9]

McCartney's operation at Mammoth featured a bathhouse where travelers soaked in the reportedly healing hot spring waters.[10] General John Gibbon noted that tourists' preference of individual bath stalls varied according to ailment.

> Should you require parboiling for the rheumatism, take No. 1; if a less
> degree of heat will suit your disease, take No. 2. Not being possessed
> of any chronic disease I chose No. 3, and took one bath—no more.[11]

Scientific authorities certified the curative powers of Yellowstone's chemical-laden hot waters.[12] Some, including British Professor Edward Frankland, proposed full development. Blissfully linking their functional and romantic attributes, Frankland argued that

the enormous advantages of an unlimited supply of natural hot
water and steam for baths and heating purposes could easily be
secured, and this without interfering with the wonders and aesthetic
beauties of this most extraordinary and interesting region.[13]

The potential human utility of Yellowstone's most vital "resource"—indeed,
its *raison d'être*—seemed irresistible. From Hot Springs, Arkansas, to Las
Vegas, New Mexico, the notion of developing and preserving hot water for
pleasure had become automatic since the mid-nineteenth century. Moreover
Niagara Falls had been rendered both an icon of the sublime and a boundless source of industrial energy.[14] In flight from the excesses of urban America, romantics intended neither to suspend civilization nor keep its amenities
from enhancing the invigorating experience of the wild.

Notwithstanding the disparaging commentary of Margaret Cruikshank in
1883, most Yellowstone visitors found George Marshall's hotel at the Lower
Geyser Basin adequate, even picturesque. Robert Strahorn found it "romantically located, at the foot of high cliffs . . . with the Forks of the Firehole
River and a pretty natural lawn in the foreground and a cold rivulet dashing
by the door on the right."[15] Another practical romantic, Marshall channeled
that lovely Firehole River into a medicinal bathhouse and laundering trough.
To complete the visitor's nature experience, he offered an earthy bill of fare
that included deer, bear, grouse, prairie chicken, and squirrel.[16]

The most endearing of the park's early hotel operators, Kentucky native
"Uncle John" Yancey enjoyed a lease on a log hotel in Pleasant Valley from
1884 until his death in 1903. His weathered countenance reminded one traveler of "the prehistoric" aspect of the park itself. So too, his hotel (fig. 37),
which, it was said,

> belongs to the primeval: its walls are of logs; its partitions and ceil-
> ings of cheese cloth. The bedrooms each contain a bed, washbowl,
> pitcher, a wooden box for a washstand, one chair, and—carpet. . . .
> When there are sheets enough to go around, [the tourist] sleeps in a
> clean bed, but if the tourists occupy half a dozen rooms, somebody
> will—but we draw the curtain over unpleasant memories.[17]

Travelers found salvation in the downstairs saloon, consisting of two barrels
covered with a slab of pine board. Urbane Carl E. Schmidt visited Yancey's
in 1901 and reported his stay to be first-rate. While incidentally noting the
nearby excellent trout fishing, Schmidt wrote at length of the evening entertainment featuring Yancey's frontier tales, southern whiskey, and fine "Red
Rooster" cigars. His refusal to give change meant that patrons invariably

Fig. 37. Yancey's in Winter, 1887. Haynes Collection, H-1896.

drank more than they had intended, quaffing Uncle John's "Old Kaintuck" from three shot glasses, which, the proprietor boasted, had never seen soap and water.[18] Such were the comforts of early Yellowstone tourism.

In 1885 McCartney, Marshall, and Yancey symbolized the rather crude state of improvements that brought W. Hallett Phillips to the park on a U.S. Senate investigation. Phillips deemed tourist infrastructure generally pathetic. He called for the demolition of "unsightly buildings" erected by locals at Mammoth Hot Springs, as well as "an eye-sore" of a bathhouse and other Improvement Company remnants.[19] He condemned the entire complex as most unbecoming of the nation's park.

Equally appalled was St. Louis lawyer and hotel proprietor, Charles Gibson. Upon his initial visit to Yellowstone in 1885, Gibson declared to the secretary of the interior, "There is not a large city in the country that does not spend annually on its park more than the nation does on this park, which is worth all the city parks put together." Harrowing park roads, argued Gibson, made hotels a questionable investment.[20] Nevertheless, on the heels of the Improvement Company's bankruptcy in 1885, Gibson and a group of Northern Pacific Railroad officials applied for and received a lease of ten acres covering the major park sites. Gibson's unnamed entity acquired

Hatch's facilities at Mammoth Hot Springs and the Upper Geyser Basin, as well as George Marshall's hostelry in the Lower Geyser Basin.[21] The group then matter-of-factly "assigned their interests" to the Northern Pacific Railroad's Yellowstone Park Association. For the next decade, a labyrinthine series of deals involving railroad holding companies, the Interior Department, and two well-connected Montana businessmen kept the park franchise in the hands of the railroad.[22]

As the 1886 tourist season opened, the Yellowstone Park Association (YPA) assumed the operation of the Mammoth Hot Springs Hotel.[23] Until construction of Old Faithful Inn in 1903, the Mammoth Hotel stood as the centerpiece of Yellowstone's built environment. St. Paul architect Leroy S. Buffington had designed this masterpiece of Gilded Age ostentatiousness in 1882 (fig. 38).[24] Loudly Victorian, the hotel boasted a Queen Anne-style tower, veranda and windows, and a garish green and red finish. One ruthless critic thought it bore "an air of discomfort" amid the austere Yellowstone landscape. Later, after a paint job, Rudyard Kipling dubbed it a "huge yellow barn."[25]

Rufus Hatch had spared no expense in the design and outfitting of the hotel interior. The U.S. Electric Light Company, which earlier in 1883 had engineered the illumination of the celebrated Brooklyn Bridge, arrived to light the piazza and corridors of the hotel. Workers dammed a nearby brook and laid pipe to bring running water to many of the rooms. Hatch imported two French chefs, a German baker, and two additional cooks from the East to prepare locally shot game on a twenty-two-foot-long stove. The hotel's entrance hall featured a long line of vermilion spittoons, a barber shop, two billiard tables, several parlors, a "ladies' department," an exhibition of local taxidermy, a Steinway grand pianoforte, and a stuffed mountain lion holding a plaque in his mouth which read, "MEET ME BY MOONLIGHT ALONE!"[26] Alice Wellington Rollins found the museumized wildlife a romantic and exotic treat. The stuffed animals, she noted, were "singularly life-like, [and] seemed to be running about at ease." It all spoke "of strange and new experience," Rollins said.[27]

And yet so very cosmopolitan. The *Livingston Enterprise* glowed that the hotel was "furnished and managed in . . . style second to nothing at the various pleasure resorts of the world." Londoner William Hardman called the hotel "simply the most remarkable product of civilization in my experience."[28] Indeed, the hotel's opening in 1883 coincided with the Gold Spike completion of the Northern Pacific Railroad—two monuments to American civilization in the midst of some of its most fearsome wilderness. The pre-

Fig. 38. National Hotel, 1884. Haynes Collection, H-1450.

tentious edifice helped to ameliorate the sublime monumentalism of the
Mammoth terraces (fig. 39). Profuse hotel imagery conveyed the idea that
civilization had arrived in the national park.

Less civilized, in retrospect, was the dumping of hotel garbage into open
steam vents and fumaroles in the vicinity of the hotel. This work happily
"[killed] two birds with one stone," according to one 1885 observer, "making [the ground] all smooth and clean around the building and at the same
time diminishing the number of pitfalls near the hotel."[29] Although crude
in modern eyes, garbage-dumping practices like this simply reflected the
urban refuse disposal pattern of the era.[30] Putting rubbish out of sight and
mind was a proper means of city beautification and must have seemed perfectly adaptable to nature. The practice produced regrettably similar side
effects: officials suspected hotel waste as the cause of a tourists' diarrhea epi-
demic in 1885.[31]

Beyond the Mammoth Hotel, the Yellowstone Park Association bought
itself a challenge. In 1888 Superintendent Moses Harris described all other
buildings as being "of a temporary character, of cheap and poor construction, and a shame and discredit to the National Park." The YPA's charge was
to increase, as Harris put it, the "appliances for comfort" available to visitors.[32] The Grand Canyon featured a "tent hotel" camp located "in thick
timber where the sun seldom penetrates, and [was] always cold and damp."

Fig. 39. Mammoth Hot Springs, 1895. Haynes Collection, H-3341.

A large dining tent—garnished, naturally, with limbs of lodgepole pine—offered the camp's only heat.[33] Situated in close proximity to the great gorge, the complex provided tourists with a convenient view of the Upper Falls. Actually, the hotel was *in* the view, violating the quarter-mile space between hotel and feature stipulated by George Vest's 1883 legislation. Still, Charles Gibson, catering to the genteel and anticipating the lazy modern, avowed that tourists would object to "climbing 300 feet" from the canyon precipice to a hotel room.[34]

In 1885, Assistant Superintendent D. W. Weimer characterized the tent hotel at the Upper Geyser Basin as "a shack and a disgrace to the park that should not be tolerated." The Firehole Hotel in the Lower Geyser Basin (nee the Marshall House) was marginally better, the walls constructed mainly of canvas, and the door, said one female traveler, "declined to shut."[35] Things changed for the better in 1891 with the construction of the popular Fountain Hotel. The hotel's picturesque location near the Fountain Geyser commanded a view of the Firehole River valley. It featured a bounty of tourist amenities: "steam heat, electric lights, and hot spring water in the baths," along with ballroom dances for military personnel and nightly bear-feeding shows.[36]

Although the tent camps of the 1880s eventually gave way to sturdier hotels like the Fountain, another park concessionaire institutionalized tent camping as an alternative form of tourist accommodation. William Wylie, a schoolteacher from Bozeman, Montana, first became acquainted with Yellowstone on a tour in 1880. Wylie then penned his own guidebook and conducted camping tours, leading his parties first "by the wayside wherever night found them," and eventually at a series of regularized, semi-permanent camp sites. Catering to both adventurous genteel romantics and visitors of more limited means, Wylie initially seemed to pose no threat to the railroad's franchise and operated with only an annual contract. But when Wylie's growing appeal allowed him to acquire a ten-year lease, the railroad's Yellowstone Park Association was not amused. Feigning concern that Wylie would "run the first class business away from the Park with the mobs he [was] taking in," the YPA predicted that Wylie would ruin the park and its hotel business.[37] They were wrong. Moreover, the popularity of "the Wylie Way" among a different sort of nature enthusiast signaled the coming democratization of national park tourism that would more fully arrive with the automobile.

To an audience less staid and more game than the hotel sort, Wylie offered a full line of amusements. The highlight was the popular nightly songfest. In the Upper Geyser Basin, a sign placed next to a piano reading, "Daisy Will Play ____," indicated the time of the Daisy Geyser's next performance. Wylie's Yellowstone commodities ranged from Yellowstone banners to wildlife skins and Indian trinkets.[38] Notwithstanding the earlier cultural indignation over the commercialization of Niagara Falls, visitor frolic and tawdry diversions became an increasingly vital part of nature tourism in America.[39] Nature could provide both moral uplift and frivolous divertissement. Yellowstone, therefore, was both the Art of God and the Daisy Geyser. The park's organic mission statement—to preserve the landscape *and* to "provide for the benefit and enjoyment of the people"—had codified the all-embracing, slightly schizophrenic American nature myth.

A secular charge to preserve the sacred invited endless contortions. In 1889, a large fire at Yellowstone Lake suspiciously coincided with the construction of the Lake Hotel. After admonishing negligent YPA workers, the superintendent recorded his anxiety over the fire evil.

> Language and art have so far failed to properly paint the beauty of
> the Grand Canon; a single fire would seriously mar its grandeur by
> destroying its fringe of forest. The shores of Yellowstone Lake have
> already been disfigured by fires. A single fire would entirely destroy
> the beauty of what bids fair to be one of the most delightful summer-
> hotel sites in the world.[40]

Predisposed to tourist development and not yet aware of the ecological benefits of fire, Yellowstone authorities judged fire of whatever origin to be a
source of debasement. The imposition of human artifice, on the other hand,
as Nathaniel Langford had forecast, *completed* the lake view. And although
the danger of a catastrophic conflagration in Yellowstone had increased with
touristic development, the compelling assumptions of benign human control
obfuscated such dilemmas.

Redesigned in the colonial style in 1903, the observation veranda of the
Lake Hotel (fig. 40, bottom image) offered the most classically picturesque
hotel view in the park.[41] Architect Robert Reamer endowed the hotel with
what became customary accoutrements of the twentieth-century tourist: golf
course, tennis courts, and boating excursions. Such ambience also evinced
the urban Arcadian myth of the turn of the century.

> [It is] a splendid, modern hotel with the woods on each side of it,
> and the most beautiful lake in the world in front of it, and within its
> doors every comfort to be desired and good living withal.[42]

Construction of the celebrated Old Faithful Inn came only after two
decades in which a series of unbecoming structures blighted the appearance
of the park's iconic geyser. In 1887, Charles Gibson's architects condemned
the first as "unsafe and liable to fall down." With Yellowstone visitors "the
most highly cultured and fastidious people in the world," warned an assistant superintendent, "such unsightlyness [sic] on the part of [slovenly?] land-
lords is utterly intolerable."[43] For their part, the railroad complained that
Yellowstone had become a questionable investment, certainly not the profit-
making venture they had envisioned. While the Northern Pacific Railroad
continued to subsidize the Yellowstone Park Association, passenger traffic
to Wonderland, not park hotels, returned a profit. "The interest on [the YPA]
investment" in Yellowstone, Olin Wheeler objected in 1894, "runs through
the entire year, the income through four months." Considering that bottom
line, he declared in 1894, the general character of improvements was good.[44]

Two factors altered the economic equation and signaled the YPA's readi-
ness to erect more suitable accommodations in the Upper Geyser Basin. The

Fig. 40. Bottom image: Lake Hotel. Wheeler, *Through Wonderland*. Courtesy Yellowstone National Park Archives. Top image: Old Faithful Inn, exterior, 1904. Haynes Collection, (H-4601).

first was a change in the burdensome quarter-mile restriction between hotels and park features. *Harper's Weekly* found the provision of the 1883 law most irritating and complained of the "unwisdom of Congress" in curbing hotel location.[45] Bowing to public pressure, Congress amended the law in 1894 to a more inviting eighth-mile. Equally compelling inspiration came from the growing number of tourists entering the park through the West gate and demanding accommodations there. Frank Haynes, who by the 1890s

operated a stage line on the park's west side, intimated to the Interior
Department his desire to construct a hotel at Old Faithful. The Northern
Pacific astutely recognized that the time had come to invest in refined accom-
modations at the park's greatest attraction.[46]

And so in 1903 Montana businessman Harry Child, by then president of
the Yellowstone Park Association, hired midwestern architect Robert
Reamer to design and oversee construction of Old Faithful Inn (fig. 40, top).
Derived from the Chicago School of Louis Sullivan and Frank Lloyd Wright,
Reamer's architectural style emphasized environmental harmony and "hon-
est" structural features. After viewing Reamer's work on San Diego's Coro-
nado Peninsula, the urbane Harry Child sought to apply this developing
American aesthetic to the transformation of Yellowstone.[47]

Constructed almost entirely out of the natural elements found in the immediate landscape, Old Faithful Inn dripped with rusticity. Reamer cleaved and
extracted and fused wild elements to the design and construction of the hotel.
An outcropping of nearby rhyolite provided the building's pillared foundation. Workers then erected the frame with Yellowstone's lodgepole pine and
trimmed porches and railings with gnarled and deformed branches, evoking and incorporating the surrounding wilderness. The rough-hewn log walls
of the inn extended upward three stories and suffused rooms with the aroma
of mountain pine. Charles Francis Adams believed the inn a human wonder so organic it looked and smelled "as though it grew there."[48]

The earthy effect permeated the lobby (fig. 41). Looking upward, the
forested architecture suggested for Victorian travelers "a giant cobweb of
woodwork, a forest of pines, a gothic cathedral." Here, according to one
guest, was "the grandeur of vast forests conquered."[49] Sunlight poured
through large dormer windows and smaller gable windows. Reamer used
lava blocks, hand-quarried from the Yellowstone landscape, to form a fire-
place forty feet tall with eight separate openings. The many staircases were
"built of hand hewn, split pine logs with baluster posts cut from locally harvested, carefully selected gnarled tree branches." Artisans forged much of the
extensive ironwork on site from Yellowstone ore.[50]

Reamer furnished the lobby in romantic accord. Heavy oak tables with
leather-blanketed tops, oak couches, a "log cabin mail box, a rustic pine
shoeshine stand," and dozens of hickory chairs graced the lobby. Behind the
wild effect hid modernity, as electric lights feigned the appearance of burning candles. Workers hewed the drinking fountain from the park's volcanic
rock. Indian rugs covered the floor—a ubiquitous and brutally ironic feature
of railroad luxury hotels throughout the expropriated West.[51] From Haynes's

Fig. 41. Old Faithful Inn rotunda, balcony, 1904. Haynes Collection, H-5200.

Indian portraits to the tepee-like eaves of Old Faithful Inn, Native American veneer appealed to Yellowstone tourists, strengthening the touristic claim Americans now held on the vanquished region of Wonderland.

Old Faithful Inn signaled a clear break from the Victorian "air of discomfort" at the Mammoth Hotel. Robert Reamer instilled national park architecture with a more sophisticated nature romanticism. Having subdued and encircled the wilderness, the modern aesthetic applied its preserved remnants to a primitivist, material reconciliation with civilization. At the Old Faithful Inn, Reamer masterfully melded the Yellowstone landscape to the *fin-de-siècle* desire to "return" to nature. One could stare at nature, sleep and smell and sit on it, and buy the work of nature's children. Here was twentieth-century nature patina, if not the thing itself.

In the last quarter of the nineteenth century, the chief complaint of Yellowstone travelers was not hotels but the primitive condition and scarcity of park roads. When Philetus Norris assumed the superintendency in 1877, roads in Yellowstone Park consisted of a few Indian trails and privately built mining roads. Bannock Indians traversed the distance from bison hunting grounds along the Clark's Fork and Shoshone Rivers northeast of the park region to their home on the Snake River plains to the west.[52] "Yellowstone Jack" Baronett, who never collected a promised reward for locating Truman Everts, found compensation nevertheless. In his search for Everts in the fall of 1870, Baronett learned of the discovery of gold on the Clarks Fork of the Yellowstone River, lying just beyond what became the northeast boundary of Yellowstone Park. Sensing a golden opportunity, Yellowstone Jack astutely erected a sturdy bridge near the junction of the Lamar and Yellowstone Rivers—the only place between the Falls region and the mouth of the Gardiner River where the Yellowstone could safely be crossed. Even at one dollar per man or animal, miners found the span a great convenience.[53] The only other road of note belonged to Yellowstone entrepreneur, prospector, and diarist A. Bart Henderson. Extending southward from the Bottler Ranch (near future Livingston), the trail wound "up and down projecting spurs, skirting the edges of high cliffs and over-hanging the tumbling river, in a manner not at all calculated to soothe the nerves of a poor rider."[54]

In 1872, from these rudiments, Nathaniel Pitt Langford proposed a formative design for what became the park's "Grand Loop" road system. Not until 1877, however, did Congress appropriate funds for road construction.[55] With a relatively generous fifteen thousand dollars, Superintendent Norris proceeded at a furious pace. Over the next five years, he almost single-handedly built in elementary form 104 miles—a full two-thirds—of the future Grand Loop. Norris's concern with park roads stemmed less from a desire to accommodate the few hundred annual park tourists he received than from a strategic motive to defend against possible Indian attack (making the Yellowstone road a harbinger of the Cold War Interstate Highway System).[56]

Most guidebook and travel-book writers noted Norris's greatest engineering feat—the road past Obsidian Cliffs. Lying on the route between Mammoth and Norris, the promontory holds one of the largest deposits of this volcanic glass in North America. To centuries of Great Plains Indians, the obsidian was sacred and useful. It proved a roadblock for Norris. In 1878 he devised a novel scheme to afford access through the area:

It was accomplished by lighting fires upon the huge masses of glass which blocked the way, and then when these had sufficiently expanded with the heat, cold water was poured upon them, causing them to fracture into fragments.[57]

Finding them evocative souvenirs of displaced Indians and Yankee ingenuity, scavenging tourists gathered "specimens" of Norris's handiwork for
years afterward.

Construction progressed throughout the park so that by 1883, Hatch's delicate Europeans visited 160 miles of attractions by coach.[58] This was no
AAA-approved ride. One hears just how bad the roads could be in this harrowing report of the stretch from Gardiner into Mammoth Hot Springs,
penned by a journalist for the *Chicago Weekly News* in August 1883.

> I shall not attempt to describe the roads; they are beyond me. I
> divided my time between holding myself on the seat with my left
> hand, and pressing my right against the driver in order that he might
> more effectively manage the brake. When the rain burst upon us I
> had a strange longing to get hold of Hare and slay him (the compan-
> ion who had urged him to ride on the outside of the coach). My only
> satisfaction was in remembering that he was on the driver's seat on
> the coach ahead without a rubber coat or an umbrella. . . . [O]ur
> troubles had only begun. It grew darker and darker, and the road
> became more precipitous and dangerous. Some of the steep aclivities
> had become slippery by the rain, and in the middle of one a wheel
> horse went down, the coach groaned and stopped, and the driver,
> holding the brake with all its strength, called to us to get off and out
> as quickly as possible before the lumbering road dragged the team
> backward. Out we all jumped in the mud, and for half a mile strug-
> gled up through sticky clay soil that clung to one's feet like pitch. . . .
> The driver told us frankly that he was afraid. He could not see the
> road, and in some places a deviation of a foot from the track would
> send the coach tumbling down into a ravine. . . . [59]

The reporter did reach Mammoth Hotel, but the experience soured his view
of the park's future. Clearly, if Wonderland was truly to be the national
pleasure ground, travel would have to be remedied. Toward that objective,
the sweeping measure of 1883 authorized the Army Corps of Engineers to
assume the design and construction of Yellowstone roads. Heading that
detail, Lieutenant Daniel C. Kingman applied military expertise and a cultivated aesthetic vision to road improvement.[60] For the next four years, Kingman engineered construction of the Grand Loop and steadfastly opposed a
park railroad and any distractions that would smack of a "Niagarized"
atmosphere. Officials and tourists hailed Kingman's proposal for a "double-
track wagon road entirely around the Park." He envisioned a road extend-

ing south from Mammoth to Norris, to Upper Geyser, east to Yellowstone lake, and north to the Grand Canyon; there would also be a new thoroughfare from Norris directly east to the Canyon.[61] Over the next twenty years, construction of Kingman's arterial design rendered Yellowstone scenery accessible and visually consumable.

During the park's first decade, the road south from Mammoth Hot Springs to Norris Geyser Basin through "Hell Gate" Canyon had been the scourge of every tourist and stage driver. George Thomas, a waiter at the National Hotel, recalled the Terrace Mountain Road as "three miles of steep, sideling, roadway that in many places looked as though a wagon might easily tip over." Kingman's design avoided that route entirely, cutting instead through Golden Gate Canyon to reach the connecting road from Swan Lake Flat to Norris Geyser Basin. In the winter of 1884 G. L. Henderson hailed the vital importance of the new road:

> The new road will save thousands of dollars to the traveling public. There will be no more swearing at the Devil's Thumb [a prominent landmark along the road], where teamsters and teams were alike helpless in the hand of the invisible demon who grasped the wheels and manacled the feet of those who were unable to ascend without stopping to breathe.[62]

Frances L. Turpin styled the Golden Gate road a "fitting entrance to such a paradise!"[63]

By 1885 Kingman's workers had reduced the outlay of time required by tourists for "doing" Yellowstone Park by one full day, as thirty tedious miles were trimmed from the Loop. That fall, *Forest and Stream,* ever the vigilant park critic, praised the "sixteen miles of splendid road" extending south from Mammoth to the geyser basins.[64] Progress demanded more. In his 1885 report to the U.S. Senate, Special Agent W. Hallett Phillips lamented that although Kingman had made great strides in his first two years, "many points of the greatest [interest] in the park cannot yet be reached, except on horseback by trails. . . . A large portion of the Park," said Phillips, "will remain to the public *terra incognita* . . . unless additional roads are constructed." For the next decade or more, officials of the Interior Department and the Army Corps of Engineers continued to urge Congress to make the necessary appropriations that would, as Superintendent Harris put it in 1886, "enable tourists to visit the principal objects of interest without discomfort, and without pasing [sic] twice over the same road."[65] The latter point was key to Victorians' need for ever-changing novelty and sensory stimulation, as well as the enduringly American obsession with efficiency.[66]

Beyond the immediate physical accomplishments of his four-year tenure, Kingman established the morally idealistic tone of Yellowstone improvement. He worked "upon the supposition, and in the earnest hope that [the Park] will be preserved as nearly may be as the hand of nature left it—a source of pleasure to all who visit it, and a source of wealth to no one."[67] Kingman's sensitive vision met with mostly positive reviews. Of the road through Gibbon River Canyon, A. B. Guptill's 1894 guidebook raved romantic:

> The road, throughout the canyon's entire length, could hardly have been better constructed to afford a more complete and thorough inspection of the wild beauty of rock and glen, and as it nears its southern exit from the pass, permits a view of one of the many charming cataracts of this region.

The new road from the Upper Basin to Yellowstone Lake, claimed Guptill, "added much to the attractiveness of the Park tour, rendering easily accessible to visitors a new and extensive region, charming in scenery."[68]

So said the guidebooks, anyhow. Upon visiting, Francis Sessions complained that the road was so narrow he had to get out of his wagon and cut down trees to allow wagons approaching from the opposite direction to pass by.[69] Charles J. Gillis in 1892 deemed it "very rough": "Twice we forded the river," complained Gillis, "and once the passengers were obliged to leave the wagon and remove a fallen tree from the way."[70] In 1887, well after Kingman's generally hailed improvements on the Gardiner River Canyon road into Mammoth, Alice Wellington Rollins found the "steep, narrow road, through cold, dull woods of uninteresting dead trees . . . almost horrid!"[71] However bothersome, the pinched character of that and other park roads reflected the romantic landscape ideal that prevailed in the design of suburban borderlands and urban parks of the East. Having learned from Olmsted, the master, landscape architects situated roads and buildings carefully, being sure not to, as Charles W. Eliot wrote in 1889, "[destroy] the very thing in search of which we left the city."[72] In 1898 Park Superintendent James B. Irwin noted how Kingman had applied that philosophy to road improvement in Yellowstone:

> Nature cannot be improved upon; the wise policy . . . has resulted in the laying out of roads interfering the least with natural conditions, and affording the sightseer with the easiest, most direct and at the same time safest routes to those wonderful sights which nature has lavishly worked in the park.[73]

Nature, of course, *was* improved upon. Road designers perforated the
Yellowstone wilderness wherever its freaks of nature dictated. That included
the Firehole River, which until the 1890s "had the right of way and seriously
objected to being made to play second fiddle to man's notions and uses."
Nevertheless, by 1901 Olin Wheeler could report that

> by dint of persistent effort and good engineering, the stream was
> finally prevailed upon to stay in the new channel provided for it at
> many places, and with the flying years the road has developed into a
> serviceable one, as well as an interesting one scenically.[74]

Pushing a river channel around to make way for a tourist road hardly equals
the mineral extraction that went on just beyond the park boundary. Yet it
does not quite square with the modern notion of an inviolable Yellowstone,
where men have artfully obscured change and enlarged the "virgin myth."
Consider Kingman's romanticized engineering, the latter-day video guides
that cast the park in eco-terms, our own postmodern blurring of nature and
nature veneer, and finally the passage of time that has further melded roads
and hotels to the Yellowstone landscape. To be sure, what we have largely
been doing here since the 1880s is to make "serviceable" both roads and
nature.

Despite Kingman's best efforts, grievances continued. Notwithstanding
W. Hallett Phillips's urgings of 1885, tourists grumbled less about access to
remote portions of the park (it seemed quite remote enough for most, thank
you) than the continued raw condition of the Grand Loop. Touring Yellowstone in 1885, Theodore Gerrish bemoaned the austere design of the road
from Norris to the Grand Canyon:

> [It was] the most provoking pine-forest I ever saw. The trees grew
> from eight to ten inches in diameter, and they grew so thickly
> together that I wondered how a rabbit could run between them.
> There were little pines to the right of us and little pines to the left of
> us, pines in front, pines in the rear. Taken together, it was the most
> piney and pining time I ever saw.

After floundering along through mud-holes, over miles of tree stumps
unevenly cut, and nearly going over the edge of a cliff, Gerrish's only comfort was in knowing he had life insurance.[75] In 1893, a beleaguered sojourner
writing for *Harper's Weekly* echoed Gerrish, urging the government to "cut
the timber back" in order to allow the sun to penetrate and dry the melting

snows from the road. "A very trifling destruction of trees would greatly enlarge the area of the sun's energy . . . [and make] the roads passable several days sooner than they are now."[76]

More vexing than mud for most of the tourist season was the pervasive dust of even improved roads. Wonderland connoisseur G. L. Henderson vented the frustrations of many an early Yellowstone traveler with this stinging critique:

> Yes, I have, very much to complain of, but I don't know who to blame, unless it be the good God who made the magnesium and igneous rocks, so friable that they are easily ground under the great coach wheels, and become a powder finer than the finest flour. From the time we left Mammoth Hot Springs, until we returned, we were traveling in one continual cloud of dust. Oh sir! it is frightful! terrible! horrible! Dust to the right of you! Dust to the left of you! Dust all over you! Dust in front of you! Dust behind you! And Dust within you! Your eyes are filled with it, your ears are filled with it, your nostrils are chuck full of it, and every time you open your mouth to speak, your mouth is filled up with it, and I believe that the brain itself is filled up with it when you try to think! Delicate people couldn't stand it! Women hate it, men curse it![77]

The resolution of these problems appeared plain to Henderson. His 1890 diatribe against park dust concluded with a commanding call to connect Yellowstone's freaks of nature with a railroad:

> We have waited ages for steam, and ages for electricity, but man is now their master, and they are his slaves. We can now harness either of them to a half dozen magnificent coaches, each coach containing 100 passengers, and make the ascent to Golden gate in ten minutes, and to Norris in an hour. We can make these giants perform the circuit from Mammoth Hot Springs, one hundred and sixty eight miles, twice a day.[78]

Henderson's declaration is curious, considering his prior lambasting of the railroad's near-monopoly of park concessions. However, the Yellowstone namer and sometime-entrepreneur saw park rail service as a desideratum for democratic development. Once improved by an independent or government-operated locomotive, the national park, Henderson prophesized, would welcome

30,000 visitors annually, instead of a paltry 3,000, as now. The
shores of Yellowstone Lake will swarm with health and pleasure
seekers, the walls of the Grand Canyon will be lined with worshippers of the Infinite.[79]

Of course it never dawns on the capitalist mind that once swarming with
worshippers, The Infinite becomes a little less so. With the modern world
before them, Gilded Age Americans, in particular, could see no such irony.

Henderson did not cry alone in the wilderness. During the summer of
1883, at the zenith of railroad acclaim in the Northwest, the *Livingston
Enterprise* waxed brightly over the possibility of a "nice little railroad
planned to take in all the points of interest" in Yellowstone. With "trains
running several times a day," the paper gushed,

> visitors to the Park could be increased a thousand fold and made
> comparatively cheap, easy and altogether delightful. In our opinion
> there are but two ways to go about it; either go to the Park and
> through it with your saddle and pack animals, or let us have railroad
> convenience to every notable point, and steamboats on the lake. The
> economy of time would pay all expenses and the time one had to
> spare could be spent at points of interest.[80]

Wearied Yellowstone pilgrims throughout the 1880s sounded the entreaty
for rail as well. In 1883 the beleaguered Margaret Cruikshank "never longed
for railroads as [she] did there." Edward Pierrepont bemoaned the Yellowstone dust and hyperbolized that, "of the thousands who have visited this
amazing region, not one can be found who will not say that a railroad in the
park is a necessity." If a railroad remained prohibited by the government,
declared Pierrepont, "much of the value of the park is sure to be destroyed."[81]
Pierrepont did not expound on the point, but the notion of *value* in this context laid bare the point of the 1872 debate—that access to nature equaled its
worth in a market economy. The issue of rail allowed some park enthusiasts to raise this thorny, and still salient, issue: If wilderness cannot be seen
through the trees, if it does not receive the gaze of tourist millions, does it
exist?

To boosters of regional development in the early 1880s, the question
seemed rhetorical, a Yellowstone railroad, axiomatic. For them, the matter
centered rather on which railroad would penetrate the bounds of Yellowstone National Park and how it would be done. The Union Pacific Railroad
briefly vaunted the possibility of beating the Northern Pacific to the park
from its southern main line across Wyoming. The aggressive Northern Pacific

would have none of it and planned the extension of its Park Branch line southward from the Cinnabar (later Gardiner) terminus into Yellowstone. In 1882 the company's survey crews reconnoitered a route linking the park's main attractions and extending all the way to its southern border.[82] The St. Paul *Pioneer Press*—a regional booster of Northern Pacific interests—in an 1882 editorial predicted big things for Yellowstone once it was made rail-accessible:

> The tourist world . . . soon tires of the old and wants a new sensa-tion. . . . What a blessing, then, will be the opening of a railroad into a region like that of the Yellowstone, combining the unique features of its geysers and its endless variety of hot springs with all the attrac-tions of a wild mountain region. . . . [83]

Despite the fact that the greatest cost of a Yellowstone tour was getting *to* Yellowstone, railroad advocates believed that park rail service would democratize tourism. In 1894 U.S. Representative Henry A. Coffeen of Wyoming put forward the grand notion that a park railroad would spread the romantic nature ideal throughout the masses: "As beholding the picturesque and attractive wonders of nature enlarges the mind, purifies the heart, and raises man to the highest and best conceptions of liberty and truth," Coffeen intoned, "so should every man, woman, and child in our land be permitted, if possible, to see the glories of this great national park in Wyoming." However, as things currently stood, he complained, a citizen must journey

> around the park, so to say, and [come] in at the back door by tedious night and day stage rides [that] are so expensive, the time and incon-veniences so great, and the season for stage travel so short . . . that the great bulk of our population must forever stay out and remain in ignorance of the scenes of the park. . . . Is this park so sacred that it should not be viewed by the common people?

The democratic thrust of Coffeen's entreaty countered the increasingly prevailing view of railroads (at least among a "great bulk" of citizens) as commandeering, monopolistic forces in American life. The Yellowstone Park Improvement Company episode exacerbated that poor image in Yellowstone. Thus, Coffeen proposed to resolve the elitist isolation of Yellowstone with a government-regulated, common access, right-of-way through the park. That, he argued, would destroy the Northern Pacific Railroad's park monopoly and allow greater access to "the common people."[84]

In addition to touristic comfort and social equality, a more compelling but ultimately self-defeating force sustained the idea of Yellowstone rail. The reserve, as Senator Trumbull offhandedly suggested in defense of the 1872 Park Act, had indeed "gotten in the way" of industrial development. Beginning in 1883, a cadre of developers worked tenaciously to reclaim a piece of Yellowstone for the surrounding extractive landscape. Actually, it was Senator Vest and General Sheridan who joined the struggle that year with their proposal to enlarge the park's eastern and southern boundaries.

Wyoming fathers were incredulous. Governor John W. Hoyt, while recognizing the economic potential of Yellowstone Park for his region, had been arguing for greater access to the reserve from Wyoming, through existing park boundaries. Restricted ingress, he complained, deprived Wyoming of the economic benefits that had accrued to Montana since the park's inception; to extend the reserve in Wyoming's direction would further injure territorial development. Noting Wyoming's "fine cattle ranges," "promising mineral districts," and "vast areas of timber" that would be rendered worthless by the park's enlargement, Hoyt asked sardonically, "Can we afford the sacrifice of all these to the possible preservation of a few more specimens of buffalo, elk, deer and mountain sheep?"[85]

As an interested participant in the debate, the governor magnanimously offered this solution: rather than enlarge the park, the government should "cut off the narrow strips which lap over upon Idaho and Montana," thereby "releasing to the people of those neighboring territories important sources of wealth" (specifically the Cooke City Mining District). After outlining a detailed program for the protection and improvement of Yellowstone Park, Hoyt offered this soaring vision of the future:

> The character of northwestern Wyoming marks it for industrial use and improvement up to the limits of the park. With beautiful valleys, grass in abundance, charming trout streams in great number, splendid forests of pine fir and spruce, deposits of coal, petroleum, asphalt, gypsum, fire clay, and mica; with good indications of lead, copper, gold and silver . . . and last of all, with a favorable climate and scenery unsurpassed on the American continent, one finds there all the requisites to a prosperous future. The day is not distant, it should be very near, when a railway will traverse that region, touching many of the resources above mentioned, and leading by easy grade up the beautiful valley of the Wind, and across the divide, to the very heart of Wonderland, and to a connection with the proposed branch of the Northern Pacific. Then look for a rapid development of many industries and the grand progress of a region as yet but little known.[86]

Like a chamber of commerce brochure, Hoyt's vision underscores once more how blithely and deeply the rhetoric of romanticism wrapped itself around the totality of the American landscape.[87] In the center of this glossy dream lies the railroad, having blissfully become the force for resource extraction and the vehicle *into* nature.

By far the greatest political pressure for rail ingress into Yellowstone came from the direction of Cooke City, Montana. Since the 1860s, miners had been prospecting the area just outside what became the northeastern boundary of the national park. In 1870 they discovered enough gold ore to draw a steady stream of miners and establish a small settlement along the banks of Soda Butte Creek. A decade later, two key events seemed to guarantee the region a prosperous future. In 1880, Jay Cooke, Jr., son of the Northern Pacific financier, visited and invested five thousand dollars in the operation, pledging to extend an NPRR branch line to ensure the town's development. So heartened were the miners that they renamed the site Cooke City. (The name stuck, even though Cooke ultimately revoked his investment and failed on the railroad promise.) Second, although miners had been prospecting an area designated by treaty as "perfectly adapted to the wild Indian," boosters clamored for its release into the public domain. In 1882, the government fueled the Cooke City boom by expropriating the region from the Crow Indians.[88]

The following year, Colonel George O. Eaton organized most of the area's mining claims into the Republic Mining Company and two years later the mine produced $95,000 worth of silver-lead bullion. Those profits were erased, however, by the town's isolation and the high cost of transportation, the solution to which appeared obvious—rail linkage with the Northern Pacific. Because of the high mountains north of Cooke City, the most practical route for a Northern Pacific Railroad rail extension lay directly across the northern tier of Yellowstone National Park.[89] For the next decade, a railroad to Cooke City drew support from regional legislators and developers and the vigorous opposition of park defenders led by George Grinnell and Senator Vest.[90]

Conservation emerged early but only as a minor theme of rail opponents. In 1883 U.S. Geological Survey scientist Arnold Hague argued against the railroad on the basis of Yellowstone's value as the "continental watershed." Flying sparks from passing locomotives, argued Hague, could ignite fires and destroy the region's forest cover, which was vital to rainfall and agricultural productivity throughout the West. As evidence of the wisdom of preserving the Yellowstone forest, Hague cited the widely publicized contemporary struggle to preserve the Adirondack wilderness of upstate New York for the long-term economic benefit of New York City.[91] This glimmer of modern ecological theory derived from the 1864 publication of George Perkins Marsh's *Man and Nature*. Introduction of the watershed concept, albeit human-centered, presaged the later efforts of ecologists to view the region as an organic whole, as more than a progression of natural curios. Although not decisive in the debate, the deployment of the watershed issue posited a utilitarian value for wilderness in the future of the greater Yellowstone region.

To defeat the railroad, opponents had to defend the visually inglorious northeastern section of the park. Rail advocates argued that in this region— which the 1883 bill would have extended and through which opponents wanted a railroad—

> there is only one single object (outside of mountains) in all that country of any interest and that is the Soda Butte Springs, a fine spring and valuable, but the most forlorn, God forsaken looking place you ever seen.[92]

The guidebooks seemed to validate their argument, invariably finding nothing of merit there beyond Soda Butte Springs and that, said mine owners, could be protected by a surrounding acre or two of ground; Interior Secretary Teller concurred.[93]

Park defenders in and out of Congress stood firm, repulsed by the very idea of a locomotive violating the sacred space of the national park. They charged the Northern Pacific Railroad as the shadowy force behind Cooke City mining partisans. The intention of the company, asserted George Grinnell, was "not to tap the mines but the Park," believing that once the precedent of rail ingress was established, the line would have been extended through the reserve to haul tourists.[94] Northern Pacific officials naturally denied such clandestine interest. At one point, conservationists even rejected a proposal to return to the public domain that section of the park desired by the mine owners (north of the Yellowstone and Lamar Rivers), in exchange for a vastly larger (two-thousand-square-mile) extension of the park on its southeastern quadrant.[95] Supported by aesthete public voices such as *Garden and Forest* magazine, conservationists refused to accept such a lopsided land swap on the grounds that the section of Yellowstone in question was vital wildlife habitat.[96] Embryonic ecology had again reared its head.

Fundamentally, however, the railroad struggle pitted the cultural and economic worth of preserved nature against the potential of extractive treasure lying outside the reserve. In 1886, the *New York World* haughtily noted that the park idea "did us credit as a people," while bemoaning the fact that traffic must go around [the Park] at considerable additional expense of time and money. Traffic . . . is a power which is in the habit of winning in the long run in this practical age. It is to be feared that the commendable and sentimental side of our nature, to use a vulgar phrase, "bit off more than it could chew" when it started out on this vast park enterprise.[97]

In the pivotal congressional debate that year, Representative Lewis Payson of Illinois put the question in epic terms: whether or not a mine, "whose output . . . will be measured by millions upon millions of dollars, shall be permitted to have access to the markets of the world." A representative of the railroad unabashedly championed the cause as populist and utterly American, asking whether "the rights of citizenship, the vast accumulation of property, and the demands of commerce . . . are to yield to . . . a few sportsmen bent only on the protection of a few buffalo."[98] In the great Yellowstone rail struggle, the duplicitous and vulgar face of late-nineteenth-century capitalism went to war with its refined inner self.

George Grinnell kept the issue on the front pages of *Forest and Stream*. Presented in starkly environmental as well as class-conscious terms, the specter of a railroad intruding upon Yellowstone must have appeared disconcerting indeed to his genteel readership:

It remains to be seen whether this magniloquent threat of "busting the Park" (promised by Railroad Commissioner Armstrong) will so alarm the Congress and the people of the United States that they will tamely submit to see their pleasure ground taken away from them, to see it cut up by railroads, to see it dotted with towns in which are machine shops, dwellings occupied by railroad hands and saloons, to see its forests and its prairies burned off, to see its game destroyed or driven out of the reservation, so that it may fall an easy prey to the hide hunters and meat butchers.[99]

With a populist attack that oddly summoned images of lower-class rabble, Grinnell implored his genteel readers to the defense of "their pleasure ground." He cast railroad forces as iniquitous and unpatriotic villains who would blight the park with the worst elements of industrialism. The conservationist then urged Americans to fight the "attempts of monopolists to seize this pleasure ground. . . . Let them be content with what they have."[100] Other publications joined the anti-rail crusade. *Harper's Weekly* complained that the citizens of Montana had no more right to deface the nation's park with a railroad than did the citizens of Washington, D.C. "to set up cigar and candy stands on the landing of the Washington Monument."[101] Amazing, is it not, to think that such a modest American visage could ever so horrify.

Persistently invoked by both rail advocates and park defenders, "the people" spoke in 1892. Officials asked visitors that season for their opinion on the issue, and they responded emphatically with a five-to-one vote against the railroad. The weighted result of the plebiscite is particularly significant since it followed what many considered a less obnoxious proposal for a quieter electric system. Many voters cited their preference for the increasingly pleasant coach tour.[102]

The railroad campaign lingered on until 1894, when the president of the Northern Pacific announced that his company had examined the Cooke City mines and declared them not worth the investment of a branch road.[103] As park historian Alfred Runte has observed, this signaled a shift in the Northern Pacific's central but ambiguous role in Yellowstone's touristic preservation. Just as the railroad triggered the creation of the park and linked it with civilization, in the end its cultivation of the American love affair with Yellowstone provoked the park's vigorous defense. Throughout the rail imbroglio, the Northern Pacific Railroad moved in the shadow of the Cooke City miners, hoping ultimately to benefit from rail ingress. But as public opinion turned decidedly against the proposal, the Northern Pacific undoubtedly saw the greater value of an undefiled park.[104]

The withdrawal of the railroad scheme signaled the elevation of Yellowstone Park to a new realm of preservation. Wonderland's heightened value within American culture would henceforth withstand overt intrusive threats to its integrity. The victory of conservationists made indelible the image of Wonderland as an inviolate sanctuary whose boundaries could not be penetrated or modified. For the first time in American life, the railroad—symbol of the machine—was halted at the garden door, significantly at a place that had redefined the garden. Defeat of railroad forces more firmly drew the line around Yellowstone Park's steaming landscape and marked it a refuge from the most egregiously foul elements of industrialism. There would be in the nation's park no steaming locomotive or "railroad hands," a little less monopoly, and, at least for now, less access for the masses.

Beyond the emphatic definition it gave to the Yellowstone aesthetic, defeat of the railroad in Wonderland anticipated twentieth-century battles waged over other special places. Some, like the 1913 struggle to save the Hetch-Hetchy Valley in Yosemite National Park from impoundment, did not enjoy the same result. Conservationists lost that battle because of Hetch-Hetchy's isolation and lack of tourist access, reinforcing the lesson learned in Yellowstone and later applied to the Grand Canyon of the Colorado River in the 1950s and 1960s: that only places Americans knew well, from visitation or

through mass media, could be kept from the indomitable growth of industrial civilization. This struggle inaugurated the political privileging of familiar and sacralized landscapes. Finally, the success of park defenders further
elevated within the conservationist movement the ideas of watershed and, to
a lesser extent, habitat protection.

No such victory comes unsullied. The success against the railroad prohibited one physical intrusion from the park; the definitive machine of the age
would not pierce the reserve. But, no railroad meant that the groove in the
Grand Loop road grew deeper, opening the way for the monoxide-exhaling
stream of auto traffic and, unwittingly, the greater access sought by Henry
Coffeen. It was, ironically, that first decade of scenery-consuming tourists
and park commodification that led to the railroad's defeat. After seasons of
increasing visitation, the sensational summer of 1883, and prolific Haynes
imagery, many in Grinnell's audience knew of where he spoke. Timing,
indeed, is everything. Had the Northern Pacific pushed for park rail a decade
before, prior to the Improvement Company fiasco, before the rise of sportsmen-conservationists and the formation of the park aesthetic, they almost
certainly would have succeeded.

The nascent conservation movement came to the rescue of Yellowstone's
palpable integrity, but tastemakers never intended to reverse the park's cultural incorporation. While the affair deepened the Yellowstone myth of
sacrosanct virgin wilderness, this was, after all, a place well punctuated and
attenuated by the hype and ritual of consumption. The human-centered
terms through which the park was saved from intrusion illustrates the
embryonic state of ecology at the turn of the century. More importantly, the
proclaimed significance of such a victory underscores the enduring limitations and illusory power of nature preservation in a commodity-driven,
anthropocentric culture. This struggle was fundamentally more cultural than
environmental: in the end, the victory against park rail said much for the
ascendancy of a refined middle-class nature aesthetic; it suggested nothing of
the innate rights of nature.

By 1903 the acculturation of Yellowstone had advanced at Mammoth Hot
Springs as well. A map of the area produced by Yellowstone Chief Engineer
Hiram Martin Chittenden (fig. 42) shows the elk-horn-enclosed studio residence of F. Jay Haynes, Ole Anderson's store offering "coated specimens"
from the Mammoth terraces, and tennis courts providing recreational
diversion for those tourists grown weary of nature. Scattered among this
growing complex of buildings were several dozen "lawn hydrants." Park
Superintendent Pitcher envisioned enormous potential for the new waterworks system at Mammoth:

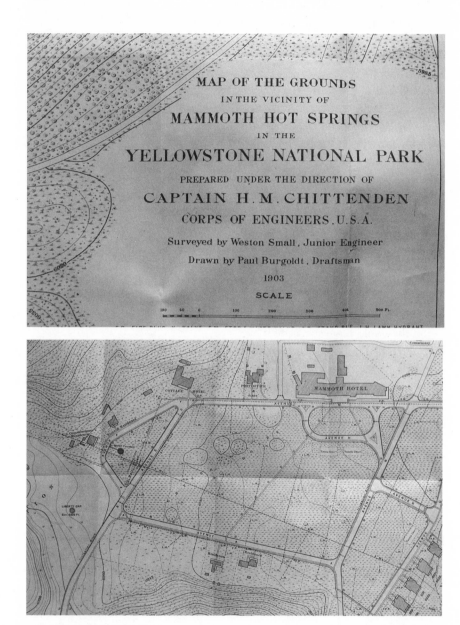

Fig. 42. Map of the grounds of Mammoth Hot Springs in the Yellowstone National Park. Prepared under the direction of Captain H. M. Chittenden, Annual Report, 1903.

It affords sufficient water to irrigate or sprinkle the entire plateau near the hotel and post of Fort Yellowstone, and the overflow from the reservoir, together with the hot water from a part of the Mammoth Hot Springs, will be utilized for the purpose of running an electric-light plant which is also in the course of construction.[105]

In his 1903 report, Superintendent Pitcher also announced that "a fair crop of grass and clover" had been planted on the plateau facing the hotel, which, he hoped, would "eventually produce a handsome lawn." Finally, the chief park authority reported that "a new system of roads and cement sidewalks about the springs" had been constructed.[106]

Celebrated urban landscape architect Warren Manning of Boston designed the new look at Mammoth. Manning imparted to the administrative and social center of the park the look of an idyllic borderland between civilization and nature. With more grace than the discomfiting National Hotel could ever deliver, Manning's aesthetic cultivation of the plateau tempered the menacing aspect of the white terraces looming in the background. His comprehensive plan for the beautification of the vicinity included extensive formal tree groves and "semiformal walks to scenic points" on the Mammoth terraces.[107] Although the plan was never fully executed, the partial transformation of Mammoth imbued the scene with the moral virtues only manicured nature could offer. As the *Gardiner Wonderland* declared in 1903: "The change that has been wrought in the face of nature on the old 'formation' at Mammoth Hot Springs is truly remarkable."[108]

The most emphatic human symbol at Mammoth was Fort Yellowstone, the origins of which extend to Superintendent Norris. In 1878, Norris constructed a residence and prisoner blockhouse on what he named Capitol Hill (fig. 27, center), the highest knoll in the Mammoth Hot Springs region from which he could "stand off the attacks of hostile Indians."[109] By 1891, with white tourists and game poachers posing the principal dangers to Yellowstone, the government began construction of a permanent headquarters for the park's military administrators. A decade later, the complex of Fort Yellowstone included a granary, hay shed, coal shed, hospital, barracks, and guardhouse (fig. 43).[110]

Fortification of Yellowstone spoke profoundly of the American desire to commandeer and defend physically from harm's way a culturally sacralized remnant of sublime nature. The manicured compound stood as a rampart between nature and civilization, a symbol of that society whose outdoor

Fig. 43. Fort Yellowstone, Mammoth Hot Springs. Haynes
Collection, H-4993.

museum required protection from itself. Fort Yellowstone answered the pleas
of genteel visitors like Henry L. Stout who in 1893 adjured for the park's
defense:

> It is the most wonderful thing on earth, and if it was anywhere in
> Europe they would build an impassable wall around it and open
> their treasuries to protect and beautify it.[111]

The garrison at Mammoth Hot Springs protected a wilderness whose transformation, orchestrated from within, was well under way. The collective and
occasionally opposed efforts of corporate concessionaires, cultivated park
authorities, and conservationist mavens fashioned the material Yellowstone
aesthetic. From the romantic masterpiece at Old Faithful to the refined garrison at Mammoth, Yellowstone's built environment featured a curious blend
of rustic natural elements and carefully delineating artifice. It complemented
well the literary circumscription of the park. Once melded to Yellowstone's
thermal landscape, richly bucolic hotels and earthy trails softened the horrific wilderness of Truman Everts and subsumed it within American culture.
A once unearthly landscape was now comfortably domesticated, its genteel
visitors properly accommodated.

The material improvement of Wonderland advanced the commodification of the park by authenticating and incorporating factitious elements of nature into the Yellowstone experience and by further imprinting already established consumption patterns. Tourists followed the Grand Loop from spring to geyser to canyon, obtaining glimpses of scenery along romantic pathways engineered by aesthete landscape architects. When taxidermic specimens of wildlife and cleaved sections of forest came in to grace the halls of Yellowstone hotels, venturing out on the chance to see the genuine article seemed a bother. For many, sleeping at the Old Faithful Inn, drinking in the fragrance of its lodgepole paneling, became synonymous with having "done" Yellowstone. The placement of hostelries in close proximity to park features further reduced Yellowstone to its attractions and melded human wonders to natural. In the end, though, formation of the Yellowstone aesthetic required balancing the genteel urge for comfort and the modern impulse toward efficiency with the nature romanticism that inspirited the landscape with cultural value in the first place. Proclaimed democratic virtue, well-bred taste, and genteel sensibility forbid the monopolistic capture and mechanistic intrusion of Wonderland's nature-enterprise, while culturally sanctioned roads and hotels manifested nature's eternal preservation *for the people.*

CHAPTER SIX

Indians, Animals, and Yellowstone Defenders

Senator Vest said to Charles the obstreperous chief of the Flatheads, "there are no more plains," and he was very near the truth. The wild Indian and the wild buffalo are in very much the same predicament.

—*Livingston Enterprise, 18 December 1883*[1]

The birds found here are apt to prove disappointing. All in all there are a good many varieties, but those usually seen are of the grosser sort.

—*Olin D. Wheeler, Wonderland, 1901*[2]

It is of greatest importance that the boundary lines of the park, in addition to being surveyed, should be so thoroughly well marked as to render it impossible for anyone to cross the line without knowing he has entered the reservation.

—*Park Superintendent Pitcher, 1903*[3]

MAKING THE YELLOWSTONE WILDERNESS visitor-friendly entailed something beyond the imposition of a romantic tourist infrastructure. It meant redefining and incorporating into Wonderland's tourist milieu the living, breathing elements of the greater Yellowstone region: wild animals and Native Americans. An increasingly visual culture rendered them as idols and effigies of nature, while park status bestowed the righteous and heavy hand of administrative government. In the last years of the nineteenth century, stewards of the Yellowstone country applied the perceptible aesthetics and taxonomic view of elite Americans to the management of wildlife and Indians. Bifurcating resources accordingly, Yellowstone authorities divided wildlife as good and bad, devised ways to keep noble animals in and evil Indians out, and similarly defined the worth of forest cover based on what side of the park line the tree stood. What flowered in Yellowstone was the management of nature by modern American rationalism.

The inexorable push of civilization reduced wildlife and natives to emblems of vestigial wilderness. Take, for example, the entwined near-extermination and touristic incorporation of Indian tribes and bison herds. Military strategy on the northern plains in the last third of the nineteenth century accelerated the slaughter of once-thundering herds of North American bison. This, General Sheridan urged correctly, would hasten the defeat of indigenous peoples who derived material and spiritual sustenance from the animal. By the 1880s the prophesy was in view, enhancing the lure of Wonderland: Railroad publicists and Yellowstone boosters fatalistically linked the vanishing Indian and the disappearing bison as paramount and now picturesque symbols of the vanquished American West. Park officials, although not recognizing the ancient ecological dynamics of the greater Yellowstone environment, vigorously enforced the Indian ban from the reserve and the containment of bison within. George Catlin's innocently contrived dream of a *"nation's park, containing man and beast"* was to be carefully defined and controlled.[4]

Sportsmen-conservationists led the movement for the preservation of select species of North American wildlife. Their efforts galvanized the movement to protect "noble" big game, which, both standing and stuffed, signified the American frontier myth they felt impelled to defend.[5] Anglo-American sportsmen affixed the language of rugged individualism, as well as the tradition of English gentility, to the democratic creations of national park and forest reserve. There, the ennobled creatures of their romanticized past might be viewed and stalked. Conceived by romantic aesthetes, sportsmen-conservationists, and park officials, the notion of wildlife preservation was particularly elastic. Animal exhibitions occurred within the bounds of Yellowstone Park, in urban zoos of the East, and in private parlors and public museums as stuffed "specimens" of the nation's cultural heritage. Aiming to extend this dilated faunal vision into the future, conservationists persevered, transforming the few surviving North American bison into the cause celebre for stronger wildlife protection measures. By the turn of the century, Yellowstone defenders had made the park a haven for choice disappearing species, and the refuge idea a compelling leitmotif of Wonderland mythology.

Even as officials fortified Yellowstone with more stringent protection, lingering concerns centered on the newly created forest reserves abutting the park. Sportsmen-conservationists applauded the designation that allowed the privilege of hunting Yellowstone's "overflow" wildlife. Yet they anguished over and fought bitterly the hunting activity of Indians, who, they charged, did not abide by the American sportsmen's code of ethics. The precise purpose of the new forest reserves was initially unclear: What activities would be allowed there? The sportsman's answer to this question raised another for park officials: How would one know when a prized elk had passed from the "wisely" used forest into the sacred space of the national park? Such anxieties sprang from a nature ethic that increasingly subdivided landscape into familiar and useable parts.

In the spring of 1903, these forest management concerns, along with a presidential act of ceremony, brought President Theodore Roosevelt to Yellowstone Park. The preeminent sportsman and conservationist of his time came to dedicate a massive stone arch at the park's north entrance. Representing conjoined myths of American nature and TR himself, this monument testified not only to the national park idea, but to the big-game-loving, national-character-building, history-denying, and forward-thinking conservation movement the president helped to lead at the turn of the century and with which he is still positively identified. The president's words there, and the arch itself, signify a paradoxical complex of beliefs that would throughout the twentieth century celebrate and bifurcate, glorify and damn, America's natural world.

The myth of a virgin Yellowstone long ago removed the park from history and humanity—especially of the native kind. Despite evidence to the contrary, that popular illusion endured—first to buttress the cultural superiority of Euro-Americans, later to support the archetypal image of unblemished wilderness we prefer in places like Yellowstone.[6] Park mythology embraced and embedded the superintendent's 1880 declaration of the natives' "superstitious awe" of the geysered landscape. Official Yellowstone's calculated expulsion of Indians necessitated in turn the suppression of the native story. Indeed, well into the twentieth century, one historian could argue that no one "of importance" lived in Yellowstone prior to creation of the park, just a "deteriorating, half-miserable-animal, half-miserable-man type . . . too despicable to be worth raiding or hunting down, even by lusty young Blackfeet, Crow, or Sioux braves hell-bent for scalps."[7]

But as other park historians have since chronicled, indigenous peoples shaped the landscape of the Yellowstone plateau and the surrounding region from prehistoric time through the arrival of Euro-Americans. To enrich their game hunting, native tribes deliberately set parcels of Yellowstone afire, thereby helping to fashion the Arcadian meadow areas tourists came to love and regenerating those cursed forests. Early explorers and officials encountered widespread evidence of Indian presence within the park, including numerous trails beaten down by the Bannocks, Arapahoes, and Shoshones (and used by the Nez Perce in their 1877 flight across the park), conically shaped lodges likely built by the Crows, various ancient archaeological sites, and freshly burned landscapes. Known as Sheepeaters for their dependence on the region's big horn sheep, the "half-miserable-animal" group of Shoshone Indians resided in the park year-round until their removal to the reservation at Fort Washakie in 1881.[8]

Having to expel Indians who did not exist, Norris exposed as subterfuge his claim that they avoided the place. He further orchestrated the negotiation of treaties prohibiting all tribes from entering Yellowstone.[9] A decade after creation of the park, officials had to pry another slice of the Crow Reservation away from the tribe in order to acquire full title to the reserve. By the time Yellowstone tourism began its steady increase in the mid-1880s, the U.S. government had legally, if not physically, contained the indigenous peoples of the region on adjoining reservations.

Supplanting the experiences of Native Americans in the Yellowstone region was a complex of imperious rhetoric and racially charged romanticism. The travel literature of the Northern Pacific Railroad and park publicists first of all assured prospective tourists that the United States government had righteously vanquished the Great Plains tribes, a conquest that further glorified the site of Custer's 1876 martyrdom. The Northern Pacific Railroad's *Wonderland* urged readers to visit the Little Big Horn en route to Yellowstone. Now that the Indians had been "whipped into a wholesome respect for the power of the Government," the visit was entirely safe and "well worth the time required," the railroad assured readers.[10] As early as 1881 the travel tomes cheerfully declared that "the Indians have gone for good and the era of fast coaches, good hotels, restaurants and bathing houses is coming on." In an 1887 interview with the *New York World,* Yellowstone concessionaire Charles Gibson reassured those tourists still anxious about the proverbial "Indian problem":

There are none [Indians] within the Park. They believe it is the abode
of evil spirits and don't like to go there. In fact, they will not even
talk about it. . . . The Northern Pacific Railroad, however, runs
through the Crow Reservation this side of the Park, and of course
there are Indians there, but they are so well guarded by the soldiers
that there is no danger to be apprehended from [sic] them.[11]

To the victor went not only land but the right to cast surviving Indians as
noble and picturesque elements of the landscape surrounding Yellowstone
National Park. As elsewhere in the West, natives assumed their place as ornamental display.[12] *Wonderland* featured innumerable images of stoically pos-
tured Indians decorating the borderland milieu (fig. 44). These Indians
played dead, lifeless objects of the tourist gaze. Artist Frederic Remington, a
frequent Yellowstone sightseer, found the Sioux "as a picture, perfect; as a
reality, horrible!" The tepees of the reconstructed Indian, as L. P. Brockett
wrote in 1891, formed "quite a picturesque feature" of the view through the
Yellowstone Valley north of the park. En route to Yellowstone with Henry
Villard in 1883, Nicholas Mohr found the distant view of "fantastic figures"
just what he and his fellow foreign guests needed for a "proper perspective
of this country and its people."[13] Indeed, their location on the borderland
between two worlds enhanced the touristic appeal of Native Americans. The
juxtaposed presentation of subdued savagery and conquering-but-refined
civilization reinforced the latter's righteousness. Indeed, Yellowstone mythology fortified such self-assuring superiority; what better signified the cultivation of the Americans than the *setting apart* of what the Indians in their
paganish fear and mundane urge to survive could not appreciate? The comments of 1883 traveler Gustave Koerner reflect the commanding dualism of
the park perimeter:

A few miles further on we saw a troop of Indians galloping near our
train and hallooing their deep 'ughs' by way of greeting. This contrast of refined and wild life was striking.[14]

Not only wild and exotic, these Indians embraced the world of their victor.
Northern Pacific advertising literature boasted of the natives' noble acqui-
escence to industrial civilization. Cheyennes, for example, "while retaining
their picturesque costume, follow agricultural and industrial pursuits, and
are independent of government aid."[15] The Indian-cum-citizen leitmotif of
Wonderland tourist culture grew more prominent over time. In 1895 the
railroad published *Indianland and Wonderland*, replete with images of
"strangely accoutered figures [and] noble red men," and balanced with the
industrious-native theme: "It would be a matter of surprise to many people

Fig. 44. Yellowstone Valley and Crazy Mountains. Courtesy Yellowstone National Park Archives.

who think that the only good Indian is a dead Indian to see the way some of the women handle sewing-machines."[16] Images of Indians huddled in front of missionary churches and government schools bolstered the claim of civilization on the march.

Ever malleable, the Wonderland Native was first and always *of nature*— the commodified nature milieu, that is. The cover of the 1903 edition of *Wonderland* featured an Indian showing the way into Yellowstone (fig. 45). Such imagery evoked the archetypal Native scout who shepherded the Euro-American explorer into the wilderness. Interestingly enough, some of the most fervent anti-Indian voices in the region suffused park features with superficial native myth. Demonstrating the shrewdness of the victor and the compliant versatility of the defeated, the normally jingoistic *Yellowstone Journal* invited tourists to Obsidian Cliff, a site "associated with a number of legends and traditions of Indian origin." Despite a fear and loathing of Indians, Philetus Norris urged tourists to visit Soda Butte, "the legendary spring of the surrounding Indian nations for the cure of saddle-galls of horse, or arrow or other wounds of warriors."[17] Some, like tourist Charles C. Howell reduced Yellowstone natives to facetious whimsy:

Fig. 45. *Wonderland, 1903*, frontispiece. Courtesy
Yellowstone National Park Archives.

It is said that when the Engineers first surveyed the (NP) Road, that
the Indian was holding a Gun, in the position of firing, and that the
Gun was Petrified and about 200 yards from the Indian stood a deer,
and the deer was petrified, and midway between the deer and Indian
was a bullet, and the bullet was petrified, and the smoke from the
rifle was petrified, and also the Blood from a wound on the Deer's
side was petrified in the most *beautiful* Colors. (The above petrified
story may possibly be somewhat exaggerated, but one can form an
Idea, and make due allowances for the rest.)[18]

Yellowstone's several "Petrified Indians" memorialized the silent, noble, and dead Indian that Americans had come to know and love (fig. 27, upper left). Both farcical and "legendary," this in-situ Yellowstone version mirrored the museumized Indian of both the exhibit hall and the cigar store.

Whether eager laborer, ready Christian, or rigidified child of nature, Wonderland Indians silently acquiesced in their demise. As J. L. Hill declared in *The Passing of the Indian and the Buffalo:*

> [T]he Indians of today can cast only a longing eye and reflect. The plains are silent to the tread of the old Indian host. . . . For the remaining Indians the painter, the museum and the art preservative alone can tell the story, even nature, the Indians [sic] God, is silent as to him and speaks not. . . . all now legend and myth.[19]

Legend and myth indeed, the vanishing Indian of Yellowstone signified and reinforced Americans' righteous conquest of the West. Lordly social Darwinism colored the pronouncements of Indian expiration:

> The Saxon has come. His conquering foot has trodden the vast domain from shore to shore. The weaker race has withered from his presence. By the majestic rivers and in the depths of the solitary wood, the feeble sons of the bow and arrow will be seen no more. . . . The Red Man sinks and fails. His eyes are to the West. To the prairies and forests, the hunting grounds of his ancestors. He says "Farewell." He is gone. The cypress and hemlock sing his requiem.[20]

Coinciding with the Indian conquest, the official declaration in 1890 of the closing of the frontier left a disquieting void in American purpose and made problematic the sustenance of national character.[21] Frederick Jackson Turner's brilliant and bombastic thesis of 1893 held that wilderness—specifically the taming of what lay beyond the frontier—was the birthright and central thrust of American history from whence all democratic goodness, physical achievement, moral strength, and racial superiority derived. Turner exemplified those Americans who championed the forces of modernity even as they looked backward and inward to resolve their *fin-de-siècle* angst.[22] With the notion swirling that America had simply become overcivilized, antimodern enthusiasts added to the pool of values represented by the national park the American creation myth of virtuous wilderness. Never mind that wilderness was evil until it was tamed or that modernity had arrived to impose bureaucratic order. These thoughts ran in circles. The four lines enclosing the wild remnant of Yellowstone Park acted as frontier; separating the sanctuary from both unsavory savages and civilization, they summoned America's origins. Pictured in stone, wood, photograph, or "legend," the petrified Indians of Wonderland stood as quaint artifacts of conquest. Like the ennobled wilderness itself, Indians were reduced to romantic emblems of a pristine past.

Transcending history, Native Americans of the Yellowstone region remained suspect villains when conditions warranted. Although the Crow had given way peacefully to the needs of the Northern Pacific and the boundaries of Yellowstone Park, some observers believed their remaining reservation too large. Expropriating the populist rhetoric of the day, Northern Pacific promoter Eugene Smalley delivered this baited attack on the perceived indolence of the Crow:

> [T]he progress of settlement and civilization up the south side of the Yellowstone Valley is stopped as by a Chinese wall. On one side of the river are new farms and the beginnings of active little towns. The axe rings and the plowman sings, and the music of industry fills the air. On the other bank all is silence and solitude. . . . Give the Indian his rights, we say, but do not let him monopolize the soil. He ought to be made to work for a living like other people. The Indian reservation system is the worst sort of land monopoly.[23]

Indian antagonists saved their greatest ire for the natives' alleged destruction of Yellowstone forest and wildlife. From the mid-1880s until the turn of the century, the ancient hunting practices of Bannock and Shoshone Indians to the west and south of Yellowstone Park proved a constant aggravation to park officials, local hunters, and conservationists. Despite the earnest paternalism of Indian agents to keep "their Indians" at bay, Bannock and Shoshone continued to set fire to select areas of the region as a means of encircling prey and regenerating feeding grounds.[24] Park stewards could not yet see the ecological value of fire that Indians knew through experience. Quite the contrary, their efforts to extinguish fire forever contributed to the final expulsion of Indians from the Yellowstone region and to the artificial suppression of wild fire for over a century. Thus is the nature of culture.

Superintendent Moses Harris declared the presence of Indians "a serious annoyance" to his cadre of soldiers charged with protecting the park. In the fall of 1888, he began demanding stricter policing of Indians caught roaming from the Fort Hall Agency in Idaho. Harris explained to the U.S. Agent in charge that, "the mere rumor of the presence of Indians in the park is sufficient to cause much excitement and anxiety" among the tourists. The reply from Fort Hall acknowledged the difficulties of controlling the Indians, but challenged the veracity of actual Indian misdeeds. "The complaints of the settlers," remarked the agent, "seem to rest more on their apprehensions on account of the presence of the Indians in said counties or vicinity thereof than on the actual wrong doing of the latter." In an uneasy Indian defense, he admitted that, "These Bannocks are bad enough," but complained, "I don't believe in making them out worse the [sic] really are."[25] There is little doubt that misapprehension and exaggeration of Indian activities exacerbated the conflict of cultures and their respective demands upon wildlife in the Yellowstone region.

The resultant storm of protest engulfed not only frenzied anti-Indian locals, but national newspapers and sportsmen-conservationists. On the northern plains in the spring of 1883, with market hunters and sportsmen about to annihilate the last great herd of bison, *The Yellowstone Journal* furiously decried the "slaughter" of "our mountain bison" by "the red ones." Wyoming resident Ira Dodge, "Collector of Wild Animals" himself, joined the fray, expressing concern for the "protection of our large game." Morally outraged, Dodge implored park officials to put an end to the "incursions of the Indians."[26]

The mainstream press joined the assault, as *Frank Leslie's Illustrated* spoke of "vanishing barbarism . . . taking a last revenge upon civilization." Condemning the agents at Fort Hall and Lemhi who could not "control their Indians," the paper took aim at the reservation system itself, which encouraged Indians to live "in idleness." Worst of all, they noted, Indians hunted "from love of game-butchery [rather] than from necessity of food."[27] Continuing a time-honored tradition, Americans projected onto the Native Other that which they hated most in themselves. Moreover, few understood the complex of Native American beliefs that emphasized material efficiency, spiritual reciprocity, and maintaining balance in nature and kinship between the animal and human worlds.[28]

In the spring of 1889, George Bird Grinnell's *Forest and Stream,* ardent defender of Yellowstone Park, began to grieve, as well. A well-educated and reform-minded liberal, Grinnell contributed much to the ethnographic study of northern plains Indians in the 1870s. He could therefore carefully distinguish the writers of *Forest and Stream* from "those who believe the Indian has no rights which should be respected." Yet Grinnell's allegiance to race, country, and the fire- and Indian-free sanctity of Yellowstone Park forced him to suggest restraints on the natives:

It is clear that these Indians ought not to be allowed to leave their reservations except in charge of some responsible white man . . . When . . . the Indian does anything antagonistic to the general welfare he must be restrained, and the Indian method of using fire as an

aid to hunting has in it an element of danger to agriculture in the
West which is most serious. It will not do at this late day to have our
only national forest preserve threatened in this way. It would be far
cheaper to supply the Indians complained of with unlimited beef
rather than have the forests of the Park perpetually endangered.[29]

Among Grinnell's colleagues, particularly his sporting friends, such paternalism seemed more than reasonable. Derived from reform advocates like
Helen Hunt Jackson, the goal of assimilating Native Americans into white
society became U.S. policy in 1886. Beyond its main provisions having to do
with land ownership, the Dawes Act demanded Indian responsibility and
respect for white laws and customs. The paramount issue of protecting
Yellowstone Park and its surrounding forests required control of natives,
Grinnell insisted. "When the Indian has been taught to comply with the
law," he argued, "he will have as much right to hunt on the borders of the
Park as anyone has. Until he has learned his lesson, he should be
restrained."[30]

Most Americans were less munificent. Letters to the editor from Grinnell's
fellow sportsmen decried "the deviltry" of Indian firehunting, and the "ruthless and indiscriminate slaughter" of game waged by the Bannock and
Shoshone. One particularly well-informed observer censured Native Americans for a reckless disregard for the future: "The Indian," he mourned,
"does not have a thought for the morrow, as by the fires he sets out he often
blockades the trail he wishes to travel the next year." There seemed to be
no limit to the sins of Indian hunters:

> I think I can safely say that these hunting parties of Indians do more
> damage (to game) than all the white men put together, with the excep-
> tion of the English pot-hunter, who desecrates the name of sportsman.
> . . . In any event, the white hunter can be dealt with whether he be a
> professional hunter, hunting for meat, horns or hide, . . . But alas!
> Who can control the Indians?[31]

Actually, the principle of control served cavalry officers rather well in governing not only Indians but wildlife. It would have been so even if park stewards of the era had been less commandeering scientists, for the cultural
framework that guided animal management sprang from enduring Western
cultural values. In Yellowstone as elsewhere, the biblical axiom of human
dominance over the hierarchical "lower" orders of nature supported the
ennobling of some species while condemning others to fearful animosity.[32]

The same categorizing cosmology of nineteenth-century science that ordered Yellowstone's geophysical features would do the same for its "grosser" birds and "noble" elk. Within that scientific paradigm, Darwin's theory that radically posited a less anthropocentric natural world ultimately was taken to reinforce human superiority and hierarchical ordering. Presumptions of the virtues of some species and the expendability of others through "natural extinction" prevailed (as did the exploitation of Darwinian concepts to fortify class and social relations). The same taxonomy castigated the "pot-hunting" of newly arrived European immigrants and extolled the sport hunting of Anglo-Saxon gentlemen.[33] Sympathy and protection for certain animal species was firmly grounded in the anthropocentric, bifurcating world view of established Americans.

In addition, the early management of Yellowstone wildlife occurred in a broader and changing cultural. In an increasingly civilized world, museums, urban zoos, and circuses offered increasing numbers of Americans their only view of the nonhuman realm.[34] Such fugitive contact with dead or living "wildlife" signaled the coming human-animal relationship that would prevail in modern life. Whether exhibited as exotic or nationalistic relics of diminished habitat, whether encased behind glass for the cultured American or performing for gawking multitudes, the containment of individual creatures diminished their Otherness. The enclosed theatrical mis-en-scene rendered wildlife comfortably and artificially natural.[35] In the 1890s, Yellowstone literature and advertising embraced the theme, promoting Wonderland as both zoological garden and living museum brimming with noble, innocent animals needing protection.

With a similar paternalism, romantic nature writers like William J. Long and Ernest Thompson Seton projected human characteristics onto what they endearingly called the "Wood Folk."[36] Their anthropomorphic literature urged readers to feel the animals' pain and share their thoughts and feelings. Inviting readers into a fictional natural world of good and evil, Seton's animal stories often cast humans, particularly sport hunters, as villains and even made victims of predators.[37] Such animistic sympathy pit the fiction writers against not only sportsmen but naturalists like John Burroughs, who disparaged them as "nature fakers." Burroughs felt the view of animals as individual creatures with human qualities and democratic rights subverted "true" natural history.[38]

Neither did outdoor enthusiasts like Theodore Roosevelt have patience for such "sentimentalism." TR and his fellow sportsmen saw in the preservation of wildlife primarily the perpetuation of the hunt. For Roosevelt, "the chase"

offered an antidote to the enervating effects of a burgeoning modern culture.[39] The adventure of man against beast inspired the rugged individualism and racial supremacy that was the legacy of Anglo-Saxon Americans and
which, TR urged, they needed in the new age. Eschewing the feminine fig-
ments of the nature fakers' imagination as well as the more spiritual bio-
centrism of John Muir, sportsmen and naturalists shared the conviction that
scientific reason and the manly frontier aesthetic should guide the protection
of select animals.[40]

No animal appealed to their eye more than the elk. This most noble of
ungulates, noted George Wingate in his 1886 hunting and sightseeing memoir, "add greatly to [the Park's] attractions."[41] Eugene Smalley typified the
sportsman's congenital admiration for and urge to kill Yellowstone's most
dominant species:

> Of all American game, the elk is justly entitled to rank first in the esti-
> mation of the sportsman. His size, splendid form, noble presence and
> magnificent antlers, excite the most hopeful enthusiasm in the hunter's
> breast, while his quickness of eye, keenness of ear and wonderful deli-
> cacy of scent, render his successful pursuit a feat to test the skill.

Smalley went on to describe the best strategies for outsmarting and bagging
an elk.[42]

Forest and Stream embodied the sportsman's ideal. A clear and determined voice in the movement to protect Yellowstone wildlife, the magazine
more fundamentally promoted the ways and means of the hunt. Although
shooting elk in the park was outlawed after the 1883 season, four years later
Forest and Stream printed a map of the park highlighting elk and bison range
areas. The elk, reported George Grinnell in 1886, had learned they were
"safe from molestation" within park boundaries and thus could be depended
on to stay within the refuge and repopulate. He predicted the "overflow"
would spill into the surrounding region and make it one of the greatest elk-
hunting grounds in the country—"just as it will be the only place in the
world where one can hope to get a shot at the almost extinct bison." Reports
of elk sightings and hunting trips in the greater Yellowstone region perme-
ate the magazine throughout the period, almost certainly contributing to
hunting within the ill-defined park boundaries.[43] Similarly loving the Yellowstone elk to death was the *Benevolent and Protective* [emphasis mine] Order
of the Elks.[44] Their growing numbers at the turn of the century came from
the same class of established, sporting Americans who read Grinnell's magazine and prized the august look of the animal.

The nobility of Yellowstone elk proved irresistible for even the most conscientious sportsman. After blaming the Bannock Indians for the near disappearance of game within the park, George Wingate reported his jubilation over a hugely successful elk hunt. Among his take were two yearlings "one-half the size of the full grown." Suddenly remembering the sportsman's code which forbid such overkill, he began to mourn. Yet, he absolved,

> it is a fact, that no matter how one may theorize, it is practically impossible during the rush and excitement of an encounter like this to stop and think, and the sportsman who can refrain from firing when a good shot at *large* game is suddenly presented, deserves to be stuffed and placed on exhibition.

The forgiven hunter then matter-of-factly describes his shooting of an antelope trophy, leaving the rotting carcass behind.[45]

Such excess aside, the conscientious sportsman's idea of Yellowstone as a haven for beseiged big game justified and extended the hunt outside park boundaries. More importantly, it supported the stewardly impulse to protect and manage the privileged animals. As Olin D. Wheeler proudly declared in 1895:

> Some day this region will be one of a few natural zoological gardens in our country. Animals, like human beings, know a good thing when they find it. . . . This will in time be a great retreat, a haven of refuge, for beasts and birds. When gone else-where, the bear and deer, the elk and antelope, the mountain-lion and buffalo, the mountain sheep and goat, to say nothing of lesser animals, will be found here, and wonderfully docile and tame.[46]

Animals, of course, once had a better thing. But Wheeler's cheerful resignation that the creatures would one day exist only in Yellowstone further sanctified the park and assigned all the "elsewheres" of their past to civilization. This view, promulgated far and wide outside the Northern Pacific Railroad advertising department, assumed the fatalism of progress.

Examined more critically, the "haven of refuge" seems less an enlightened creation of American culture than an artificial constriction of vast habitat.[47] At the turn of the century, cultural savants fancied Yellowstone a virtuous place of innocence "where animals have been intrusted [sic] with self-government." In this republican paradise, extolled *Recreation* magazine, animals would fear humans no more, thereby "[converting] Yellowstone Park into an Eden for all lovers of nature."[48] This America-Before-The-Fall theme would repeat itself throughout the national park system, offering images that fear and loathing and national progress could never allow. In the tumultuous 1890s, a society increasingly unsure of its ability to maintain order could at least return to a paradise of elusive—and illusory—harmony. A few like Frances Lynn Turpin recognized it as an apparition: in Yellowstone, she observed dryly, "birds and beasts . . . fancy man their friend, [and] have no conception of the cruel bold [sic] thirsty creature he is."[49] Prairie dogs who got plugged by nature-loving romantics from atop the NPRR observation car knew it.[50] Inside the park, unruly tourists revealed how imperiled a sanctuary it was. Writing for the *Magazine of Western History*, Francis Sessions recounted how his party, waiting impatiently for the fog to clear from the Grand Canyon, amused themselves by throwing stones at an eagle's aerie full of young.[51] That one of Yellowstone's cultured tourists would boast of an assault on a living national emblem in a public journal screamed of the necessity—and perhaps the ultimate futility—of the national park idea.

The targets of greatest enmity and gunpowder were those who throughout the West came under the despicable heading of "vermin": mountain lions, wolves, and coyotes. In 1884 virile champion of progress Eugene Smalley worried over a problem forced by the otherwise benign extirpation of bison: the increasing assault of wolves upon cattle who supplanted bison as their prey on the Great Plains. Wolf poisoning, he brightly resolved, would become a "profitable industry."[52] Until the late 1890s, Smalley and others in the local press decried (and exaggerated) the de facto protection afforded wolves through the anti-hunting measure of 1883:

> There is one class of hunters privileged to prey on the game of
> Yellowstone National Park, and . . . are not prosecuted simply
> because they are as closely under the protection of the Government
> as the rarest of the wild creatures of the park. The big park is
> infested with wolves and coyotes in larger numbers than ever before,
> and they are said to be slaughtering the game animals of the park.[53]

Clearly the national park could not offer asylum to such creatures. Centuries of Euro-American myth, the harsh economic realities of cattle ranching in the region, and the privileging of noble ungulates in Wonderland all fostered universal antipathy, fear, and mass extermination of the predators. Beginning around the turn of the century and lasting into the 1930s, the federal government sanctioned and led the effort to poison and shoot the wolves and coyotes of the greater Yellowstone region.[54] Although one local resident believed the "two-legged coyotes" (pot hunters) equally responsible for the

decline in big game, the vast majority of park defenders found wolves, coyotes and Indians more convenient villains.[55] By 1892 Georgina Synge could
speak of the perceptible decline in the Yellowstone predator population:

> "It's a wolf!" I shrieked, "and it wants to eat us!" And we seized our
> sticks and made a terrific noise to frighten the monster. . . . The cay-
> otes [sic] and wolves are much scarcer than they were, as the cattle-
> men have poisoned and killed them in large numbers, owing to their
> depredations among the young calves, etc. The mountain lion also,
> a horribly savage beast, something like a small panther, has been
> trapped and hunted down to a large extent, and is not often seen.[56]

Reflecting their somewhat mercurial image in American folklore and popular culture, the bears of Yellowstone elicited mixed reactions.[57] They amused
the tourists as they feasted on the open garbage pits of several park hotels;
the 1901 *Wonderland* guidebook boasted of "quasi pet" bears feeding from
the dumps "where they can be seen and photographed without difficulty."
Wonderland's bears, glowed the Northern Pacific Railroad, lived "in unity"
with humans.[58] Not everyone shared the bear's new warm and fuzzy image.
Sportsman George Grinnell believed the close proximity of bears and park
civilization simply proved how "bold and careless these generally wary animals may become if not hunted." In 1889 A. M. Matoon found the creatures
"very numerous . . . extremely bold and . . . sometimes quite troublesome."
A few years later, the increasing number and danger of human-bear encounters prompted one official of the Interior Department to suggest that "steps
could be taken to rid the ground of a few of the most troublesome of the
beasts."[59]

Authorities purified their peaceable kingdom with perfectly American
methods: by capturing and caging the unruly or superfluous animals behind
bars. Beginning in the 1890s, officials relocated a number of bears to the
Smithsonian Institution's Zoological Garden in Washington, D.C. In 1891
Arnold Hague wrote to Superintendent Anderson of one "ugly cuss" of a
bear who "no doubt . . . [thought] shooting in the Yellowstone Park prefer-
able to trapping."[60] This was likely the same ursine specimen who, although
nicknamed "Lucifer" on account of his ornery disposition, nevertheless
served as a fine "ornament" for zoo visitors, according to the Washington
press.[61] The seizure of wild animals proved an adventure for man and beast
and literally broke the heart of one bear: an attempt to remove one of the
"very troublesome" bears loitering around the Fountain Hotel ended when
"he died of a rupture of the heart in his struggles to escape." In other cases,

caged beasts awaiting transport to the east became either too numerous or vexing and had to be shot before transfer.[62]

Capture and shipment of Yellowstone wildlife was not limited to bears. An 1893 list of animals requested by the Smithsonian and the United States National Museum includes bison, moose, elk, antelope, mule deer, wolverines, gray wolves, mink, marten, beaver, otter and porcupine.[63] The Department of the Interior noted that said specimens were wanted dead or alive:

> The hunter should be authorized and instructed to capture for the Institution, any living animals in the following list, especially the larger ones, suitable for exhibition; and also, if desired, and within such limits as you may be pleased to prescribe, be authorized to shoot such animals as may be required to complete the Government's collection of natural history specimens.[64]

Fittingly enough, P. T. Barnum's former animal-keeper, W. H. Blackburn, managed the animal display at the Zoological Garden.

The preservation of Yellowstone wildlife in a controlled environment satisfied a variety of turn-of-the-century upper- and middle-class interests: scientific curiosity, exotic performance, and benevolent paternalism. Still, a certain ambivalence over the containment of wildlife nagged the conscience of some animal lovers. Writing for *The Century Magazine* in 1900, nature writer Ernest Thompson Seton labored to assuage his discontent:

> The real plan is to restore the natural conditions. We are slowly grasping the idea, taught by the greatest thinkers in all ages, that the animals have an inalienable right to the pursuit of happiness in their own way as long as they do not interfere with our own happiness. And if we must for good reasons keep them in prison, we are bound to make their condition tolerable, not only for their sakes, but for our own, because all the benefit that we can get out of them in bondage is increased in proportion as we slacken their bonds within the limits of judicial restraint.[65]

For all the anthropomorphisms that Seton and other nature romantics affixed to wildlife, the moral claim of animals had limits even for them. If in fact animals possessed inalienable rights, they clearly remained subordinate to those of men. Moreover, Seton's hopes notwithstanding, the construction of "buffalo houses" only signified the ultimate futility of such paternalism. Alas, the Zoological Garden was not Yellowstone Park, which itself resembled less the boundary-less place it had once been. Both places displayed and memorialized animals as symbols of class and conquest. Whether in Yellowstone Park or in urban zoos, the exhibition of wildlife testified to the decline of their numbers and habitat and the wisdom of their keepers.[66]

No animal's fate was more closely tied to American ascendancy than the bison. Extinguished from the eastern half of the continent by 1840, forty million North American bison still blackened the Great Plains and fed the material, spiritual, and cultural needs of Indian tribes. As they had for centuries, the Plains Indians continued to revere and hunt the bison.[67] The Oregon Trail and the Union Pacific Railroad, however, divided the bison into southern and northern herds and by 1872 the number had been reduced to just seven million. In 1871 the discovery by an eastern tannery of the commercial value of bison hides brought market hunters by the hundreds to chase down the remaining animals. By 1882, five thousand hunters and sportsmen stalked the last great bison herd on the northern plains.[68] During the peak of the slaughter, an average marksman could take down sixty a day. In just a few months, the Northern Pacific Railroad carried no fewer than two hundred thousand hides out of Montana and North Dakota.[69]

Neither hunter nor sportsman could resist reports of the slaughter. Until the tide of public opinion shifted in the 1890s, Wonderland's imagery of living or slain animals (fig. 46) and its typically lurid text invited all comers:

> The antelope, buffalo, and elk, which have occasionally been seen
> since we crossed the Missouri River, . . . now appear in greater num-
> bers; and either from the windows or platforms of the moving train
> we may test the accuracy of our aim and the range of our six-shoot-
> ers by firing at the retreating herd.[70]

In the late 1870s, a group of gentlemen hunters led by Howard Eaton of Pittsburgh arrived in the Badlands region of the Little Missouri River. The men renamed the area Pyramid Park and transformed it into a "sportsman's paradise."[71]

With market hunters, sportsmen, and Indians all on the hunt for the last bison, by the time Theodore Roosevelt arrived at Pyramid Park for his first hunt in September 1883, virtually none could be found.[72] The bison market had been reduced to bones (fig. 47). Thrifty scavengers gathered the remains and shipped them off to the fertilizer and sugar processing industries.[73] While the bison's demise stunned and saddened genteel Easterners like Roosevelt, most observers portrayed its passing as a righteous fait accompli and a harbinger of progress. Some mourned the loss but blamed

Fig. 46. (1) Head of Mountain Sheep; (2) Brought Low at Last;
(3) How He Stopped Him; (4) Head of Antelope; (5) Black Tail Deer
Camp; (6)Moose Killed in Bitter Root Mountains. Wheeler, Sketches,
1895. Courtesy Yellowstone National Park Archives

Fig. 47. The End, 1883. Martin S. Garretson, 1913. F. Jay Haynes Collection. Courtesy Montana State University Library, Bozeman.

the Indians: "If the Redman had been a man of foresight," declared J. L. Hill, "he would have seen what his wholesale slaughter would result in, and would have been moved by common impulse to kill sparingly."[74] Until the 1890s, its extermination seemed a foregone conclusion among both the sympathetic and the jingoistic. As Eugene Smalley put it in 1884:

> Viewed, therefore, from the standpoint of the rationalist and optimist, the buffalo must rapidly disappear before the rapid march of the ox and cow, just as the Indian disappears before the march of his superior, the Caucasian. His bleached bones and moldering horns which now dot the prairies will fertilize the soil over which he was wont to roam in times of old, and he will go to dwell forever with the mastodon as one of the extinct species of an ancient and honorable race.[75]

Indeed, cultural ennoblement and conservationist sympathies nearly arrived too late for the bison. In this, the bison's final hour, the American sportsman's irrepressible impulse to subjugate nature gave way to his love for it. Concerned for the future of the last vestiges of American wilderness, General Phil Sheridan helped lead the anti-monopoly movement in Yellowstone; Buffalo Bill Cody championed the cause of the bison he once slaughtered by the dozen; and Theodore Roosevelt, in his 1886 book, *Hunting Trips of a Ranchman,* waxed softly that the "true still-hunter should be a lover of nature as well as of sport, or he will miss half the pleasure of being in the woods."[76] George Bird Grinnell's review of Roosevelt's book that year sparked a friendship that would bear lasting fruit for wildlife conservation. Grinnell and the future president began discussing the formation of a sportsmen's organization to promote the preservation of game. Although they discussed matters, said TR, "about which we knew very little," the two men were unsentimentally clear on the intended purpose of such a group:

> We wanted the game preserved, but chiefly with the idea that it should be protected in order that there might be good hunting which should last for generations.[77]

In 1887 Roosevelt proposed to Grinnell the formation of a club of prominent and worthy sportsmen to "promote manly sport with a rifle." Assuming the mantle of frontier heroes, the Boone and Crockett Club boasted among its esteemed membership Yellowstone defenders George Vest and William Hallett Phillips. Looking to their secondary mission of preservation, they extended honorary membership to scientist Arnold Hague, a sensitive soul who proudly claimed to have never shot an animal. Almost immediately the club turned to conservation matters and helped to defeat the Cooke City railroad scheme in Yellowstone Park.[78]

But in the late 1880s, even Grinnell and Roosevelt held out little hope of saving the bison. Grim field reports from such authorities as William T. Hornaday, chief taxidermist for the National Museum, supported the widespread belief that the bison was an extinct species—"Gone but not forgotten," as Grinnell eulogized. After noting its "complete destruction," the conservationist described the recent construction of a bronze memorial to remember the beast. Mounted over the Missouri River Union Pacific Railroad bridge at Council Bluffs, Nebraska, the metal totem glorified the bison as artful nostalgia:

> The largest bronze casting ever made in one piece in this country . . . is a huge buffalo head. . . . To old-timers it will recall the days in the early history of the road when the trains thundered past far-stretching herds of bison, and cockney sportsmen fired from car window and platform into the great stupid beasts. . . . but [now] one may pass and repass from East to West and see no sign of bison save the mounted heads which ornament some of the stations, and this bronze cast over the Missouri bridge.[79]

By the late 1880s, observers presumed the bison very nearly extinct—making trophy heads and robes all the more valuable among Wonderland tourists. Harry Yount, later the first gamekeeper of Yellowstone Park, found the sale of bison tongues quite lucrative while they lasted. On her way home from Yellowstone in 1892, Georgina Synge stopped in Livingston to purchase a bison robe. After decrying the slaughter which led to the exorbitant prices being forced upon her, Synge purchased a robe of "this exceedingly stupid beast" for sixty dollars.[80] The bison head, by far the most desirable relic, fetched an average five hundred dollars in Livingston from exceedingly covetous tourists. Emblems of a glorious past, bison heads ornamented the Victorian parlors of the nation and city streets throughout the Northwest. Yellowstone Superintendent George Anderson noted in his 1892 report: "The great value placed upon them by sportsmen and taxidermists makes their protection difficult."[81] The chain of poachers, entrepreneurs, and consumers had reduced the number of moving bison heads in Yellowstone National Park to between 150 and 400 animals.[82]

And so the saga went, until the winter of 1893–1894, when Cooke City resident Edgar Howell brought infamy to Yellowstone bison poaching and began to reverse the animal's free-for-all annihilation. Early that winter,

Howell set up camp in the Pelican Valley of the park with the intention of shooting the small bison herd that wintered there. Hopeful of "skinning out the heads, and hanging the scalps safely in trees to wait the spring," Howell and his partner planned to "take the trophies out on packhorses and realize from $100 to $300 apiece for their troubles." In March, Park Superintendent George S. Anderson received reports of suspicious activity in the region and sent a small detachment of soldiers led by Scout Felix Burgess to investigate. Anderson described the events of March 13:

> On the morning of the 13th, very soon after starting, [the soldiers] came across some old snowshoe tracks which they could scarcely follow, but by continuing . . . they soon came across a cache of six bison scalps suspended above the ground, in the limbs of a tree. Securing these trophies, the party continued down Astringent Creek to its mouth and then turned down Pelican. They soon came across a newly-erected lodge, with evidences of occupation, and numerous tracks in the vicinity. Soon after this they were attracted by the sight of a man pursuing a herd of bison in the valley below them, followed by several shots from a rifle. After completing the killing, the culprit was seen to proceed with the removal of the scalps. While thus occupied with the first one my scouting patrol ran upon him and made the capture.[83]

Military officials of the park had been apprehending poachers for years, but lacked authority to do anything more than expel the violators. Only a second fortuitous encounter made the Howell capture any different: while escorting Howell back to Fort Yellowstone, Burgess and the soldiers met another party concerned for the protection of the bison. Fate and George Grinnell had sent Emerson Hough, field correspondent for *Forest and Stream,* photographer Frank Jay Haynes, and Yellowstone guide T. E. "Billy" Hofer to investigate poaching activities in the park. Hough immediately wired the story of Howell's capture to Grinnell, who printed it along with several of Haynes's graphic images, sensationally captioned, "The Butcher's Work" (fig. 48).[84]

The story provoked widespread indignation and Grinnell sensed an opportunity to put an end to Yellowstone poaching. With the political force of the Boone and Crockett Club's esteemed membership, Grinnell pressed for immediate legislation to protect park wildlife. On March 26, just thirteen days after the incident, Representative John F. Lacey of Iowa introduced a bill designed "to protect the birds and animals in Yellowstone National Park,

Fig. 48. The Butcher's Work, *Harpers Weekly*, 1894. Courtesy Library of Congress.

and to punish crimes in said park. . . ." Congress quickly passed the Lacey Act and President Benjamin Harrison signed it into law on May 7, 1894.[85] Following the legislation that created the park and the imposition of the cavalry in 1886, the Lacey Act (formally the National Park Protective Act) proved to be the third administrative milestone in Yellowstone's early history. The law provided authority and clear federal jurisdiction to enforce the law. With a full-time U.S. commissioner appointed to the park to adjudicate criminal offenses, penalties were stiffened and meted out; anyone caught poaching wildlife now faced a fine of up to one thousand dollars and two years in jail. As Grinnell later recalled, "This [Lacey Act] was the ultimate reward of a number of men who, for a dozen years, had been working for the protection and betterment of the Yellowstone National Park."[86] Moreover, the law established the framework for future wildlife protection policy in all national parks.

Despite its ultimate impact, the Lacey Act did not supersede capitalism's law of supply and demand. Bison numbers in Yellowstone continued to fall, dwindling to an all-time low of about twenty-five in 1900. The fewer there were, the more intense the desire to have one. In 1901 *Recreation* magazine explained how its enduring value as an ornamental commodity—even among those ostensibly seeking its preservation—continued to endanger the bison:

> Buffalo heads are in great demand. Fine ones command extravagant prices. Buffalo skins are eagerly sought by museums and wealthy people, and I was told last summer that in the neighborhood of the Park purchasers had paid as high as $2 a pound for buffalo steaks. The very bones of these animals are in demand, for anatomical specimens for museums; hence a wild buffalo is looked on as a small fortune walking around without an owner.[87]

Naturally, Superintendent Anderson received numerous requests for the heads of Ed Howell's infamous bison kill. Bison defenders Grinnell and William Hallett Phillips each sought the whereabouts of the legendary and mysteriously missing trophies.[88]

The bison fetish continued. With increasing tourist fascination in the animal after the 1894 incident, the Yellowstone Park Association constructed an enclosed menagerie of buffalo and elk on Dot Island in the middle of Yellowstone Lake. At the turn of the century, excursions aboard E. C. Waters' steamboat the *Zillah* landed passengers for a guaranteed view of four bison specimens imported from a Texas ranch.[89]

In 1895 the Smithsonian Institution and the U.S. Cavalry schemed to hold and breed bison in a pen they located on Alum Creek in the Hayden Valley. Bales of hay deposited inside the enclosure would draw the bison in, officials thought; once inside, the soldiers were to close the gates and begin domesticating the animals. The bison failed to cooperate, largely because the Yellowstone Park Association cut the hay from the Hayden Valley and "drove the buffalo from their old home."[90] The entrapment of the park's remaining wild herd never materialized. In 1902, however, pressured by a number of organizations like William T. Hornaday's American Bison Society, the U.S. Congress authorized the purchase of privately owned bison cows and bulls from other areas of the West to begin breeding a new Yellowstone herd. Until 1905 bison authority Charles J. "Buffalo" Jones managed the animals in an enclosure situated on the well-guarded grounds of Fort Yellowstone. After several years of successful growth, officials relocated Yellowstone's "Buffalo Ranch" to the Lamar Valley where they amused tourists well into the 1950s.[91] Once preserved, the assemblages of Yellowstone bison appeared as docile creatures in a paradisiacal home, happy to amuse the visitors. One Haynes view of the Yellowstone bison herd bears the caption, "Buffalo In Enclosure, Nearly As Tame As Domestic Animals" (fig. 49).

Fig. 49. Buffalo in Enclosure, Nearly as Tame as Domestic Animals. F. Jay Haynes, *Portfolio of Wild Animals of Yellowstone Park* (St. Paul: Haynes Publishing, 1904). Courtesy Montana State University Library, Bozeman.

At its core perhaps, the enclosure of Yellowstone's wild animals aspired to restore a sense of human-animal kinship that had been lost through the development of urban industrial civilization. But the common ground of the national park contained not only animals but the divergent impulses of Americans that sparked wildlife preservation: the empathy of romantic nature fakers, the managing paternalism of modern science, and a general sense—felt most acutely by sportsmen—that Yellowstone and other vestiges of wildness recapitulated the American frontier myth. The nascent culture of conservation affixed to the bison and noble ungulates of Yellowstone the benevolence and grandeur that it wanted to see as it looked back on the Frontier. Preservation of the innocent is a beguiling image. And yet entrapment, fetishization, and display of a particularly beseiged species reveals both the conscience of Americans and an unconscious, unholy impulse to mask a history of exploitation. Most fundamentally, the containment and idolatry of select wildlife bespoke the essential modern desire to *see* that which is preserved; and to see it in the broad sense as cultural possession. The "exceedingly stupid" bison was saved not through any effort of its own, but through the magnanimity of enlightened stewardship. It exists not for its sake but for ours.

Throughout the 1890s, white poachers and troublesome Indians left park defenders still concerned for the vulnerability of wildlife. The sportsmen's *Forest and Stream* and Boone and Crockett Club, along with the watershed- and timber-conscious American Forestry Association, agitated for the designation of a forest reserve surrounding the park.[92] On March 3, 1891, Congress responded by establishing the Forest Reserve Act, which authorized the president to set aside "forest reserves," although for unspecified purposes. President Benjamin Harrison immediately created fifteen such reserves—later given the less preservationist moniker of "national forests." One of them abutted Yellowstone Park on its southern and eastern borders. Within a few years the Teton Reserve and an expansion of the Yellowstone Park Timberland Reserve embraced about half the area Phil Sheridan had recommended for the park proper years before. Conservationists, who deemed these lands of vital importance to wildlife, and forestry advocates concerned for the long-term health of forestry in the West, rejoiced over the new federal status.[93]

What sort of protection the reserves would be afforded was a matter of considerable debate within government and the conservation movement for nearly a decade. Although initially ambivalent about the level and types of use that should be allowed in the national forests, John Muir ultimately led those forces who believed that they merited preservation status equal to the national parks. By the turn of the century, Muir had parted company with efficiency- and utilitarian-minded conservationists of the Progressive movement. Led by the nation's premier forester Gifford Pinchot and his White House ally Theodore Roosevelt, the Progressives established the "wise"—later "multiple" use—policy that guided the management of the nation's forests for at least the next century. The resources of the national forests, said Pinchot, should be privately developed but wisely overseen by skilled government experts with an eye to providing the "greatest good for the greatest number" far into the future. Like corn and wheat, trees would be "harvested" for the highest possible sustainable yield.[94]

Few in the West advocated Muir's vision of the national forests as spiritual havens of wildness. Even within the Progressives' multiple use framework, the very withdrawal of more public lands drew objection. Led by Pinchot, the new American forestry experts defended the national forests mostly on economic grounds, arguing that broad forest cover was essential to maintenance of the continental watershed—the wellspring for long-term development of the West.[95] Speaking of the "slur" of "sentimentalism" being leveled at advocates of forest conservation, William Hallett Phillips in 1886 rejoined that the forests "serve an important economic end . . . by regulating and equalizing the precipitation of moisture and by retaining the snows whereby the streams are fed. For the cultivation of the Yellowstone Valley" to the north, argued Phillips, "the maintenance of this great forest preserve, is indispensable."[96] Evoking the mid-nineteenth-century image of the West as "The Great Desert," Yellowstone engineer Hiram M. Chittenden further silenced the detractors:

> The great value of these forest growths is their agency in the conservation of a water supply for the surrounding country. A glance at the map will show that the park is in the midst of a vast region extending far into the surrounding states. The reclamation of these vast desert wastes, and their conversion into productive lands can be accomplished by irrigation alone, and for this purpose the abundant streams which descend from the mountains are the indispensable water supply.[97]

Multiple-use disciples would eventually apply long-term thinking and scientific expertise to the vigorous development of water and timber resources in the national forests. In the spring of 1903, however, lingering opposition to the designation prompted President Theodore Roosevelt to defend the reserves on a visit to Yellowstone National Park. Wyoming sheep and cattle ranchers, along with the governor of the state, feared the 1902 expansion of the forests would lead to enlargement of the national park itself, or in some other way inhibit the agricultural and industrial development of the region. Gifford Pinchot had no stronger advocate of the new scientific approach to resource conservation and development than the president. Roosevelt quelled the fears of local residents by pitching their economic self-interest:

> The preservation of the forest is of course the matter of prime importance in every public reserve of this character. In this region of the Rocky Mountains and the great plains, the problem of the water supply is the most important which the homemaker has to face. . . . and nothing is more essential to the preservation of the water supply than the preservation of the forests. Montana has in its water power a source of development which has hardly yet been touched. The water power will be seriously impaired if ample protection is not given the forests; therefore this Park, like the forest reserves generally, is of the utmost advantage to the country around from the merely utilitarian side.[98]

In 1905 the forest-as-crop concept became symbolically clear when President Roosevelt transferred control of the national forests from the Department of the Interior to Agriculture.

As for wildlife, though park officials believed the authority of the Lacey Act should have been extended to the reserves, sportsmen-conservationists intended the Yellowstone reserves as a sporting repository for the big game who strayed from the park.[99] Elk, too, would be harvested. In his 1903 remarks made at the park, Roosevelt made that plain. The national forest, he proclaimed, was a place wherein America's frontier myth, like the timber yield itself, might be sustained in the modern age:

> Here all the wild creatures of the old days are being preserved, and
> their overflow into the surrounding country means that the people of
> the surrounding country, so long as they see that the laws are observed
> by all, will be able to insure to themselves and to their children and
> to their children's children much of the old time pleasures of the
> hardy life of the wilderness and of the hunter in the wilderness.[100]

But with hunting prohibited in the park, how would a conscientious sportsman or tourist know when they had, as Owen Wister put it, penetrated "the sacred line" of forest into the "sanctuary"?[101] The perceptible division of nature proved vexing. In 1903 Superintendent Pitcher brightly proposed to saw a dividing line between the sacred park and the prosaic forest: "It is exceedingly desirable," wrote Pitcher, "that a wide swath should be cut along the entire boundary line wherever timber exists, and also that additional monuments should be set up wherever the country is open."[102] This would serve humans. As for bison, their fear of civilization would provide all the motivation necessary to stay within the national zoological paradise. As one early enthusiast predicted, "settlement of the surrounding country" would eventually chase and keep the bison within the park.[103] Indeed it came to pass; with increasing development of the greater Wonderland region, Yellowstone wildlife increasingly migrated away from threatening forces and stayed near the refuge.[104]

Park officials never heeded Pitcher's proposal to literally sever the forest. Patrolling the national forest became easier in 1905 with the establishment of the paramilitary National Forest Service. In the meantime, authorities took Pitcher's suggestion to erect a monument marking the boundary line of Yellowstone National Park at the park's most heavily traveled northern entrance. On April 24, 1903, President Roosevelt, acting on the other clear purpose of his Yellowstone trip that spring, laid the cornerstone of what became known as the Roosevelt Arch. A fifty-foot-high structure built of Yellowstone's columnar basalt rock, engineer Chittenden located the arch at the edge of the town of Gardiner so that visitors would pass under it as they entered the official bounds of the park (fig. 50). There would be no missing the passage from civilization into the national nature asylum.

Fig. 50. Theodore Roosevelt Arch, n.d. Haynes Collection,
H-5422.

In his remarks after the laying of the cornerstone, Roosevelt urged the
American people to protect the park by "assuming ownership in the name
of the nation and jealously safeguarding and preserving the scenery, the
forests, and the wild creatures." As only TR could, he cloaked the protection and management of the "Nation's Nature" as nothing less than a patriotic mission. The "essential democracy" of Yellowstone and the national
forests, argued the president, distinguished them from the hunting preserves
of the Old World, which had been the exclusive province of the rich.[105] Officials later punctuated that message by inscribing across the top of the arch-
way the republican and fundamentally anthropocentric purpose of the
Yellowstone Park Act:

FOR THE BENEFIT AND ENJOYMENT OF THE PEOPLE

The Theodore Roosevelt Arch looms now as a grand and fitting symbol
of the Yellowstone myth created during the Wonderland era. With its
Romanesque evocation of American idealism, the arch reinforced the image

of Yellowstone's Immaculate Conception by enlightened statesmen. The stone barrier also, however, exposed the need to partition nature from a culture that resisted bounding. For "the people," nature would be managed by the expertise of elites whose demarcation of nature and civilization went beyond symbolism: Superintendent Pitcher noted that flanking the gateway, workers had constructed a fence

> which extends for about 4 miles along the northern boundary of the
> Park. This fence has long been needed, and it now affords a means of
> keeping stock of all kinds off that section of the park in the vicinity
> of Gardiner and Cinnabar, thereby saving for the antelope, deer, and
> elk the grass which they badly needed in the winter.[106]

For two decades such paternalism had guided the management of wildlife and Indians in Yellowstone. And why not, for as Roosevelt thundered, nature here was possession. Just as literateurs had given order and meaning to the thermal features of the landscape, so did official Yellowstone and its conservationist defenders impose upon the forest a beguiling fiat of discipline and division. "The first duty of the human race," Gifford Pinchot declared, "is to control the earth it lives upon."[107]

Feeding the winter elk, enclosing the bison from poachers, imaging and vilifying the native Other—all of this poked holes in the illusion that nature and culture had been separated with lines on a map. Yellowstone Park had been created by market capitalism, colored by romanticism, and firmly organized by science. From the later impulse came the dominant strain of conservation theory which aspired to preserve, dissect, and extend forever a wilderness purified of natives, fire, and other predators. That the prophecy of vanishing bison and Indian had nearly come to pass simply proved American dominance and the fatalism of progress. Even as they looked to the future of nature, sportsmen-conservationists saw it chiefly as hardy Americana. As such, they cast the bison as a disappearing icon of national conquest, divided good animals from bad, and exploitable forest from sacred. With proper management, urged the conservationists, that which was noble within this modern-day peaceable kingdom would last forever. With enough rugged sportsmen, the elk population would be controlled. Remove the unruly bears and peace would reign. Sufficient barriers would safeguard the sanctuary. Although the stupid bison and the noble elk felt much of this for the illusion that it was, for the early lights of the conservation crusade it was quite real. With modern angst creeping in, the expert management of the Yellowstone region offered firm evidence of a benevolent and cultivated nation tenaciously clinging to its premodern myths.

CHAPTER SEVEN

From Wonderland to Ecosystem

Everyone should see Manhattan, the Grand Canyon, Walt Disney World . . .
Yellowstone National Park, Beverly Hills . . .

—*Glamour, April 1995*[1]

[Yellowstone's] virgin wilderness . . . is a living reminder of what our country
was like before it was civilized and developed.

—*Yellowstone: The First National Park (a video guide), 1990*[2]

THE CULTURAL AND ECONOMIC FORCES that shape environmental history have an uncanny knack of rearing themselves into the future. In the late nineteenth century, romantic assumptions undergirding the Wonderland myth promised sanctifying, museumlike preservation of Yellowstone Park. And so, it would seem, that has come about. Picking up the trail of park popular culture in contemporary video guides, we learn that Yellowstone's "virgin wilderness" has stood pat—a "landscape unchanged."[3] (Such static immutability would make it the only such place in the world.) These guidebook descendants summon as well the nationalism that moved nature to the center of American culture in the nineteenth century, proclaiming Yellowstone an "American triumph" and reinforcing its paradigmatic role in the preservation of "our most precious, irreplaceable, most unique areas."[4]

Yellowstone Park is now, as it was in the late nineteenth century, both ideal and place. One is in better shape than the other. The qualities affixed during the Wonderland era—the romantic sublimity and exoticism of its attractions, the efficiency with which one may see them—keep Yellowstone on the list of must-see American places, just behind Disney World. Increasingly in the past century, Yellowstone's place as the first and largest of federal parks has also made of it the emblem of American wilderness, signifying our national creation myth. And in an age of increasing global environmental anxiety, Old Faithful is a comforting metaphor of the foresight of nature-loving Americans. The image still glows but the actual landscape is under duress: In late 1995, the World Heritage Committee, an international treaty organization, added Yellowstone Park to its short list of "World Heritage Sites in Danger" because of a variety of ecological threats.[5]

The designation was prompted less by forces within as from beyond park borders. Just as the reserve has come to symbolize the wisdom of environmental preservation, the declining integrity of lands surrounding it reveals both the precarious ecological health of the planet outside and the limitations of the park-making project. Less intellectually malleable as Yellowstone but every bit the "American triumph," five national forests that nearly encompass the park possess a bounty of extractive resources. They represent the utilitarian half of Wonderland rhetoric, the near side of the American frontier. Here, the Forest Service applies the multiple-use philosophy of Gifford Pinchot to encourage and oversee large-scale corporate logging, hardrock mining, grazing, oil and gas exploration, agriculture, and recreation.

Throughout the Yellowstone region there is much that would please the entire cast of the late-nineteenth century—park defenders, boom proponents, and wise-use conservationists. Ever-increasing numbers of sightseers tour the national park with greater efficiency and in greater air-conditioned comfort than G. L. Henderson could have dreamed; subdivisions of new homes now sprawl over Paradise Valley north of the reserve; thousands of mining claims and numerous clearcuts mark the surrounding forests. This chapter will survey the current demands Americans make of the greater Yellowstone region and find them, not surprisingly, well rooted in the Wonderland era. From the controversy over the 1988 park fires to struggles over Cooke City gold mining, the issues swirling around the management of Yellowstone summon the ghosts of western history. Black hats and white, this is familiar stuff.

Yet if this study has argued anything, it is that the hats are mostly gray.[6] The story of Wonderland is far more interesting than a crudely simple *good-versus-evil* thing. Yellowstone's present reflects its enigmatic formative years as a park—most acutely the dangers and delusions of dividing sacred lands from profane and commodifying that which we hold dear. Alas, today's Yellowstone is laden with myth and trapdoors to the past. The final hope here is to urge a look beyond the popular imagery of our own time, to both cultural history and the current health of the land to understand what in nature is really being preserved beyond what we see. What does it mean to call a place that receives three million people a year "virgin"? Patriarchal frontier myth—now melded to twentieth-century environmentalism—seems to insist on the term. More importantly, can any place whose biological condition is linked to the endangered well-being of the earth outside be more than ephemeral visual gratification? The threats to a place that exists in both the American mind and in nature are insidious and real. They will in these last pages pose a final question: if *Yellowstone,* for Muir's sake, is now less than sacred, to what nature can we flee?

Since its establishment in 1916, the National Park Service has persevered in the impossibly difficult challenge of balancing the preservation of Yellowstone's environment with the needs and desires of human visitors. Park administrators work in the context of tight budgets, changing politics, increasing numbers of tourists, and evolving ideas about the management of nature. In the 1970s, biologists conducting a landmark study of the habitat of the Yellowstone grizzly bear concluded that its range extended over more than five million acres, of which little more than two million were encased inside the boundary of the national park. Determination of the grizzly's vast range ultimately led scientists to conceive the idea of the Greater Yellowstone Ecosystem.[7]

The wide reach of the ecosystem, though defined not by economic but by earthly forces, ironically recalls the all-embracing packaging of Wonderland. Dynamic and complex in definition, the ecosystem extends broadly in four directions from the park boundary, taking in nearly eighteen million acres (fig. 51). The region encompasses six national forests, two national parks, other parcels under state and federal control, and some private lands. Environmental organizations, led by the Greater Yellowstone Coalition (GYC), argue that the biophysical health of Yellowstone Park must be viewed and managed within this bioregional context, not the lines of arbitrary political boundaries established in 1872. The term has reached a surprising level of acceptance in the region's vernacular: during a 1989 visit, President George Bush noted the international significance of "greater Yellowstone, one of the last intact ecosystems."[8]

Despite the reference, the president almost certainly did not imply support for managing the region as an ecosystem. Promoted by the Greater Yellowstone Coalition, such a strategy would represent a true paradigm shift away from the century-old multiple-use tradition. Ecosystem management adds "intrinsic" values of resources ("without reference to their usefulness") to the extrinsic, economic-human orientation of traditional management. The central goal of the ecosystem approach is to maintain the "long-term viability of natural processes," as opposed to the protection or extraction of particular species and resources. If implemented, Yellowstone managers would have to consider the needs of humans alongside, not before, those of other species.[9] The tenets of ecosystem management would strike at the anthropocentric heart of the organic park mission branded in the Roosevelt Arch: "FOR THE BENEFIT AND ENJOYMENT OF THE PEOPLE."

Although the Department of the Interior did not immediately embrace the concept, the idea that Yellowstone Park ought to be managed as an ecosystem extending well beyond its borders gained greater acceptance in the 1970s and 1980s. By 1991, environmentalists greatly anticipated a *Vision for the Future* document that was to propose a framework for inter-agency coordination based loosely on the principles of ecosystem management. Designed to preserve the "naturalness" and ecological integrity of the region while allowing for "biologically sustainable" economic development, the draft document drew the wrath of pro-business groups throughout the area. Although the *Vision* plan would have excluded private lands from management, the Wyoming Multiple Use Coalition feared a "superpark" and derided its ideas as a "land grab."[10] Wyoming political leaders joined the fray, fearing the *Vision* plan would hinder the "wise orderly development and the multiple uses of almost everybody's land." A Montana State University economist, among others, not only opposed it but called for the privatization of Yellowstone Park.[11] When the Park Service released the final draft of *Vision for the Future,* most of what would have been ecological

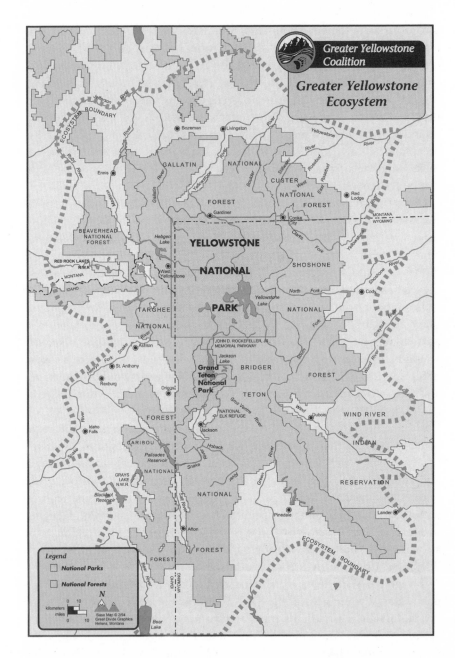

Fig. 51. Greater Yellowstone Ecosystem Map, 1990. Courtesy Greater
Yellowstone Coalition, Bozeman, Montana.

strides forward had been gutted for "political considerations," according to Lorraine Mintzmeyer, regional director of the Park Service at the time and coauthor of the original document.[12] Mintzmeyer's sudden and suspicious removal from her position signals the political and ideological distance that ecosystem management must yet cross before its institutionalization.

The bitterly polarized debate over ecosystem management summoned the memory of those who feared that the establishment of national forests a century earlier would "lock up" those resources and oppress economic liberty. Journalist Micah Morrison saw the 1990s struggle in such epic terms: "the independent man struggling against the elements, versus the New West of environmentalists, special interests and bureaucrats."[13] Echoing Senator John Ingalls' 1883 castigation of government involvement in the "show business" of Yellowstone, in 1991 one local entrepreneur saw it as "a business, by any measure." To pretend Yellowstone is "unspoiled wilderness" is an utter "charade," he declared rightly. (There has always been a refreshingly brutal candor in the antigovernment critique.) This merciless critic called for the National Park Service to surrender the park to "private contractors, allow them a profit incentive, and make way for . . . COMMON SENSE."[14] The "value of wilderness," Micah Morrison proclaimed, "is defined by mankind." Right he is. Opponents of park privatization leaned once more on the economic value of preserved, publicly managed nature, just as park defenders of the Wonderland era had done. Clean air, wildlife, and open space, argued the director of the U.S. Fish and Wildlife Service, are "an extremely valuable commodity [sic] to [Wyoming]."[15] Americans on the whole are too pragmatic, too industrious, too anthropocentric a bunch to ever accept the notion of the intrinsic worth or rights of nature, however defined.

That did not prevent the passions of the nation from being aroused by the most spectacular Yellowstone event of the century—the 1988 conflagration that burned nearly one million acres of forest, almost forty percent of the park. That summer's televised images of forest fire encroaching on Yellowstone's most celebrated icons—Old Faithful and its historic Inn—shocked and horrified Americans. Viewers could easily side with local residents and business people who were outraged at park officials for deliberately, they charged, letting the fires get out of hand. Implemented in 1972, the "let-burn" policy of the National Park Service mandated that natural fires like the ones sparked that hot and dry summer be allowed to run their course. The policy was part of a multifaceted effort initiated in the 1960s to restore all national parks to a semblance of pre-European conditions.[16] But conditions in 1988 were unprecedented. The hottest and driest summer in Yellowstone history, combined with weeks of high winds and a century of fuel lying on the forest floor spread the flames out of control. Increasingly defensive and desperate park officials finally called in firefighters and military personnel to protect life and property.

The fires sparked a legitimate debate regarding fire policy in Yellowstone. A number of ecologists argued that the "let-burn" policy's denial of Yellowstone fire history inevitably led to the 1988 inferno. Officials implemented the plan, they said, without recognizing the native Indians' use of fire and the vital role it served in not only recycling nutrients through the ecosystem, but periodically clearing the forest of excess fuel. In pre-*managed* Yellowstone, natural and cyclic Indian fires "created a mosaic pattern of forest growth, encouraging a wide distribution of ages of plants and trees."[17] When park officials expelled Indians and suppressed all flame for more than a century, they disrupted a thousand-year-old pattern of human-ecological succession in Yellowstone. With mature lodgepole pines assuming a greater dominance, the "monotonous" forest cover decried by Wonderland tourists a century ago assumed new meaning. Moreover, the policy effectively created an unprecedented forest of matchsticks. A fire of this magnitude simply waited for the right weather conditions. Ultimately, the denial of history and cultural imperialism have been real culprits in the 1988 holocaust.

Notwithstanding the merits of the let-burn policy, the inherent sensationalism of the story and horrific televised images did not promote understanding of Park Service intentions. Walls of flame engulfed the nation's preeminent nature park and threatened surrounding civilization, arousing widespread indignation toward park officials. Image-driven journalism left one to conclude that Yellowstone had been destroyed by government negligence. Television newsman Tom Brokaw stood amid a charred wasteland, declaring grimly, "This—is Yellowstone Park."[18] *Time* called it "an environmental Armageddon" and cited the concerns of Wyoming U.S. Senator Malcolm Wallop that the fires were a "catastrophe" for the tourist industry.[19] One observer of the media coverage of the fires aptly called the event "the Park Service's Vietnam."[20] Indeed, the language of war abounded that summer: *Newsweek* described the brave but "losing battle" of firefighters and Army personnel and the ultimate "[engagement] in all-out war to save the park itself." This was "destruction," pure and simple. Further, mourned *Newsweek,* "no amount of second-guessing will change the blackened woods back to green." The magazine cited "forestry experts[']" predictions of "100 to 300 years" for nature to "repair" the damage.[21]

With the specter of Bambi and Mom-and-Pop motels on the run, Americans and grandstanding politicians found it very easy to blame everybody's favorite villain—the incompetent government bureaucrat. Local residents called for the head of the Park Service and the park superintendent. Few would have ventured a look in the mirror of history. Not surprisingly, mainstream coverage of the fires failed to note the prehistoric (pre-1872) but suppressed use of fire by natives. *Newsweek*'s yearning to "repair" the park sounds as if they were covering the burning of something inanimate, something like . . . an outdoor museum. This event appalled us so, not just because fire encroached upon our civilization, but because we have been culturally conditioned to see Yellowstone in static, iconographic images. A cultural monument, it appeared, had been ravaged by an enemy we should have been able to beat. And like the Vietnam myth, defeat seemed to be self-inflicted.

On the contrary, as some publications quietly reported the following spring, the fire began regenerating the health of the Yellowstone forest the day it started. Although not conducive to the same tabloid coverage of the fire evil, the signs of Yellowstone's renewal were everywhere: popped seeds of the lodgepole pine's serotinous cones lay about, ready to take hold; the next year's wildflower growth in the burned-over forests were brilliant; meadows appeared greener and more lush than anyone could remember. Fire, as Park Service officials had hypothesized, brought new life to Yellowstone.[22]

While reaction to the 1988 apocalypse surpassed anything since the capture of poacher Ed Howell, the more destructive phenomenon of timber-cutting outside park boundaries has proceeded apace—quietly out of view of most Americans. Superintendent John Pitcher's 1903 proposal for bounding Yellowstone with a swath of cleared forest has been eerily manifested a century later. Massive clear-cutting of the adjoining Targhee National Forest—carried out by private companies, subsidized by federal tax dollars and encouraged by the Forest Service's multiple use policy—has resulted in a stark dividing line between park and forest (fig. 52). Intensive lumber extraction has emphatically answered the fears of nineteenth-century development proponents that the nation's first forest preserve would effectively be "locked up" as an extension of Yellowstone Park. On the contrary, timber "harvesting"—the happy euphemism used by Forest Service and timber company officials—has accelerated to a level that Yellowstone Ecosystem activists argue is nonsustainable, based on the growth rate of Rocky Mountain forests.[23] Playing to the shifting paradigm, the Forest Service considers its timber-cutting and road-building program part of "ecosystem management,"[24] pointing out how dangerously pliable that term can be.

Rather than repeat itself verbatim, history in the Yellowstone region seems

Fig. 52. Targhee Forest/Yellowstone Park Border, 1990. Photo by Tim
Crawford. Courtesy Greater Yellowstone Coalition.

inclined to return in ominous new forms. That is the case in the mountains
surrounding Cooke City, Montana, site of the late nineteenth century's most
protracted struggle over park integrity. The focus of intensive gold mining
for decades, the mountains in the New World Mining District were by the
1980s heavily scarred by roads and an accumulation of orange-colored toxic
mine tailings (fig. 53). Poisonous mining byproducts oozed downward
toward the Stillwater River, while a nearby tailings pond from the same
abandoned mine leached heavy metals into Soda Butte Creek—the one trib-
utary that flows across the dividing line and into Yellowstone Park. With the
residue of precious metals leaking into the nation's crown jewel, in 1989 the
Environmental Protection Agency (EPA) conducted an immediate cleanup of
the most affected area using federal Superfund money. The EPA action
underscored once more Yellowstone's significance; never before had the
agency "intervened on behalf of a wildland with no immediate threat to public health or human safety." There are an estimated one thousand abandoned
hard-rock mines in the Greater Yellowstone Ecosystem, the effects of which
may likely never be fully remediated.[25]

The environmental hazards posed by past hard-rock mining are owed in
large part to the carte blanche privileges afforded to mine operators by the

Fig. 53. New World Mining District, Cooke City Montana. Photo by Tim Crawford. Courtesy Greater Yellowstone Coalition.

federal Mining Law of, ironically enough, 1872—the year Yellowstone National Park was born. Enacted along with other measures of the period to induce development of public lands in the West, the 1872 Mining Law requires the U.S. government to buy or "patent" land for the ridiculously archaic price of five dollars per acre. Paying no royalties to the government, companies must only demonstrate some proof of valuable mineral deposits. With a national debt in the trillions, from 1992 to 1995 alone the United States government sold $15.3 billion worth of precious metals on public lands for $16,015. Outrageously antiquated from an ecological perspective as well, the 1872 Mining Law supersedes virtually all requirements for environmental protection on public lands.[26]

In 1990, under license of the Mining Law, a Canadian-controlled minerals corporation proposed a major redevelopment of the New World Mining District near Cooke City. The project would have entailed the construction of several open-pit gold, silver, and copper mines, a cyanide-based

processing mill, and a tailings pond the size of seventy football fields and
up to one hundred feet high to hold toxic byproducts. In return for a song
to U.S. taxpayers, Noranda, Inc., the Canadian entity that controlled the
claim, hoped to extract a minimum $600 million worth of precious metal.
Despite the stigma of foreign ownership, Noranda's project drew local support because of the promise of high-paying, year-round jobs in an area economically dependent on seasonal tourism.[27] "I support anything that provides
a good living for the people that work there as long as they are concerned
about the environment," said Patricia Crabb, who with her husband owns
the All Seasons Mine Company Motel and Restaurant. "I'm sure they will
be," she resolved. "We're supposed to be good stewards of the environment,
but that doesn't mean we have to lock it all up."[28]

Environmentalists claimed the New World Mining project posed numerous environmental threats, including water quality degradation in the Clark's
Fork of the Yellowstone River and Soda Butte Creek, which flows into the
Lamar River of Yellowstone Park. Project opponents also claimed that the
expansion of mining activity would disturb grizzly bear habitat, and worse,
bring the potential for a major toxic disaster in the event of an earthquake—
a very real possibility, they argued, in the seismically active Yellowstone
region. Noranda protested that state-of-the-art technology would prevent
such a catastrophe and securely impound the mine tailings forever.[29] They
projected the "sort of technological confidence," the *New York Times* feared,
"that chills the blood."[30]

Most people in the region agreed, believing the mine to be a major threat
to a sustainable tourist economy. "We've seen the boom-and-bust economies,"
said Jim Barrett, who headed the Beartooth Alliance opposed to Noranda's
plans. "Now we've got a viable recreation- and tourist-based economy here.
. . . There's no such thing as a good mine in this place," he declared in
1995.[31] John Graham, an outfitter and leader of hunting and fishing excursions into the mountains of the Yellowstone region, felt similarly threatened.
"Our clients are up here for a quiet wilderness experience, and that mine
would ruin it," said Graham. "People don't come up here to listen to a bunch
of machinery. . . . I just can't see them giving a permit to people to mine gold
to make necklaces and wrecking that whole country up there."[32]

Clearly, this majority response to the project illustrated an ongoing but
profound shift in definitions of commodification and aesthetic perceptions
of nature in the region from a century ago. The blissful juxtaposition of the
natural and the technological sublime, commonplace in Wonderland culture,
no longer appeals to the tourist eye. With the widening sprawl of civilization, coexistence of the mechanistic and the natural in a place like Yellow-

stone now repulses. In the postmodern era where only constricted or contrived nature is readily available to most Americans, here, of all places, nature must be wide and pure. We expect Yellowstone to represent our natural wilderness heritage as it appeared in its "virgin" state, not as it looked a century ago. Stated pragmatically, the expansion of mining in the region, as most local entrepreneurs saw it, would damage the patina and the business of nature. Yellowstone, President Clinton, later said, "is more precious than gold."[33]

The struggle raged for several years, despite the opposition of the Yellowstone Park superintendent, Mike Finley, President Clinton's secretary of the interior Bruce Babbitt, and major national and international environmental organizations. After flying over the area himself in 1995, President Clinton announced that he was "very worried" about the mine. "No amount of gain that could come from [the mine] could possibly offset any permanent damage to Yellowstone," he declared.[34] In a deal straight from the Clinton Department of Compromise, in August 1996 the White House Council on Environmental Quality brokered a deal that sent Noranda packing—for a price. In exchange for giving up its New World mining rights and cleaning up historic pollution at the site, the corporation would receive $65 million worth of federally owned lands elsewhere in the West.[35] The company retained veto power on whatever the government offered. More worrisome for some observers was the precedent the deal seemed to set: Could anyone holding one of the more than six thousand remaining mining claims in the Yellowstone Ecosystem make the same demand?[36] At least one thing seemed clear from the episode: after repeatedly failed reform efforts, the principles of corporate capitalism that undergird the 1872 Mining Law are as politically sacred as the Yellowstone Park Act. Inspired the same year with the overlapping purpose of western development, the guardians of each statue are every bit as tenacious as their ancestors.

The Greater Yellowstone Ecosystem holds other attractive underground resources, both within and beyond the park. Exploratory drilling for oil and gas has been extensive throughout the surrounding national forests. Oil and gas development involves not only the clearing of a large drilling site, but, as with the harvest of timber, construction of roads into formerly roadless areas. Road building brings a number of associated negative impacts, including erosion and sedimentation of vital watersheds, "disturbance corridors" for the penetration of noxious weeds, fragmentation of wildlife habitat and migration routes, and greater access for poachers. Rural subdivisioning for housing and development of high-impact tourist facilities such as ski resorts and golf courses are posing similar problems.[37]

The laundering of dirty tourist garb in the crater of Old Faithful ended a century ago. One might presume, then, that at least the geysers would be safe. However, the geothermal activity responsible for Yellowstone Park's three hundred geysers and thousands of hot springs is connected to a larger underground plumbing system that scientists have determined extends beyond the park perimeter. In the late 1980s, that hydrological network became attractive to the outside world once again. In 1991, in spite of National Park Service warnings, the Department of the Interior acquiesced to a proposed subsurface development of related geothermal resources on private land lying just north of Mammoth Hot Springs, outside the park boundary. Based on experience elsewhere in the world where geothermal resources have been developed, environmental groups argued that tapping into the region's geothermal network posed a clear risk to Yellowstone's geyser basins and hot springs.[38] Even Old Faithful may not be as "locked up" as we believed.

Long thought to be functional only for laundering, it turns out that Yellowstone's more than ten thousand thermal features harbor an amazing number and variety of microorganisms of great interest to academic researchers and enormous value to the biotechnology industry. With their unique capacity to thrive at scalding temperatures and extremes of acidity and alkalinity, these living thermophiles and their catalytic enzymes have proven useful and environmentally friendly in a number of applications, including DNA fingerprinting, conversion of organic waste into ethanol, pulp and paper processing, gold and copper mining, acid mine drainage and reclamation, food processing, and various genetic-engineering projects. Dozens of researchers and private labs mining Yellowstone's microorganisms "liken the vast, largely untapped microbial ecology to the incredible biodiversity of the Brazilian rainforest."[39]

Like the rainforest, the discovery of microbic treasure in Yellowstone has prompted declarations that the utilitarian represents the "greater value" of the park. Curiously, even the Park Service director thought "the microbe rush in Yellowstone [proved] the intrinsic worth of national parks."[40] Actually, leaving the microbes be would verify their intrinsic value. Biotech companies reaped hundreds of millions of dollars in profits from the microbes in the first few years of exploration. But because there was no policy on biotic mining in national parks, the U.S. Treasury and the always-strapped Yellowstone budget had not accrued a dime in royalties as of 1997.[41] No matter the price, Park Superintendent Mike Finley worried about precedent and perception: "People will get the idea we're auctioning off what the park is supposed to preserve," he said.[42]

In the late nineteenth century, conservationists argued successfully that the Cooke City Railroad had to be defeated and the national forests established in order to protect the watershed that was vital to farmers and ranchers. Neither conservationists nor ranchers of the era could see that cattle would never properly adapt to the arid climate of the West and that their congregation near biologically critical riparian areas would harm water quality. Even as hunters, they could not recognize that wild ungulates would struggle to compete with millions of non-native cattle and sheep for forage; nor did they mourn for the native bison supplanted by cattle herds. They had little or no memory of the tall grasses that thrived on the plains and mountain meadows before livestock ground down the rangelands beyond recognition and allowed the invasion of noxious weeds. Sheep ranchers could not predict that their domestic herds would be the likely culprits that later ravaged the Yellowstone bighorn sheep population with a bacterial eye infection. They certainly did know and participate in the near-extermination of wolves that occasionally preyed on their property. These are some of the legacies of livestock grazing in the Greater Yellowstone Ecosystem.[43] And because myth— and the corporate cowboy lobby—is stronger than fact, grazing fees on public lands throughout the West continue to be appallingly low. It costs a human tourist one hundred times more for the privilege of touring Yellowstone than it does a rancher to graze one cow on the adjoining national forest.[44]

Ranching clearly is too large a part of western myth and reality to disappear. Moreover, many ranching families in the Greater Yellowstone Ecosystem and throughout the West acknowledge that part of their economic woes are rooted in bad environmental practices. Beginning in the 1980s, cattlemen's groups began working with environmentalists on strategies for better stewardship, including Holistic Resource Management, conservation easements, and watershed planning—all of which begin with an understanding of the western environment before the arrival of cattle. And because they are so mythically connected to this landscape, ranchers represent one of the best hopes for defending it. Ecosystem defenders have found common ground with ranchers (the two groups are not mutually exclusive) on such threats as the postmodern "ranchette," a 20-acre subdivision offering Old West veneer to the wave of new arrivals who began flooding the region in the 1980s.[45] Prospective land owners north of the park are invited to "Own a Piece of Paradise . . . in many cases only minutes away from national forests or parks."[46]

Likewise, an agricultural system ill-suited for the climate and soils of the Rocky Mountains has had negative impacts on the fringe areas of the

Yellowstone Ecosystem. The standard "monoculture of cultivated plants" that is modern agriculture has largely supplanted the diverse and dynamic vegetative life that evolved and once thrived there. For most of the twentieth century, farmers relied increasingly on fertilizers, pesticides, and hydrothermal dam projects that increasingly threatened aquatic life and the integrity of watersheds throughout the region. Popular belief has long held that the yeoman farmer cannot survive without the appurtenances of corporate farming. The ecological health of the Yellowstone region, say environmentalists, may well not survive with them.[47]

A similar dissonance between what-we-think and what-is prevails with regard to park wildlife. The realities of altered populations and constricted biodiversity belie the popular paradisiacal image that derives from the turn of the last century. Elk seem quite at home on the streets of downtown Gardiner. As the tourist passes through town and under the Roosevelt Arch, she is greeted by a sign indicating "Wildlife Exhibit Ahead." Moments later a few bison enter the windshield view. Especially in winter, when wildlife moves down from the high country, tourists are likely to be rewarded with intimate, zoolike images.[48] Playing on the virgin myth, the Yellowstone concessionaire's 1988 promotional literature heralded "wildlife roaming as free as when the world was young."[49]

Well, not quite. What appear to be healthy populations of Yellowstone's most famous and noble species obscure the changes wrought among park fauna by more than a century of human activity and management. Wildlife reported in large numbers by Theodore Roosevelt on his 1903 visit are now scarcely to be found, among them mule deer, white tail deer, pronghorn antelope, big horn sheep, and beaver.[50] Throughout the ecosystem, the rural sprawl of an expanding population and excessive road building to serve timber companies pose the most insidious and tenacious threats to their continued survival.

The elk are doing very well; some believe too well. Their expanding number is the result of more than a century of shifting human manipulation and may now be an ecological threat itself. The policy of "natural regulation" adopted by park officials in the 1970s brought an end to the deliberate thinning of elk each year; since then, the population of the park's northern range has soared—from thirty-one hundred in 1968 to more than twenty thousand in 1995. Charles Kay, a wildlife biologist at Utah State University, believes the dominance of elk is to blame for the decline in species diversity and a host of related woes: the erosion of stream banks, the disappearance of woody shrubs, the inability of aspen shoots to grow and mature, and the increasing grass-dominated monoculture of grazing areas. "What [the Park

Service] is changing this into is a lawn. There's more to an ecosystem than grass," says Kay.[51] With comparative evidence from other regions where the only difference seems to be the elk population, scientists make a compelling case. They argue that park officials cling to current policy because of elk politics; tourists love to see them and hunters and outfitters in surrounding areas love the overflow. (Poachers would also hate to see a change; an aphrodisiac and medicinal cure-all on the Asian market, Yellowstone elk "horn" now fetches $5–12 per pound.)[52] Kay puts the issue squarely: "If you want lots of elk and bison to make the tourists happy, it's not a nature park, it's a theme park—it's entertainment. So you might as well let Disney run it."[53]

The issue bespeaks the larger internal conflict of park officials who are charged with fulfilling the mission inscribed across the Roosevelt Arch. FOR THE BENEFIT AND ENJOYMENT . . .. Of course Yellowstone is entertainment; it has been primarily that from the start. The perpetual struggle of park managers is to incorporate what they can of developing ecological practice within the lowest common denominator mindset of tourism: what we think visitors want or will accept.

As demonstrated in the 1988 Yellowstone fire episode, park officials must also balance the needs of the park with the desires and fears of local residents. The gray wolf comes to mind. Scientific thought on the vital ecological role of wolves has been changing since the day Aldo Leopold saw the "green fire die" in the eyes of a hunted New Mexican wolf.[54] Victim of cultural abomination in the Wonderland era, the gray wolf's sixty-year absence in Yellowstone is certainly one major reason for the abundance of elk. (Strangely enough, a park guidebook available in 1991 at the Visitor Center listed the wolf as one of the native species still to be seen.)[55] For several decades independent ecologists called the wolf the ecosystem's "missing link" for its vital role as the "preeminent predator in the region." Nevertheless, various Park Service proposals in the 1980s and 1990s to reintroduce the animal faced vehement opposition from nearby Montana ranchers who feared depredations to their cattle.[56] Opponents refashioned the evil wolf myth to support their cause; one rancher at a 1991 meeting on the issue vilified the wolf as "the Saddam Hussein of the animal kingdom."[57]

Opposition continued into the spring of 1995, months after wolves were finally reintroduced into the Yellowstone Ecosystem. U.S. Representatives Helen Chenoweth (R-Idaho) and Barbara Curbin (R-Wyoming) damned "this misguided experiment [that was] being forced on our states" and requested a hearing on the issue before the House Committee on Resources. Renee Askins, executive director of the Wolf Fund, which worked for the return of wolves, provided key testimony at the hearing:

If I were a rancher I probably would not want wolves returned to the
West. If I faced the conditions that ranchers face . . . I would want to
blame something, to fight something, even kill something. The wolf
is an ideal target . . . [but] wolves aren't the cause of the changes
occurring in the West any more than the rooster's crow is the cause
of the sun's rising, but they have become the means by which ranchers
can voice their concern about what's happening around them. . . .
Emotions, not facts, have controlled the Yellowstone wolf debate.
Wolves have never been just wolves: the wolf is the devil's keeper,
the slayer of innocent girls, the nurturer of abandoned children, the
sacred hunter, the ghostly creature of myth and legend. In short,
wolves are symbolic; restoring wolves to Yellowstone is a deeply
and profoundly symbolic act.[58]

And so the deed was done. Over the vehement protests of cattlemen and
politicians, wolves returned to Yellowstone. Among the few human-ecological events more amazing to behold than this one is the simultaneous ennoblement of the wolf in popular culture. In the nature stores and malls of
America, shoppers found posters, puzzles, coffee mugs and calendars depict-
ing a kinder, gentler wolf—often in association with Yellowstone. Even "The
Three Little Pigs" was rewritten from the wolf's point of view![59]

Although never eliminated from Yellowstone Park, grizzly bears have
faced their own struggle. After the garbage-dump-feeding era ended in the
mid-1960s, officials moved to restore the natural patterns of grizzly bear
feeding and migration. They worked, however, in the face of threats from
within and outside the park, most egregious among them excessive road
building throughout the Yellowstone Ecosystem. Restoration of critical habitat in the Fishing Bridge area was slowed due to the park's mid-1990s budget
crisis.[60] The grizzly will certainly survive in museumized form: in 1991, park
officials welcomed visitors to a "glossy new exhibit entitled 'Bears—Imagination and Reality'"; the display was fittingly located at Grant Village—site
of a tourist development that destroyed prime grizzly bear habitat.[61]

Park wildlife continue to be vulnerable to unpredictable forms of assault.
In the 1994 season, park officials labeled the accidental or deliberate introduction of lake trout into Yellowstone Lake a "biological disaster." Because
lake trout feed on Yellowstone's world-renowned native cutthroat species,
biologists predicted a 70 percent loss in cutthroat numbers over the next
century without human intervention. More frightening is the potential magnitude of the disaster throughout the food chain: forty-two Yellowstone
mammal and bird species feed on the cutthroat. In a culture where every-

thing can be quantified, park officials estimated the 1994 value of the Yellowstone fisheries at more than $36 million. With the lake trout control program costing one-quarter that amount over a thirty-year period, saving the cutthroat carries a "good cost-benefit ratio."[62] On occasion the commodification of nature comes in handy.

In another ironic twist, ranchers are increasingly raising the bison as a more environmentally friendly and lucrative alternative to cattle and, like the Indian tribes of old, wasting precious little of the animal. Throughout the West, bison has become an "exemplar of gourmet dining, high fashion and low kitsch." Restaurants serve bison prime rib and burgers, while trendy gift shops feature high-priced bison golf putters and purses.[63]

Attractive once more as commodity and repopulating private reserves, bison on the periphery of Yellowstone Park are more vulnerable than they have been in a century. Cattlemen and Montana livestock officials claim that bison carry the disease brucellosis that causes cattle to abort their calves. This belies several facts, most notably that there is no documented case of bison infecting cattle in the wild (the infecting bacteria dies as soon as it meets sunlight). Cattle introduced the disease into the region in the first place.[64] And there is this: elk also carry brucellosis, yet because elk are of enormous value to the hunting and tourism industries, no official has ever suggested hunting down elk who stray over the line, nor have elk ever infected cattle.[65] As with wolves, however, fear and the sacred cow carried the day. In the winter of 1995–1996, Montana officials shot 450 bison on the northern edge of Yellowstone Park. In the fall of 1996, park officials themselves—charged with protecting the animal—began rounding up bison herds migrating toward the park's northern boundary and shipping them off for slaughter. Nearly one-half the bison population had been shot dead by the spring of 1997.[66] "This is a struggle between the park and agribusiness and we're losing badly," said John Varley, Yellowstone's chief scientist. Varley believed the bison slaughter program was in part retaliation for the successful reintroduction of the wolf.[67]

Thus, although elk are welcome to migrate onto the public lands beyond the park, the same traditional migration corridor for bison is now closed. Wolves are free to roam Yellowstone, but remain vilified and vulnerable in Paradise Valley to the north. The bison controversy is not about brucellosis any more than the wolf conflict was about sheep predation. Fundamentally, these struggles are founded on the economics of agribusiness that have made ranchers desperate for villains, and a segregationist culture that long ago tore asunder the world of wolves and elk. Once before, we slaughtered bison with great efficiency and made the Great Plains safe for cows and democracy.

Americans may cringe at the spectacle of the contemporary bison kill, yet our national soul clings to the myth of the West that has brought it on. What is this about, beyond the unquenchable urge to tame, to *control* that which resists the rule of men?

Environmentalists find outrageous the treatment of "our bison" as just so many "livestock in a corral." Indeed, to believe such spectacle an "injustice" to the mission and history of the park—and to label them *ours*—supports our righteous and patriotic indignation.[68] And yet the present conflict brings the history of Yellowstone bison full circle. The ancestors of the present herd were once enclosed within pens and early park officials always intended the bison to stay within the refuge. Except for noble big game, Yellowstone animals *were* to stay put in the imaginary corral. Congressional park defenders promised that Yellowstone could be altered "if it got in anybody's way," and once more it has. We sanctioned the park, and the park only, as a peaceable kingdom.

Inside the reserve, bison contend with an increasing number of ogling tourists. Their determination to view this emblem of the West creates urban-like traffic jams at the height of the tourist season (fig. 54). In the winter, the visitor gaze often forces the bison to use precious bodily energy trying to avoid a human encounter.[69] For some bison, that energy means the difference between survival and death in the spring. In the early 1990s, greatly expanding winter visitation brought increased pressure upon wildlife.[70]

Despite predictions to the contrary after the 1988 fires, tourist numbers, winter and summer, are growing. In the landmark year of 1883, tourism topped five thousand for the first time; by 1994 visitation exceeded three million—an average of five thousand passing through park boundaries *every hour* during the summer season.[71] With every tourist who passes through the gate, the Yellowstone myth grows while the landscape itself shrinks by absorption. And while the rhetoric of consumption has been toned down from the sumptuousness of the Victorian era, Wonderland advertising still entices with touristic rusticity and cosmopolitan gratification:

> Yellowstone has it together—all in one spectacular place: Old Faithful Geyser, . . . [t]he Grand Canyon of the Yellowstone, crowned by a waterfall higher than Niagara. Wildlife roaming as free as when the world was young. Accommodations in grand old hotels or in rustic cabins. Old West things to do like stagecoach rides and steak cookouts, and all-West things to do like superb fishing and cruises on a high-mountain lake. You can even sightsee by scenicoach with a driver/guide, so you can pay more attention to what you came for.[72]

Fig. 54. Buffalo Jam, 1990. Photo by Tim Crawford. Courtesy Greater Yellowstone Coalition.

What "you come for" still begins (and ends, for many) with Old Faithful and its rustic and elegant lodgings. In the commodity-consumption tradition, tourists in 1988 were urged to not "miss the new etched-glass windows in the lounge" of Old Faithful Inn, nor the lobby of Old Faithful Lodge which "offers geyser views and a cafeteria."[73] Since 1903 the touristic trappings have become wonders equal to the geothermal environs of the Upper Geyser Basin.

The efficiency of the late-nineteenth-century Wonderland tour has improved markedly. Whereas the average Yellowstone visit in the 1880s lasted a week or longer, it is now done in less than forty-eight hours.[74] Obviously, the automobile has much to do with this increased efficiency, although its current rule as the dominant mode of park travel did not always appear certain. In 1900, the *Livingston Enterprise* offered a sarcastically dim view of the ludicrous notion of autos in Yellowstone:

> [I]t is but a fancied advantage to be able to travel by gasoline amid the wonders of nature. There are some things so incompatible that one cannot regard them without somewhat of a mental wrench. An

automobile camping party in the wilderness, for instance, is a prospect that it takes a minute or so to realize the incongruity of and that doesn't seem to be a thing of joy.[75]

As elsewhere in America, autos had their way with Yellowstone, accompanied by more roads. Following roadways, of course, are the tourists:

> Yellowstone National Park has the dubious distinction of possessing its own freeway interchange, part of a new bypass road built to help relieve congestion at Old Faithful. Visitors wishing to see Yellowstone's most famous geyser turn off at a grade-separated interchange and drive to one of several large parking lots more reminiscent of a suburban shopping center than the popular image of a wilderness national park. Thousands converge to watch the hourly eruption, the estimated time of which is communicated to visitors on electronic displays at convenient locations along the roads and paths leading to the geyser cone. After the eruption, most visitors can count on traffic delays and carbon monoxide fumes as cars leave the lots.[76]

In the postmodern world, the profanation of the sacred is so commonplace that scenes like this are irritating, but assumed as the price of a worthy display. After all, the best attractions at Disney World require even longer waits among larger crowds. While visitors are encouraged by Park Service literature to get off the main highway in the "as if" explorer mode, most of us remain fixed on the main attractions.[77] The road less traveled may be more romantic, but discovery implies toil.[78]

Yellowstone National Park, it seems, is forever and inextricably linked to its Wonderland roots. Notwithstanding the rigorous antimonopoly crusade against the Yellowstone Park Improvement Company, most concessions in the park are still managed by one corporation. TW Recreational Services, by all reports a gracious and professional concessionaire, has held the franchise since 1979 and, partly because of a controversial clause in park concession policy, will likely continue to do so. The "preferential right" held by current concessionaires gives them the right to match the highest bid of any possible competitor while competing for renewal of their contract, effectively shutting out the competition. Treading the path of George Vest, in the early 1990s Congress struggled unsuccessfully to revoke that provision, as well as to obtain a modest increase in the small fees private concessionaires pay to the government for the privilege of operating in the national park.[79]

In light of the $70 million generated by Yellowstone concessionaires in 1995 and a shrinking park budget, obtaining a larger share of concession fees has become a particularly pressing issue. By 1996 the park budget had reached such a crisis that managers began considering measures once unthinkable: closing facilities, laying off additional staff (beyond the current twelve percent unfilled positions), and a shortening of the summer season.[80] That year, Alaska Senator Frank Murkowski offered an audacious but less-than-novel solution to administrator woes: corporate sponsorship of all national parks. Why not? Corporate dollars have done wonders for auto racing. The Greater Yellowstone Coalition rejected the idea out of hand. Go figure; those ungrateful environmentalists. In what could have been an analysis of the Northern Pacific Railroad's control of Yellowstone a century ago, the GYC said that such underwriting would allow corporations "to use this country's national parks as a tool in public relations games and even to hide environmentally destructive records."[81] Corporations may have to continue deploying nature camouflage as they do now—through television and magazine advertising, nature programming, nature calendars, and other insidious forms.

A century after the Wonderland era, the inexorable growth in visitor numbers prompted park officials to begin studying possible solutions to the tourist impact upon Yellowstone's environment and the related decline in the quality of the sightseer's experience. Discussions include a possible ceiling on the number of visitors allowed per season and limitations on the exploding number of snowmobilers. Yellowstone Superintendent Mike Finley put the issue squarely in the context of other activities in the ecosystem:

> Visitation to national parks, just like extractive industries of timbering and mining, is not without consequence and cannot be sustained with unlimited growth into the future.[82]

There was also a short-lived and ironic proposal to study the feasibility of an electric monorail transport system in Yellowstone Park.[83] Proponents of the rail project would have implemented, with modern technology, essentially the same design that was fought so vigorously by park defenders a century ago. Too un-American to ever receive serious consideration, it would have improved both the quality of the visitor experience and air quality in Yellowstone.

The grand view of the Greater Yellowstone Ecosystem in the late twentieth century summons the futuristic vision of Wonderland promised by its most zealous boosters in the late nineteenth century: mining (despite the defeat of the New World Mine), timbering, ranchette-building, grazing, and, as Colgate Hoyt prophesied in 1870, "right in the heart of all this noise and wrestless [sic] life . . . that marvelous region [of the] National Park."[84] Hoyt, Olin D. Wheeler, Eugene Smalley, and Frank J. Haynes would likely be pleased. Perhaps like no other place in America, we seem to have it all here. Americans impounded, arranged, and classified the Yellowstone wilderness even as we damned its surrounding (and as we now know, connecting) "resources" to the exploitative designs of an expanding market economy. Three million visitors a year can't be wrong. The environmental problems facing Greater Yellowstone dissolve before the tourist gaze. We do not see them, nor would we want to.

Long after Americans have reduced the park to a sedative from modernity, we insist on the innocence of Yellowstone. It is, finally, myth and innocence and greatness and idealism that makes Yellowstone National Park so awfully American. And it is the charge of this and future generations to carry on the work of cultural and political elites of the late nineteenth century who made of Yellowstone something *separate*: apart from its prehistoric past; disconnected from the earth surrounding it; elevated above the ranked animal world; and mythically disengaged from the prosaic and profaned world in which Americans live.

Proponents of ecosystem management tenaciously aspire to put Humpty together again. With human presence in the region becoming more and more dominant, the challenge is daunting. The extreme difficulties ecosystem advocates face expose the insidious defects inherent in the original act of Yellowstone's preservation. We sealed off the spectacular for our sensuous, psychic gratification and patriotic possession; the rest we left to unfettered, (though later *managed* and unfettered) extractive exploitation. Modest restraint and regulation in the second half of the twentieth century have not altered the status of Americans as the greatest super-consumers of the planet's resources. The vulnerability of even a culturally sacralized refuge like Yellowstone Park, along with the general degradation of the biosphere outside, offer sobering testimony to the unquenchable urges of consumption and the deficiencies of border making on the American landscape.

In the end, of course, there are no alternatives. Yellowstone National Park must and will endure. It seems to me as improbable as it is imperative that we reenvision Yellowstone as a place unknown. Can we imagine Yellowstone before it was reduced to Old Faithful t-shirts? Before the tastemakers of Wonderland grooved the path to Inspiration Point? It is hard to comprehend a time when only Native Americans shaped the Yellowstone landscape, when there were no lines in the wilderness and this wild place of vitality and might belonged only to the earth. A humbling notion it is. One returns to Truman Everts, who escaped from Yellowstone with not only a desire for Yellowstone's taming, but with respect for its power. And it is that humble spirit, less than the romantic aesthetic or strategy of managerial stewardship that came to dominate, that Americans need to reinstill in ourselves if Yellowstone is to endure as more than icon. That humility is at the spiritual core of the nineteenth-century sublime.

The need to reimagine and revere nature as sacred is upon us with fierce urgency. Herein lies the peril and deception of national parks and wilderness: Are not all lands irreplaceable in the truest sense of the word? We must extend reverence beyond the boundary of Yellowstone and other culturally privileged places. Indeed it seems essential that we begin to dissolve the lines between the sacred and the profane. For that to happen elsewhere, it must happen in the Greater Yellowstone Ecosystem. Yellowstone is both cultural myth and environmental paradigm. As such, the region and its people bear a burden of symbolism and responsibility that is global in scope. Leading the way once again, environmentalists there are now working to extend the concept of ecosystem to the macro level. They argue that the vast region from Yellowstone to the Yukon, while fragmented, was formerly of one piece and remains ecologically linked.[85]

Yellowstone is a place of precedent—first national park, birth of wildlife conservation, the first park to test a let-burn fire policy, first to reintroduce wolves. So what happens here—if the notion of regional ecosystem can be a contagion strong enough to disrupt the forces that oppose it—may well signify whether and how well the global ecosystem survives. In the meantime, renewing a sense of the sacred will matter most where we least expect: in the wonderlands of our own ecosystem, in our own backyards.

Notes

Preface

1. Aubrey L. Haines, *The Yellowstone Story: A History of Our First National Park*, 2 vols. (Mammoth, WY: Yellowstone Park Museum Association, in cooperation with Colorado University Associated Press, 1977); Richard A. Bartlett, *Yellowstone: A Wilderness Besieged* (Tucson: University of Arizona Press, 1985); and Lee H. Whittlesley, *Yellowstone Place Names* (Helena: Montana Historical Society, 1988), 19.

2. The work of esteemed scholars of cultural myth has gone before me and clearly shaped my thinking. In particular: Henry Nash Smith, *Virgin Land: The American West as Symbol and Myth* (Cambridge: Harvard University Press, 1950); Leo Marx, *The Machine In the Garden: Technology and the Pastoral Ideal in America* (New York: Oxford University Press, 1964); Richard Slotkin, *The Fatal Environment: The Myth of the Frontier in the Age of Industrialization, 1800–1890* (New York: Atheneum, 1985); Annette Kolodny, *The Lay of the Land: Metaphor as Experience and History in American Life and Letters* (Chapel Hill: University of North Carolina Press, 1975), and *The Land before Her: Fantasy and Experience of the American Frontier, 1630–1860* (Chapel Hill: University of North Carolina Press, 1984).

Chapter One

1. Truman C. Everts, "Thirty-Seven Days of Peril," *Scribner's Monthly*, November 1871, 17.

2. Nathaniel Pitt Langford, *The Discovery of Yellowstone Park: Journal of the Washburn Expedition to the Yellowstone and Firehole Rivers In the Year 1870*, with a foreword by Aubrey L. Haines (Lincoln: University of Nebraska Press, 1972; reprint from original 1905 edition published by the Haynes Foundation), 97. Originally "Wonders of the Yellowstone," in *Scribners Monthly* May, June, 1871.

3. Ferdinand Vandiveer Hayden, Report to the U.S. House of Representatives Committee on Public Lands, 1872, quoted in *Ferdinand Vandiveer Hayden and*

the *Founding of Yellowstone National Park,* U.S. Department of the Interior Geological Survey Publications (Washington, DC: Government Printing Office, 1980), 24–25. Hereafter cited as *Hayden and the Founding.*

4. The Yellowstone Organic Act of March 1, 1872, U.S. Statutes at Large, vol. 17, chap. 24, 32–33.

5. Whittlesley, *Yellowstone Place Names,* 166, states that prospector A. Bart Henderson used the name first in his diary July 24, 1871, followed by a *New York Times* article in October 1871, "The New Wonderland." Aubrey L. Haines, *The Yellowstone Story: A History of Our First National Park* (Yellowstone Library and Museum Association in cooperation with Colorado Associated University Press, 1977), vol. 1, 354, n54, recalls that the name was borrowed from the story, "Alice's Adventures Underground," written by Charles Lutwidge Dodgson in 1862 for the amusement of a child companion. As Haines notes, the little girl for whom the story was written later wrote of her visit to the Yellowstone Wonderland.

6. Haines, *The Yellowstone Story,* vol. 1, 132.

7. Joel Janetski, *Indians of Yellowstone National Park* (Salt Lake City: University of Utah Press, 1987), 82–83; see also Joseph Weixelman, "The Power to Evoke Wonder: Native Americans and the Geysers of Yellowstone National Park" (master's thesis, Montana State University, 1992).

8. Philetus W. Norris, *Annual Report of the Superintendent of the Yellowstone National Park to the Secretary of the Interior for the Year 1880* (Washington, DC: Government Printing Office, 1881), 35. The canard that Indians were afraid of and spent little time in Yellowstone descended as fact far into the twentieth century; see, for example, Michael D. Yandell, ed., *A Photographic and Comprehensive Guide to Yellowstone National Park,* National Parkways Guide Series (Casper, WY: World-Wide Research and Publishing Company, 1976), 7. More often Indians are simply not mentioned at all: see National Park Service, *Official Yellowstone Map and Guide* (Washington, DC: U.S. Department of the Interior, 1991).

9. Merrill Beal, *The Story of Man in Yellowstone* (Caldwell, ID: Caxton Printers, 1949), 84–91; and Haines, *The Yellowstone Story,* vol. 1, 237–38.

10. Haines, *The Yellowstone Story,* vol. 1, 218–19, notes that the Cowan tourist party harassed by the Nez Perce in 1877 falsely believed even then that the Indians' "superstitious fear" of the place would have kept the Nez Perce safely away from the park. So although Norris did not invent the notion, he stamped it with authority.

11. Michael V. Sheridan, *Personal Memoirs of Philip Henry Sheridan,* (New York: D. Appleton and Company, 1904), vol. 2, 550–51.

12. Bridger quote in *Personal Recollections and Observations of General Nelson A. Miles* (Chicago: Werner Co., 1897), 137; quoted in Haines, *The Yellowstone Story,* vol. 1, 57–59. Haines thoroughly recounts what is popularly known as the "era of discovery" in chapters 3 and 4.

13. Langford, *The Discovery*, xxix.

14. Peter Koch, "Discovery of the Yellowstone National Park: A Chapter of Early Exploration In the Rocky Mountains," *Magazine of American History*, June 1884, 512.

15. For excellent discussions of the picturesque, see John R. Stilgoe, *Borderland: Origins of the American Suburb, 1820–1939* (New Haven: Yale University Press, 1988), 22–24; John Sears, *Sacred Places: American Tourist Attractions In the Nineteenth Century* (New York: Oxford University Press, 1989), chap. 5; and Paul Shepard, *Man in the Landscape: A Historic View of the Esthetics of Nature* (New York: Alfred A. Knopf, 1967), 125–26. For the first explication of the sublime, see Edmund Burke, *A Philosophical Enquiry Into the Origin of Our Ideas of the Sublime and Beautiful* (1757); on the American sublime, see Sears, *Sacred Places;* Shepard, *Man in the Landscape*, 157–65; Elizabeth McKinsey, *Niagara Falls: Icon of the American Sublime* (New York: Cambridge University Press, 1985); and Philip Terrie, *Forever Wild: Environmental Aesthetics and the Adirondack Forest Preserve* (Philadelphia: Temple University Press, 1985), 17–18.

16. Osborne Russell, *Journal of a Trapper*, ed. Aubrey L. Haines (Portland: Oregon Historical Society, 1955), 26–27.

17. Portions of Henderson's journal are reprinted in *The Yellowstone Interpreter*, vol. 2 (1964); quoted in Haines, *The Yellowstone Story*, vol. 1, 79.

18. Charles W. Cook, David E. Folsom, and William Peterson, *The Valley of the Yellowstone*, ed. Aubrey L. Haines (Norman: University of Oklahoma Press, 1965), cited without page number by Haines in *The Yellowstone Story*, vol. 1, 99.

19. Haines, *The Yellowstone Story*, vol. 1, 101.

20. T. J. Jackson Lears, *No Place of Grace: Antimodernism and the Transformation of American Culture, 1880–1920* (New York: Pantheon, 1981), 57–58, 304–305.

21. Estwick Evans, *A Pedestrious Tour of Four Thousand Miles through the Western States and Territories during the Winter and Spring of 1818* (Concord, NH: n.p., 1819), 6, 102; quoted in Roderick Nash, *Wilderness and the American Mind*, 3d ed. (New Haven: Yale University Press, 1982), 56.

22. Shepard, *Man In the Landscape*, 181–82.

23. Everts, "Thirty-Seven Days," 3.

24. Ibid., 12–13.

25. McKinsey, *Niagara Falls*, 31–32.

26. Everts, "Thirty-Seven Days," 9.

27. Shepard, *Man In the Landscape*, 169, describes fire as one of the "supremely mutable, symbolic, iconic forms" of the sublime that could arouse the same compelling and terrifying response as that provoked by a yawning cataract.

28. Everts, "Thirty-Seven Days," 10.

29. Ibid., 2; for a complete analysis of themes in Christian pilgrimage, see Vic-

tor Turner and Edith Turner, *Image and Pilgrimage in Christian Culture* (New York: Columbia University Press, 1978).

30. Everts, "Thirty-Seven Days," 11.

31. The theme of wilderness and redemption is explored in Perry Miller, *Errand Into the Wilderness* (New York: Harper and Row, 1956); and Kolodny, *The Lay of the Land*.

32. Whittlesley, *Yellowstone Place Names*, 103–105, 107; Whittlesley, 105, citing the *Helena Independent*, 6 February 1887. Everts, incidentally, lived to be a grand old man.

33. Sears, *Sacred Places*, chapters 1–6.

34. Everts, "Thirty-Seven Days," 17.

35. Haines, *The Yellowstone Story*, vol. 1, 105.

36. James MClellan Hamilton, *History of Montana: From Wilderness to State-hood*, ed. Merrill G. Burlingame (Portland: Binfords and Mort, 1957), 220–24; and Haines, *The Yellowstone Story*, vol. 1, 105.

37. Haines, *The Yellowstone Story*, vol. 1, 108–135.

38. Louis C. Cramton, *Early History of Yellowstone National Park and its Relation to National Park Policies* (Washington, DC: Government Printing Office, 1932), 107.

39. Nathaniel Pitt Langford, "Travels in Montana," *New York Times*, 22 January 1871, 8.

40. Nathaniel Pitt Langford, "The Wonders of the Yellowstone," *Scribner's Monthly*, June 1871, 114.

41. The Grand Canyon of Arizona most likely provided the inspiration for the Washburn party to name what had been known to trappers and prospectors as the "Fourth Canyon" (on the Yellowstone River, from Livingston, Montana.) See Whittlesey, *Yellowstone Place Names*, 65.

42. For Americans' interest in the exotic, see Howard Mumford Jones, *The Age of Energy: Varieties of American Experience, 1865–1915* (New York: Viking Press, 1971), 13.

43. Langford, "The Wonders," May 1871, 10, 13, 16.

44. Ibid., 7.

45. Langford, "The Wonders of the Yellowstone: Second Article," June 1871, 128.

46. Katherine E. Early, *"For the Benefit and Enjoyment of the People": Cultural Attitudes and the Establishment of Yellowstone National Park*, no. 1 of the *Georgetown Monograph in American Studies Series* (Washington, DC: Georgetown University Press, 1984), 69.

47. Langford, *The Discovery*, x-xi.

48. Haines, *The Yellowstone Story*, vol. 2, 31; and Bartlett, *A Wilderness Besieged* (, xi.

49. Langford, *The Discovery*, with Haines, 117–18.

50. For a late-nineteenth-century example of the myth's promulgation, see

John Hyde, *Official Guide to the Yellowstone National Park: A Manual for Tourists* (St. Paul, MN: Northern News Co., 1888), 10; contemporary versions include *Geysers of Yellowstone,* produced, written and edited by Russ Finley, video cassette, 52 minutes, Finley Holiday Films, 1992; *Yellowstone: The First National Park,* written, produced and directed by Dan Goldblatt, video cassette, 52 minutes, America's Natural Playground Series, 1990; and Hugh Crandall, *Yellowstone: The Story Behind the Scenery* (Las Vegas, NV: KC Publications, 1977), 40.

51. Yellowstone historian Aubrey Haines was the first to expose the myth. Further developing the intimate connections between the railroad and the park are Bartlett, *A Wilderness Besieged,* passim; and Alfred Runte, *Trains of Discovery: Western Railroads and the National Parks* (Flagstaff, AZ: Northland Press, 1984), 19–21.

52. Other explorers in the 1860s with less influence had previously suggested some kind of a park. Haines, *The Yellowstone Story,* vol. 1, 90, 103, notes the ignored park suggestions of Thomas F. Meagher, acting territorial governor of Montana in the 1860s, and the 1869 Cook-Folsom party. For his part, Hedges recommended in 1870 only ambiguous "appropriation to the public use." See Cramton, *Early History,* 107.

53. Sydney Smith, *Edinburgh Review* (1820); quoted in Alfred Runte, *National Parks: The American Experience,* 2d ed. (Lincoln: University of Nebraska Press, 1987), 32.

54. For discussions of cultural nationalism and national parks, see Runte, *The American Experience,* chap. 1; and Nash, *Wilderness,* chap. 4; and for a broader analysis of nature and America's cultural identity in the nineteenth century, see Barbara Novak, *Nature and Culture: American Landscape and Painting, 1825–1875* (New York: Oxford University Press, 1980).

55. McKinsey, *Niagara Falls,* chapters 1–3.

56. Runte, *The American Experience,* chapter 3.

57. Langford, "The Wonders," May 1871, 9.

58. Observers of, and participants in the project of western development applied the term universally throughout the nineteenth century. The historiographical reference is to Smith, *Virgin Land.*

59. See, for example, Nash, *Wilderness,* 96–100.

60. Henry David Thoreau, "Walking," *The Atlantic Monthly,* June 1862, based on an 1851 lecture entitled, "The Wild," in Thomas J. Lyon, ed., *This Incomparable Lande: A Book of American Nature Writing,* (Boston: Houghton Mifflin, 1989), 172–94; George Catlin, *North American Indians: Being Letters and Notes on Their Manners, Customs, and Conditions, Written During Eight Years' Travel Amongst the Wildest Tribes in North America, 1832–1839* (Minneapolis: Ross and Haines, 1965 reprint; first printed in London, 1841), vol. 1, 261; and George Perkins Marsh, *Man and Nature; or Physical Geography as Modified by Human Action* (New York, 1864).

61. See Peter J. Schmitt, *Back to Nature: The Arcadian Myth in Urban America,* with a foreword by John R. Stilgoe (New York: Oxford University Press, 1969; reprint, Baltimore: Johns Hopkins University Press, 1990), 56–70 (page reference is to reprint edition); Alan Trachtenberg, *The Incorporation of America: Culture and Society in the Gilded Age* (New York: Hill and Wang, 1982), 143; and Hans Huth, *Nature and the American: Three Centuries of Changing Attitudes,* with an introduction by Douglas H. Strong (Berkeley: University of California Press, 1957; new edition, Lincoln: University of Nebraska Press, 1990), 123 (page reference from new edition).

62. Clifford Edward Clark Jr., *The American Family Home, 1800–1960* (Chapel Hill: University of North Carolina Press, 1986), 24, 114.

63. Huth, *Nature and the American,* 48, 60, 78.

64. On preserved nature as a capitalist social construct, see, for example, Carolyn Merchant, *Ecological Revolutions: Nature, Gender, and Science in New England* (Chapel Hill: University of North Carolina Press, 1989), 250–51.

65. For a probing analysis of Hayden's role in and vision of the West, see Peter B. Hales, *Transforming the View: William Henry Jackson and the Transformation of the American Landscape* (Philadelphia: Temple University Press, 1988), 95–97; on page 69, Hales notes that sometimes the Survey results bore personal fruit: typical for men of high position, Hayden was not above accepting $10,000 from a major landholding company in exchange for "glowing" reports about its region. For an excellent biographical portrait of Hayden, see William H. Goetzmann, *Exploration and Empire: The Explorer and the Scientist in the Winning of the West* (New York: Alfred A. Knopf, 1966).

66. Haines, *The Yellowstone Story,* vol. 1, 141–42.

67. *Hayden and the Founding,* 8.

68. Ibid., 9–10.

69. F. V. Hayden, *Preliminary Report of the United States Geological Survey on Montana and Portions of Adjacent Territories: Being a Fifth Annual Report of Progress* (Washington, DC, 1872), 108. Hereafter, Hayden, *Preliminary Report.*

70. *Hayden and the Founding,* 8.

71. Whittlesey, *Yellowstone Place Names,* 104.

72. Ferdinand Vandiveer Hayden, "The Wonders of the West—II: More About the Yellowstone," *Scribner's Monthly,* February 1872, 388–89.

73. Robert Strahorn, *Montana and Yellowstone Park* (Kansas City: Millett and Hudson, 1881), 109.

74. Letter in *Records of the Department of the Interior Geological Survey, Letters Received by F. V. Hayden, 1871,* Record Group 57, National Archives, Washington, DC; cited by Haines, *The Yellowstone Story,* vol. 1, 155.

75. Bartlett, *A Wilderness Besieged,* 2.

76. Senate Debate, 42d Congress *Congressional Globe* (Washington, DC: Government Printing Office), 697. Runte, *The American Experience,* argues in

chapter 3 that the creation and survival of all national parks and wilderness areas
has continued to depend in the twentieth century on their "worthlessness."

77. U.S. Congress, House, *Committee on the Public Lands, The Yellowstone
Park*, H. Report 26 to accompany H.R. 764, 42d Cong., 2d sess., 27 February
1872, 1–2.

78. Haines, *The Yellowstone Story*, vol. 1, 170.

79. Langford recalled that in the famous campfire discussion, the party had
spoken only of protection for the area's "decorations"—its geysers, springs, and
Grand Canyon. Notwithstanding the dubious argument that the discussion led
to the creation of the park, the notion of limited protection would have been consistent for its time, and in fact was advocated by several members of Congress
during the 1872 debate. Langford, with Haines, 117–18; and Hayden, "The Hot
Springs and Geysers of the Yellowstone and Firehole Rivers," *American Journal of Science and Art* 3 (1872): 176; cited by Nash, *Wilderness*, 112.

80. Joe Frantz, "The Meaning of Yellowstone," *Montana: The Magazine of
Western History*, Summer 1972, 11.

81. Hales, *Transformation of the American Landscape*, 109.

82. Nathaniel Langford, *Annual Report of the Superintendent of the Yellowstone National Park for the Year 1872*, U.S., 42d Cong., 3d sess., Ex. Doc. 35,
February 4, 1873, 9.

83. Hayden, *Preliminary Report*, quoted in Runte, *The American Experience*,
33.

84. F. V. Hayden, "The Hot Springs and Geysers," 176.

85. *The Organic Act*, U.S. Statutes at Large, vol. 17, chap. 24, 32–33.

86. *Nevada Territorial Enterprise*, March 22, 1872.

87. Langford, *Annual Report*, 9; *Scribner's Monthly*, Editorial, May 1872,
120; and Walter Trumbull, 1871, quoted in Runte, *The American Experience*,
33.

88. *John L. Stoddard's Lectures* (Boston: Balch Brothers, 1898), vol. 10, 208.

Chapter Two

1. Colgate Hoyt, "Roughing It Up the Yellowstone," ed. Carroll Van West,
Montana: The Magazine of Western History, Spring 1986, 35.

2. Frank Jay Haynes to Charles Fee, General Passenger Agent for the Northern Pacific Railroad, 1879; quoted in Freeman Tilden, *Following the Frontier
with Frank Jay Haynes: Pioneer Photographer of the Old West* (New York:
Knopf, 1964), 11–12.

3. Industrialist Asa Whitney first proposed to Congress in 1853 a railroad
extending from Lake Michigan to the Pacific shore that would secure the future
control of the territory and certain passage to Far Eastern trade routes. In 1868
Josiah Perham, who had received the charter, died in poverty, having lost con-

trol of the company before his death. See Leonard Bertram Irwin, "Pacific Railways and Nationalism in the Canadian-American Northwest, 1845–1873" (Ph.D. diss., University of Pennsylvania, 1939), 9–10.

4. Slotkin, *The Fatal Environment,* 287; and Matthew Josephson, *The Robber Barons: The Great American Capitalists, 1861–1901* (New York: Harcourt, Brace and Company, 1934), 97.

5. Quoted in Bartlett, *A Wilderness Beseiged,* 121; see also Edward Chase Kirkland, *Industry Comes of Age: Business, Labor, and Public Policy, 1860–1897* (New York: Holt Rinehart, 1961), 6–7; and Trachtenberg, *The Incorporation,* 121.

6. The Northern Pacific carried an increasingly beleaguered image throughout the period. Many attacks focused on the excessive land grant given the company by the U.S. government and the incestuous relationship between railroad and government officials; see "The North Pacific Job," *New York World,* 28 January 1881, and "The Attacks Upon the Northern Pacific," *The Daily Statesman,* 26 January 1882.

7. Olin D. Wheeler and the Northern Pacific Railroad, *Wonderland '96* (Chicago: Rand McNally, 1896), 47–48.

8. Trachtenberg, *The Incorporation,* 21–22; and Slotkin, *The Fatal Environment,* 285.

9. Despite the Jeffersonian intentions of the 1862 Homestead Act to secure individual farmers with arable plots, corporate control of the trans-Mississippi West escalated dramatically in the last quarter of the nineteenth century. Indeed, laws such as the Homestead Act and the 1872 Mining Law served perversely to concentrate land and wealth into the hands of speculators and corporations. See Slotkin, *The Fatal Environment,* 284–85; also see Smith, *Virgin Land,* (190–93; and Trachtenberg, *The Incorporation,* 19–22, who notes that only one-tenth of all new farms settled between 1860 and 1900 were established under the Homestead legislation; the rest were bought from land development and railroad companies.

10. John Ise, *The United States Forest Policy* (New Haven: Yale University Press, 1920), 322.

11. *Report of the Commissioner of the General Land Office for the Year 1867* (Washington, DC, 1867), 135–36; quoted in Smith, *Virgin Land,* 180.

12. David M. Emmons, "The Influence of Ideology On Changing Environmental Images: The Case of Six Gazetteers," in *Images of the Plains: The Role of Human Nature in Settlement,* eds. Brian W. Blouet and Merlin P. Lawson (Lincoln: University of Nebraska Press, 1975), 125–36.

13. See Leonard Bertram Irwin, "Pacific Railways and Nationalism in the Canadian-American Northwest, 1845–1873" (Ph.D. diss., University of Pennsylvania, 1939), 127–28; Northwest quote from "The Northern Pacific Country," *The Pioneer Press,* 11 October 1883.

14. Undated advertisement, in Northern Pacific Railway Company Records,

Annual Reports, 1870–1968 (St. Paul: Minnesota Historical Society), microfilm, reel 5, p. 16.

15. Ibid., reel 5, p. 15; and Irwin, "Pacific Railways," 120–21.

16. Olin D. Wheeler and the Northern Pacific Railroad, *Sketches of Wonderland* (Chicago: Rand McNally, 1895), 13–14.

17. Edward W. Nolan, *Northern Pacific Views: The Railroad Photography of F. Jay Haynes, 1876–1905* (Helena: Montana Historical Society, 1983), 3.

18. Ibid., 4.

19. Ibid., 6–10.

20. F. Jay Haynes to Lily V. Snyder, 9 October 1876, F. Jay Haynes Papers, Montana State University Library Special Collections, Bozeman (hereafter Haynes Papers).

21. Unidentified [Fargo, North Dakota] clipping, in Lily V. Haynes Scrapbook, Haynes Papers.

22. Gilbert Fite, *American Farmers: The New Minority* (Bloomington: University of Indiana Press, 1981), 236–38, 130.

23. F. J. Haynes to Lily V. Snyder, 11 October 1876, Haynes Papers.

24. F. J. Haynes to Lily V. Snyder, 16 October 1876, Haynes Papers.

25. F. J. Haynes to Lily V. Snyder, undated letter, Haynes Papers.

26. F. J. Haynes to Lily V. Snyder, 29 October 1876, Haynes Papers.

27. Slotkin, *The Fatal Environment*, 327.

28. Ibid., 413–31; Thomas A. Clinch, "The Northern Pacific Railroad and Montana's Mineral Lands," *Pacific Historical Review* 34 (Fall 1965): 323–35; Ise, *U.S. Forest Policy*, 4; and William S. Bryans, "A History of Transcontinental Railroads and Coal Mining on the Northern Plains to 1920" (Ph.D. diss., University of Wyoming, 1987), 128–58. Ironically, in just a few years, it would be the railroad and its subsidiary "improvement" companies that would face charges of monopolization of everything from mining to Yellowstone Park.

29. H. N. Maguire, "The Black Hills and American Wonderland," *The Lakeside Library* vol. 4, no. 82 (Chicago: Donnelley, Loyd and Co., 1877), in *Western Americana, Frontier History of the Trans-Mississippi West, 1550–1900*, no. 3444, 277–312 (New Haven, CT: Research Publications, 1975), microfilm, Denver Public Library.

30. F. J. Haynes to Lily V. Snyder, 5 December 1877, Haynes Papers.

31. Frank J. Haynes to Lily V. Haynes, October or November 1877, Haynes Papers. In January 1878 Lily went to work as his retoucher and studio manager, positions she held, apparently with some reluctance, for the better part of two decades; see Nolan, *Northern Pacific Views,* chap. 1.

32. If Frank Haynes gave much thought to the drama of this changing landscape, he did not record it. He scrupulously documented his travel, business transactions and the like, yet apparently wrote nothing about his subject matter or artistic sensibilities. Although his inventory reflects an aesthetically attentive eye, Haynes viewed himself primarily as a businessman who happened to

make a very successful living operating a camera. His obsession with the business side of his work prompted Haynes's wife Lily to lament years later, "Sometimes it seemed as if he cared too much for the success of his undertakings and was too attentive to business regardless of everything else." Lily V. Haynes Diary, 29 December 1885, Haynes Papers.

33. Nolan, *Northern Pacific Views,* 14–16. Although Haynes's request for "official photographer" status was never formally approved by railroad officials, he began printing the self-designation on all of his materials shortly after he and Fee met. As further testimony to the importance of their affiliation, one year after Fee left the Northern Pacific in 1904, Haynes severed his association with the railroad.

34. See Hales, *Transformation of the American Landscape.*

35. Patricia Limerick, *The Legacy of Conquest: The Unbroken Past of the American West* (New York: W. W. Norton and Company, 1987), 105, 129.

36. The best work on the vanishing Indian myth is Brian W. Dippie, *The Vanishing American: White Attitudes and U.S. Indian Policy* (Middletown, CT: Wesleyan University Press, 1982).

37. Burton M. Smith, "Politics and the Crow Indian Land Cessions, 1851–1904," *Montana: The Magazine of Western History,* Autumn 1986, 24–28.

38. Thomas P. McElrath, *The Yellowstone Valley: What It Is, How to Get There: A Handbook for Tourists* (St. Paul: Pioneer Press, 1880), 94–95.

39. *Livingston Enterprise,* 4 August 1883, 2.

40. F. Jay Haynes to Lily V. Haynes, 16 September 1881, Haynes Papers.

41. Haynes returned to Yellowstone every summer for the rest of his life and eventually passed his various concessionaire enterprises on to his son Jack, who continued the work of "Haynes Picture Shops" in the park until 1968. See Nolan, *Northern Pacific Views,* and Bartlett, *A Wilderness Beseiged,* 155.

42. F. J. Haynes to C. H. Warren, 30 October 1887, Haynes Papers; and Nolan, *Northern Pacific Views,* 106.

43. H. Austin et al. to Department of the Interior, 1881, Haynes, F. Jay—Letters Concerning Appointment As Photographer, manuscript file, Yellowstone National Park Archives.

44. *Helena Daily Herald,* 28 February 1872.

45. Frederick Schwatka and John Hyde, *Through Wonderland with Lieutenant Schwatka* (St. Paul: Northern Pacific Railroad, 1886), 22–26.

46. "The Clark's Fork Country," *The Yellowstone Journal,* 10 March 1883, 1.

47. Ibid., 1.

48. The Arapooish letter is found reprinted in much of the Yellowstone literature of the late nineteenth century; I quote from I. Winslow Ayer, *Life in the Wilds of America, and Wonders of the West in and beyond the Bounds of Civilization* (Grand Rapids, MI: Central Publishing Company, 1880), 347–48.

49. Ibid., 348.

50. Burton M. Smith, "Politics," 24–28; for additional background on the Crows and Yellowstone, see Haines, *The Yellowstone Story*, vol. 1, 20–29; and Mark H. Brown, *Plainsmen of the Yellowstone: A History of the Yellowstone Basin* (Lincoln: University of Nebraska Press, 1961), 431–32.

51. Charles S. Fee and the Northern Pacific Railroad, "A Romance of Wonderland," advertising circular (St. Paul: Northern Pacific Railroad, 1889), Haynes Papers.

52. Hyde, *Official Guide*, 18–19.

53. F. Jay Haynes, *Catalog, Northern Pacific Views* (Fargo, Dakota Territory: Haynes Publishing, 1883), 31, Montana Historical Society Archives, Helena.

54. *Catalog of Northern Pacific and National Park Views* (Fargo, Dakota Territory: F. J. Haynes, Publisher, 1884), 9, 16, Montana Historical Society Archives.

55. See, for example, George Dimock's probing discussion of Carleton Watkins's nature-corporate work in northern California, *Exploiting the View: Photographs of Yosemite and Mariposa by Carleton Watkins* (North Bennington, VT: Park-McCullough House, 8 July 1984), 10–18, published transcript, University of New Mexico Fine Arts Library, Albuquerque.

56. John F. Kasson, *Civilizing the Machine: Technology and Republican Values In America, 1776–1900* (New York: Penguin Books, 1976), 174.

57. *The Complete Works of Ralph Waldo Emerson*, ed. Edward Waldo Emerson, vol. 1 (Boston: Centenary Edition, 1904), 451–55; quoted in Kasson, *Civilizing the Machine*, 121.

58. Marx, *The Machine In the Garden*, 251–52.

59. Trachtenberg, *The Incorporation of America*, 17.

60. William M. Thayer, *Marvels of the New West* (Norwich, CT: Henry Bill Publishing Company, 1891), 499.

61. McElrath, *The Yellowstone Valley*, 98–99.

62. Randall E. Rohe, "Hydraulicking In the American West: The Development and Diffusion of a Mining Technique," *Montana: The Magazine of Western History*, Spring 1985, 18–35. For a good succinct description of hydraulic mining, see Rodman Wilson Paul, *Mining Frontiers of the Far West, 1848–1880*, Histories of the American Frontier Series (1963; reprinted, Albuquerque: University of New Mexico Press, 1974), 29–30.

63. L. P. Brockett, *Our Western Empire: Or the New West Beyond the Mississippi* (Philadelphia: Bradley, Garretson and Company, 1881), 107.

64. Hamlin Garland, *Boy Life On the Prairie* (Lincoln: University of Nebraska, 1961); quoted in John B. Jackson, *American Space—The Centennial Years: 1865–1876* (New York: W. W. Norton and Co., 1972), 55.

65. Since John Winthrop's call to not let "suffer a whole Continent . . . to lie waste without any improvement," Americans had been working to ease the

rough conditions of nature. In Federalist Paper Fourteen, James Madison argued that the nation would overcome democracy's presumed natural limits by "improvements" of nature. In his 1833 inaugural speech, Andrew Jackson touted the "improvements which art can devise or industry execute," as evidence of the righteousness of transcontinental conquest. See John Winthrop, *Conclusions for the Plantation In New England* (1629), in *Old South Leaflets,* 9 vols., (Boston, 1895), vol. 2, no. 50, 5, quoted in Nash, *Wilderness,* 31; James Madison, *Federalist Paper 14,* quoted in Alan Trachtenberg, *Brooklyn Bridge: Fact and Symbol* (University of Chicago Press, 1965; reprinted 1979), 10; and Andrew Jackson Inaugural Speech, March 1833, quoted in Nash, *Wilderness,* 41.

66. Thanks to Alan Trachtenberg for his great study and the title, previously cited.

67. U.S. Senate *Congressional Globe,* 42d Cong., 2d sess., 30 January 1872, 697, quoted in Alfred Runte, *The American Experience,* 52.

68. "The Preservation of the Yellowstone Park," *Yellowstone Journal,* 6 May 1882, 2.

69. F. Hess to Congressman C. C. Carpenter, forwarded to Interior Secretary Teller, February 22, 1883; and J. J. Hoyt to Secretary Schurz, 1879, Department of the Interior, file microcopies of Record Group 62, records relating to the Yellowstone National Park, Patents and Miscellaneous Division, Letters Received, 1872–1886 (hereafter cited as RG 62, P&M, LR, 1872–1886), National Archives, Washington, DC.

70. Haines, *The Yellowstone Story,* vol. 1, 214.

71. Bartlett, *A Wilderness Beseiged,* 121–23.

72. P. W. Norris to Interior Secretary Samuel J. Kirkwood, 1 October 1881, RG 62, P&M, LR, 1872–1886.

73. Bartlett, *A Wilderness Beseiged,* 123.

74. Ise, *U.S. Forest Policy,* 87.

75. Haines, *The Yellowstone Story,* vol. 1, 259–60; Norris made himself vulnerable to charges of egotistical authoritarianism by, for instance, naming a score of park features after himself.

76. Herman Melville, *Moby-Dick,* a Norton Critical Edition, ed. Harrison Hayford and Hershel Parker (New York: W. W. Norton and Co., 1967; first published in America 1851), chap. 42.

77. Schmitt, *Back To Nature,* 147 (page reference from reprint edition).

78. Nolan, *Northern Pacific Views,* 172.

79. Jones, *The Age of Energy,* 296.

80. "Tap the Rockies" is a popular advertising campaign proffered by the Coors Brewing Company in the 1990s in which gigantic humans are shown bounding overtop sparkling mountain tops. The Coors Brewing Company has a less than sparkling environmental record.

Chapter Three

1. "The Preservation of the Yellowstone Park," *Yellowstone Journal*, 6 May 1882, 2.

2. Marta Weigle and Peter White, *The Lore of New Mexico* (Albuquerque: University of New Mexico Press, 1988), 52; Beal, *The Story of Man In Yellowstone*, 162; G. Edward White, *The Eastern Establishment and the Western Experience: The West of Frederic Remington, Theodore Roosevelt, and Owen Wister* (New Haven: Yale University Press, 1968), 94. White notes that two of the West's notable part-time residents—Theodore Roosevelt and Frederic Remington—established ranching operations in the northern West in 1883. One of these events likely produced the word *dude*, which *Webster's* attributes to the year 1883.

3. Uncle Rufus earned his endearing Wall Street appellation from the paternal advice he offered to "anyone who would listen." *New York Times*, 24 February 1893, 1.

4. The term originates with Haines, *The Yellowstone Story*, chap. 14.

5. Biographical information on Henry Villard—his political background in Bavaria and rise to wealth and power in the U.S. through the famous "Blind Pool" scheme—can be found in the following sources: Robert S. Macfarlane, *Henry Villard and the Northern Pacific* (New York: Newcomen Society of North America, 1954), 9–10; Nicolaus Mohr, *Excursion through America,* Ray Allen Billington, ed., and LaVern J. Rippley, trans., The Lakeside Classics Series (Chicago: R. R. Donnely and Sons Co., 1973), xxv-xxvii; and "Romantic Career of Henry Villard," *Semi-Weekly East Oregonian,* 12 June 1883, in Northern Pacific Railway Company Records, clippings scrapbooks (St. Paul: Minnesota Historical Society, microfilm), reel 4 (hereafter Northern Pacific Records); and James B. Hedges, *Henry Villard and the Railways of the Northwest* (New York: Russell and Russell, 1930), 55–90.

6. "Henry Villard," *Washington Chronicle,* 19 August 1883, in Northern Pacific Records, clippings scrapbooks, reel 4.

7. Mohr, *Excursion through America,* xxxii; and *The Memoirs of Henry Villard* (Cambridge: Riverside Press, 1904), vol. 2, 308.

8. Invitation in Northern Pacific Records, Villard Excursion file, reel 1.

9. "Villard's Voyagers," *Chicago Tribune,* 29 August 1883; and Macfarlane, *Henry Villard and the Northern Pacific,* 17.

10. Thomas J. McCormack, ed., *Memoirs of Gustav Koerner, 1809–1896,* vol. 2 (Cedar Rapids, IA: Torch Press, 1909), 681, 697–98; and Lord Charles Russell, *Diary of a Visit to the United States* (New York, 1910), 46, quoted in White, *The Eastern Establishment,* 47. Until well into the twentieth century, the inordinately high cost of western travel—even without frills—served to keep out "the scum of the earth," one tourist noted in *Land of Sunshine,* 1 (October 1894): 99, in Earl Pomeroy, *In Search of the Golden West: The Tourist in Western America* (New York: Knopf, 1957), 9.

11. Mohr, *Excursion through America,* xli-xlv.

12. Oswald G. Villard, *Fighting Years* (New York: n.p., 1939), 34–62.

13. "Villard's Guests," *Livingston Enterprise,* 28 August 1883.

14. *Livingston Enterprise,* 8 September 1883.

15. Mohr, *Excursion through America,* xlviii-xlix.

16. In Northern Pacific records, Villard Excursion file, reel 1.

17. "Livingston: Railroad Town On the Yellowstone," *Montana: The Magazine of Western History,* Autumn 1985, 84–86; and John C. Hudson, "Main Streets of the Yellowstone Valley," *Montana: The Magazine of Western History,* Autumn 1985, 63–64.

18. "The Decorations At the Depot," *Livingston Enterprise,* 7 September 1883.

19. "Age of Excess" borrowed from Ray Ginger, *Age of Excess: The U.S. from 1877 to 1914* (New York: Macmillan, 1965); Yellowstone and Adirondack car reference from the *Livingston Enterprise,* 17 September 1883, 3. The preservation effort for the Adirondacks roughly paralleled that of Yellowstone. See Terrie, *Forever Wild.*

20. McCormack, ed., *Memoirs of Gustav Koerner,* 691.

21. Mohr, *Excursion through America,* 132–44.

22. Charles Lord Russell of Killowen (Late Chief Justice of England), *Diary of a Visit to the United States of America in the Year 1883* (New York: U.S. Catholic Historical Society, 1910), 74–75. The Gray Cliff spectacle is early evidence of what Dean MacCannell calls the "conquering spirit of modernity" expressed in tourist culture. See MacCannell, *The Tourist: A New Theory of the Leisure Class* (New York: Schocken Books, 1976; reprint 1989, with a new introduction by the author), 3 (page reference from 1989 edition).

23. Harry L. Fine, "Gold Creek, Montana," *Western Express: Research Journal of Early Western Mails* 16 (July 1966): 11. Fine notes that Gold Creek was the site of the first gold discovery in Montana Territory. The region was also an important trading center until the arrival of the Northern Pacific diminished its importance.

24. George W. Irvin, "When General Grant Drove Northern Pacific's Last Spike," *Denver Times,* 2 February 1902, 16; and George N. Hillman, *Driving the Golden Spike* (n.p., 1932), 21, in F. Jay Haynes Papers, Montana State University Library Special Collections, Bozeman; and Edward W. Nolan, "'Not Without Labor and Expense': The Villard-Northern Pacific Last Spike Excursion, 1883," *Montana: The Magazine of Western History,* Summer 1983, 7.

25. Irvin, "When General Grant," 16; and "The Last Spike," *Livingston Enterprise,* 10 September 1883.

26. "Redman's Welcome To Villard," *Livingston Enterprise,* 28 March 1884.

27. Mohr, *Excursion through America,* lxiv. Though Villard had counted on a $300,000 investment in the Gold Spike excursion to bolster his sagging fortunes, the Northern Pacific in fact lost nearly twenty-five points on the stock market while he was gone. As the *Livingston Enterprise* commented, the Gold

Spike Special was for Villard "a sort of Belshazzar's feast." He resigned the presidency of the Northern Pacific in January 1884. Long-time friends abandoned
him, and Villard suffered a partial nervous breakdown. Scorned on Wall Street,
Villard was pitied and praised in the West as a fallen hero. See *Railroad Gazzette*,
(1883): 609, cited by Dietrich G. Buss, *Henry Villard: A Study of Transatlantic
Investments and Interests, 1870–1895*, Dissertations in *American Economic History*, ed. Stuart Bruchey, (New York: Arno Press, 1978), 145, 151–57; Macfarlane, *Henry Villard and the Northern Pacific*, 18; Oswald G. Villard, *Fighting
Years*, 62; and *Livingston Enterprise*, 29 December 1883. Several years later Villard reemerged as a force in the business world, yet never regained the esteemed
position of public favor he enjoyed in September 1883.

28. *Helena Daily Herald*, 13 September 1883.

29. On the myth of abundance, see David M. Potter, *People of Plenty: Economic Abundance and the American Character* (Chicago: University of Chicago
Press, 1954).

30. Mohr, *Excursion through America*, 256–58.

31. Bartlett, *A Wilderness Beseiged*, 124, 128.

32. Senate Report 911, 47th Cong., 2d sess. (S.N. 2087), 1–11; and *Report of
the Secretary of the Interior on the Administration of Yellowstone National Park*,
Senate Executive Document 47, Part 3, 48th Cong., 1st sess. (S.N. 2162), 3.

33. Hiram Martin Chittenden, *The Yellowstone National Park*, edited and
with an introduction by Richard A. Bartlett (Norman: University of Oklahoma
Press, 1964), 109–110.

34. Senate Executive Document 10, 47th Cong., 2d sess. (S.N. 2073); and C. T.
Hobart to Henry F. Douglas, forwarded to Secretary Teller July 28, 1882, Record
Group 62, Patents & Miscellaneous, Letters Received, 1872–1886, microfilm,
reel 2, National Archives, Washington, DC.

35. Haines, *The Yellowstone Story*, vol. 1, 270; *Avant-Courier*, 28 December
1882; and Bartlett, *A Wilderness Beseiged*, 131.

36. Richard A. Bartlett, "The Senator Who Saved Yellowstone Park," *The
Westerners Brand Book* 16 (New York, 1969), 49–52.

37. W. H. Randall to Hon. John D. White, January 28, 1883, RG 62, P&M,
LR 1872–1886, microfilm, reel 2.

38. *Congressional Record*, 47th Cong., 2d sess., Senate, 3270, 3488.

39. Secretary Teller to Superintendent Conger, 15 January 1883, Yellowstone
National Park Archives, microfilm, Letter Box 1.

40. *Congressional Record*, 47th Cong., 2d sess., Senate, 3193–95, 3482–83.
The complete history of the military administration of Yellowstone Park is found
in H. Duane Hampton, *How the U.S. Cavalry Saved the National Parks* (Bloomington: Indiana University Press, 1971).

41. Assistant Superintendent to Superintendent Conger, letter, 20 November
1883, Yellowstone National Park Archives, microfilm, Letter Box 9, Document
1384; and L. B. Cary to Frank Hatton, Esq. , February 2, 1884, forwarded to
Teller, RG 62, P&M, LR 1872–1886, microfilm, reel 2.

42. Quoted in Hampton, *How the U.S. Cavalry*, 66.

43. Superintendent Conger to Secretary Teller, November 6, 1882, RG 62, P&M, LR 1872–1886, microfilm, reel 2.

44. "About the Northwest," *Livingston Enterprise*, 10 January 1884.

45. *New York World*, 17 August 1883; and William Hardman, *Trip to America* (London: T. V. Wood, 1884), 137–38.

46. Hardman, *Trip to America*, 102–103.

47. *Livingston Enterprise*, 6 June, 31 July, and 22 August 1883.

48. Haines, *The Yellowstone Story*, vol. 1, 282; and *Livingston Enterprise*, 13 August 1883.

49. *Livingston Enterprise*, 23 August 1883.

50. Edward Pierrepont, *From Fifth Avenue to Alaska* (New York: G. P. Putnam's Sons, 1885), 238; and "The Abductors," *Chicago Weekly News*, 30 August 1883, 1.

51. Hardman, *Trip to America*, 149.

52. "In Yellowstone Park," *Chicago Weekly News*, 23 August 1882.

53. Hardman, *Trip to America*, 159–60, 171.

54. Margaret Cruikshank, "Notes On the Yellowstone Park" (1883), Yellowstone National Park Archives, manuscripts file, 18, 34–35.

55. Due to excessive costs incurred by his guests and because he "got on the wrong side of the market" during the trip, Hatch claimed to have lost $10,000 on the excursion; in *Livingston Enterprise*, 5 September 1885.

56. Paul A. Hutton, "Phil Sheridan's Crusade for Yellowstone," *American History Illustrated*, 19 February 1985, 11.

57. P. H. Sheridan, Jas. F. Gregory, and W. H. Forwood to Brig. Gen. R. C. Drum, Adjutant General, 1 November 1882, typed manuscript, RG 62, P&M, LR 1872–1886, 7–8.

58. Quoted in John R. Cook, *The Border and the Buffalo* (Topeka, 1907), 113.

59. David A. Dray, *The Buffalo Book: The Full Saga of the American Animal* (Athens: Ohio University Press, 1974), 104–105.

60. Reprinted in the *Chicago Evening Journal*, March 19, 1883; quoted in Hampton, *How the U.S. Cavalry*, 61.

61. For a good and broader discussion of wildlife and sportsmen, see Thomas R. Dunlap, *Saving America's Wildlife* (Trenton, NJ: Princeton University Press, 1988), 5–17.

62. J. Schuyler Crosby, Governor, Montana Territory to N. G. Ordway, Governor, Dakota Territory, 7 February 1883, manuscript file, Yellowstone National Park Archives.

63. Lewis Sabo, "When Wagon Trails Were Dim," *Pacific Northwesterner* 28 (Spring 1984): 23–24; and Peter Wild, *Pioneer Conservationists of Eastern America* (Missoula, MT: Mountain Press Publishing Co., 1986), 70, 78. Grinnell later organized and named the Audubon Society for Grandma Audubon.

64. John F. Reiger, *American Sportsmen and the Origins of Conservation* (New York: Winchester Press, 1975), 99.

65. Andrew Giarelli, "An Indian Understanding of the Nature of Things," manuscript file, University of Wyoming American Heritage Center, Laramie.

66. "Their Last Refuge," *Forest and Stream,* 14 December 1882, 383, quoted in John F. Reiger, "George Bird Grinnell and the Development of American Conservation, 1870–1901" (Ph.D. diss., Northwestern University, 1970), 141.

67. "The Park Grab," *Forest and Stream,* 4 January 1883, 441.

68. *The National Cyclopedia of American Biography* (New York: James T. White and Company, 1921), 297–98.

69. *New York Times,* 21 April 1883; and Thomas C. Reeves, *Gentleman Boss: The Life and Times of Chester Alan Arthur* (New York: Alfred Knopf, 1965), 355–58.

70. *Omaha Daily Bee,* 19 June 1883; *Forest and Stream,* various stories in the spring and summer of 1883; the fuss over Arthur's trip is striking, not only in light of today's excessive governmental perks, but also because all members of the expedition paid their own costs—unlike the other two celebrated Yellowstone trips that summer.

71. "Washington: President Arthur Will Spend His Vacation Entirely in the West," *Chicago Tribune,* 16 July 1883.

72. Lears, *No Place of Grace,* 28–30, 300–307.

73. P. H. Sheridan to Senator Vest, April 9, 1883, in P. H. Sheridan Papers, box 42; quoted by Thomas C. Reeves, "President Arthur in Yellowstone," *Montana: The Magazine of Western History,* Summer 1969, 20.

74. Sheridan's account was later compiled with 150 of Haynes's views of the excursion, and forwarded by the photographer to each of the participants as a memento of their journey. M. V. Sheridan, *Journey through the Yellowstone National Park and Northwestern Wyoming, 1883. Photographs of Party and Scenery along the Route Traveled, and Copies of the Associated Press Dispatches Sent Whilst en Route,* (New Haven CT: Research Publication, 1975), microform, *Western Americana, 1550–1900: Frontier History of the Trans-Mississippi West,* reel 292, no. 2926.

75. "The President," *Chicago Tribune,* 9 August 1883.

76. Sheridan, *Personal Memoirs of Philip Henry Sheridan,* vol. 2, 540–42. The festivities at Fort Washakie were abbreviated when Senator Vest proposed to the Indian leaders the final abolition of tribal living and an allotment of lands to individual Indians in severalty. What became official policy in 1887—the General Allotment, or Dawes Act—apparently met some resistance that day.

77. M. V. Sheridan, *Journey through the Yellowstone National Park,* 24.

78. "The President Lost in Reverie," *Chicago Tribune,* 13 August 1883.

79. M. V. Sheridan, *Journey through the Yellowstone National Park,* 27 August and 31 August, 35,40.

80. On the historic role and motivations of conservationist-sportsmen, see

Thomas R. Dunlap, "Sport Hunting and Conservation, 1880–1920," *Environmental Review* 12 (Spring 1988): 52–58; Dunlap, *Saving America's Wildlife,* 8–13; and Reiger, *American Sportsmen.*

81. M. V. Sheridan, *Journey through the Yellowstone National Park,* 15 August and 25 August, 19, 31.

82. Vest, "Notes of the Yellowstone Trip," *Forest and Stream,* 3 November 1883.

83. M. V. Sheridan, *Journey through the Yellowstone National Park,* 27 August, 35; and Eugene Field, *Sharps and Flats,* ed. Slason Thompson (New York: Charles Scribner's Sons, 1900), 60–62, 68–70, 74–75, 197.

84. James Deay to Superintendent Conger, 31 August 1883, Yellowstone National Park Archives, Letter Box 9, Document no. 1367; Margaret Cruikshank, "Notes on the Yellowstone Park," 28; and D. E. Sawyer to Superintendent Conger, 12 September 1883, Yellowstone National Park Archives, Letter Box 9, Document no. 1554.

85. "Going to Kidnap the President," *Livingston Enterprise,* 27 August 1883; and Hardman, *Trip to America,* 175.

86. George Thomas, "My Recollections of Yellowstone Park, 1883," typed manuscript, manuscript file, Yellowstone National Park Archives, 7.

87. "The Passing of Arthur," *Chicago Inter-Ocean,* 5 September 1883.

88. Reprinted in *The Northwest,* September 1883, 13.

89. *Livingston Enterprise,* 23 August 1883.

90. Ibid., 27 August and 31 August 1883.

91. "Uncle Rufus Interviewed—He Makes Some Startling Disclosures," *Chicago Tribune,* 27 August 1883.

92. "The Abductors," *Chicago Weekly Tmes,* 30 August 1883.

93. Special Agent Scott Smith to Interior Secretary Teller, September 1883, RG 62, P&M, LR 1872–1886.

94. Chittenden, *The Yellowstone National Park,* 116.

95. *Livingston Enterprise,* 14 December 1883; 29 January 1884; and 4 February 1884.

96. P. H. Conger, *Annual Report of the Superintendent of the Yellowstone National Park to the Secretary of the Interior for the Year 1883* (Washington, DC: Government Printing Office, 1883), 6; and L. B. Cary to Frank Hatton, February 2, 1884, RG 62, P&M, LR 1872–1886.

97. Rufus Hatch to Secretary Teller, May 29, 1884, RG 62, P&M, LR 1872–1886.

98. Bartlett, *A Wilderness Beseiged,* 146–47.

99. *Livingston Enterprise,* 26 March 1884.

100. Haines, *The Yellowstone Story,* vol. 2, 33.

101. After the first decade in which the Park existed in relative obscurity, visitors more than quadrupled that season to an estimated 5,000 and rose steadily to 10,000 by 1897; Haines, *The Yellowstone Story,* vol. 2, 478.

102. "English Writings about the Park," *Livingston Enterprise,* 19 August 1883, reprinted from the *London Daily Telegraph.*

103. *Livingston Enterprise,* 29 June 1883, 21 July 1883, 20 September 1883, and 5 September 1883, 1; *Catalog: Northern Pacific and National Park Views* (Fargo, Dakota Territory: F. Jay Haynes Publisher, 1884) Montana Historical Society Archives, Helena; and "Life Among the Rockies," undated clipping, Scrapbook no. 3, Yellowstone National Park Archives, 18.

104. "The Yellowstone Park," *Forest and Stream,* 20 December 1883, 401–402.

105. Lieutenant Kingman to Chief of Engineers, 1 November 1883, Department of the Interior, Patents & Miscellaneous Division, Letters Received, 1883–1884, National Archives, Washington, DC.

Chapter Four

1. Ashley Cole, "The Yellowstone National Park," *The Manhattan,* August 1884, 144.

2. *Congressional Record,* 47th Cong, 2d sess., 14, pt. 4, 3488.

3. "Alice's Adventures in the New Wonderland," *The Northern Pacific Railroad, the Wonderland Route to the Pacific Coast,* advertising brochure, in F. Jay Haynes Papers, Montana State University Library Special Collections, Bozeman (hereafter Haynes Papers).

4. For discussions of the transformation from a culture fixated on work to one that encouraged leisure, see John A. Jakle, *The Tourist: Travel in Twentieth-Century North America* (Lincoln: University of Nebraska Press, 1985), 67; David Strauss, "Toward a Consumer Culture: 'Adirondack Murray' and the Wilderness Vacation," *American Quarterly* 36 (Summer 1984): 270–86; Daniel Rodgers, *The Work Ethic in Industrial America, 1870–1920* (Chicago, 1974, 1978); John Higham, "The Reorientation of American Culture in the 1890s," in John Weiss, ed., *The Origins of Modern Consciousness* (Detroit, 1965); and Ann Douglas, *The Feminization of American Culture* (New York, 1977).

5. On the ability of words to mediate unknown landscapes, see Paul Shepard, *Man In the Landscape.* Dean MacCannell, *The Tourist,* notes that in the modern tourist world the act of naming is the first step in transforming a site into a tourist "sight. " By far the best exploration of Yellowstone nomenclature is Lee H. Whittlesey's *Yellowstone Place Names.* Whittlesey notes that names derive from six sources: "fur traders; gold prospectors; early explorers; government surveyors; local use by Park employees and visitors; and recognition of local use by Park officials."

6. Nathaniel Pitt Langford, *The Discovery,* (24, 28. The explorers borrowed Devil's Den from its famous Gettysburg namesake, where one of the party had served.

7. William Tod Helmuth, "The Yellowstone National Park and How It Was Named," 7 August 1892, in G. L. Henderson, Ash Scrapbook: Miscellaneous Newspaper Clippings Collected by George L. Henderson from 1882–1905, Yellowstone National Park Archives and Research Library (hereafter YNPARL).

8. Whittlesey, *Yellowstone Place Names,* xvii, 71, 126, 162.

9. Whittlesey, *Yellowstone Place Names,* xvii; and G. L. Henderson, "Naming a Geyser," Ash Scrapbook, YNPARL.

10. John Muir, "The Yellowstone National Park," *Atlantic Monthly,* April 1898, 516–17.

11. Philetus Norris, *Annual Report, 1880,* 14.

12. Ray Stannard Baker, "A Place of Marvels," *The Century Magazine,* August 1903, 491.

13. For a piercing discussion of the consignment of intellectual and emotional sovereignty in the tourist world, see Walker Percy, *The Message In The Bottle: How Queer Man Is, How Queer Language Is, And What One Has To Do With The Other* (New York: Farrar, Straus and Giroux, 1975), 54–55.

14. A. B. Guptill, "Yellowstone Park," *Outing,* July 1885, 256.

15. Olin D. Wheeler, *Yellowstone National Park: Descriptive of the Beauties and Wonders of the World's Wonderland* (St. Paul: W. C. Riley, 1901), 52; and A. B. Guptill, *All About Yellowstone Park: A Practical Guide* (St. Paul: F. Jay Haynes Publishing, 1894), 13.

16. John Hyde, *Official Guide;* W. W. Wylie, *Yellowstone National Park; or the Great American Wonderland* (Kansas City, MO: Ramsey, Millett and Hudson, 1882), 9–11; Wheeler, *Wonderland '96,* 56; *Sketches of Wonderland,* 26.

17. For an excellent discussion of this paradox in the nineteenth-century tourist world, see Sears, *Sacred Places,* 137.

18. George W. Wingate, *Through the Yellowstone Park on Horseback* (New York: O. Judd Co., 1886), 79; Alice Wellington Rollins, "The Three Tetons," *Harper's New Monthly Magazine* 74 (1887): 878–80; and Francis Gibson, pocket diary kept on a trip through Yellowstone, 7–27 August 1882, 44–45, manuscript file, YNPARL.

19. Myra Emmons, "From New York to Heaven," *Recreation,* December 1901, 433.

20. Muir, "The Yellowstone National Park," 522.

21. Baker, "A Place of Marvels," 485.

22. On the fascination with wilderness, see Roderick Nash, *Wilderness,* 141–60. Sawtell, quoted in Strahorn, *Montana and Yellowstone Park,* 159.

23. Henderson, "National Park Manual: Wonderland Condensed," Scrapbook no. 1, YNPARL.

24. Norris, *Annual Report, 1880,* 20.

25. Hyde, *Official Guide,* 28.

26. Francis C. Sessions, "The Yellowstone Park," *Magazine of Western History* 6 (1890): 436.

27. Wingate, *Through the Yellowstone Park,* 68; and Rollins, "The Three Tetons," 872.

28. Edward Pierrepont, *From Fifth Avenue to Alaska* (New York: G. P. Putnam, 1885), 243.

29. "The Yellowstone National Park," *Harper's Weekly* 37 (1893): 719; Pierrepont, *From Fifth Avenue,* 243; and Guptill, *All About,* 13.

30. "Among the Terraces," *New York Herald,* 26 April 1888, in Ash Scrapbook, YNPARL; and "Senator Conkling at Mammoth, 1883," *New York Herald,* 24 April 1888, Ash Scrapbook, YNPARL.

31. Henderson, "National Park Manual: Wonderland Condensed," Site nos. 27, 44, 45, 64, 70, and 71, YNPARL; and Whittlesey, *Place Names,* 99, 149. On the fashion of Orientalism in Victorian culture, see Howard Mumford Jones, *The Age of Energy,* 297.

32. Henderson, "National Park Manual," site nos. 30, 31, YNPARL.

33. Ibid., site nos. 68, 33.

34. L. P. Brockett, *Our Western Empire,* 1260.

35. George Thomas, "Recollections of the Yellowstone National Park, 1883," 7, typed manuscript [photocopy], manuscript file, YNPARL; William Hardman, *Trip to America,* 154; and "Boiling: The Geysers in the Yellowstone National Park," *Brooklyn Daily Eagle,* 15 August 1883, in Northern Pacific Railway Company Records (St. Paul: Minnesota Historical Society), clippings scrapbooks, microfilm, reel 4 (hereafter Northern Pacific Records).

36. Wingate, *Through the Yellowstone Park,* 112. For a germane discussion of sacred-secular pilgrimage, see Victor and Edith Turner, *Image and Pilgrimage In Christian Culture* (New York: Columbia University Press, 1978), 240–42.

37. Rudyard Kipling, *From Sea to Sea: Letters of Travel,* vol. 2 (New York: Doubleday and McClure, 1899), 98; quoted in David Harmon, ed., *Mirror of America: Literary Encounters with the National Parks* (Boulder: Roberts Rinehart, 1989), 58.

38. J. H. Dawes, "The Yellowstone Park; A Paper Read March 16th, 1891, before the Buffalo Historical Society," 9, in Haynes Papers; Rollins, "The Three Tetons," 884; and Thomas, "Recollections," 9.

39. Whittlesey, *Place Names,* 98. For the first two decades of the park's life, Hell's Half Acre remained the tourist's preferred name for the site. Midway's eventual popular victory in the titling struggle may have been aided by the famous Midway Plaisance, the mile-long walkway of amusements at the 1893 World's Columbian Exposition in Chicago.

40. A. M. Mattoon, "The Yellowstone National Park, Summer of 1889," 21, typed manuscript (photocopy), manuscript file, YNPARL.

41. Olin D. Wheeler, *Sketches,* 39.

42. Hyde, *Official Guide,* 64.

43. Stanley quoted in L. P. Brockett, *Our Western Empire,* 1252–1253; and W. F. Hatfield, *Geyserland and Wonderland* (San Francisco: Hicks-Judd Co., 1901), 73.

44. Wylie, *Great American Wonderland,* 45; "The Yellowstone Park," unmarked Pittsburgh publication, 6 November 1902, Acc. no. 296 (N213p-Yel), Eaton Ranch Collection, University of Wyoming American Heritage Center, Laramie; and Lispenard Rutgers [Henry Erskine Smith], *On and Off the Saddle* (New York: G. P. Putnam's Sons, 1894), 7; and Hardman, *Trip to America,* 155.

45. The original term belongs, of course, to Ralph Waldo Emerson; *The Complete Works of Ralph Waldo Emerson,* ed. Edward Waldo Emerson, vol. 1 (Centenary ed. Boston, 1903–1904), 365–75. For a brilliant analysis of this central theme of American letters, see Perry Miller, *Nature's Nation* (Cambridge: Harvard University Press, 1967).

46. On the natural-technological sublime, see Marx, *The Machine In the Garden;* and Kasson, *Civilizing the Machine,* 172–75 (page reference is to reprint ed.).

47. Guptill, *All About,* 69–71; William M. Thayer, *Marvels of the New West: A Vivid Portrayal of the Stupendous Marvels In the Vast Wonderland West of the Missouri River* (Norwich, CT: Henry Bill Publishing, 1891), 78–79; and Wylie, *Great American Wonderland,* 43.

48. Sessions, "The Yellowstone Park," 439.

49. Major Sir Rose Lambart Price, *A Summer On the Rockies* (London: Sampson Low, Marston and Co., 1898), 177; Henry M. Field, *Our Western Archipelago* (New York: Charles Scribner's Sons, 1895), 226; Hyde, *Official Guide,* 67; and Margaret Cruikshank, "Notes," 22–23.

50. Rutgers [Smith], *On and Off the Saddle,* 10; Thayer, *Marvels,* 76; Theodore Gerrish, *Life In the World's Wonderland: A Graphic Description of the Great Northwest* (n. p., 1887), 215; and Guptill, *All About,* 47.

51. Thomas, "Recollections," 10; Hyde, *Official Guide,* 76; Guptill, *All About,* 54; Rutgers [Smith], *On and Off the Saddle,* 10.

52. E. V. Smalley, "The Yellowstone National Park," *The Northwest,* May 1887, 3, 1; and Mattoon, "The Yellowstone National Park," 18.

53. Cruikshank, "Notes," 21–25, *passim;* and Synge, *A Ride Through Wonderland,* 82.

54. Park Archivist Lee H. Whittlesley reported to the author that Smalley stole this account of the Evangeline directly from G. L. Henderson, correspondence dated 24 August 1994.

55. E. V. Smalley, "The Yellowstone National Park," *The Northwest,* July 1884, 4.

56. In the Pittsburgh area, for example, there were the following "works" or furnaces: Isabella, Carrie, Lucy, Christy, and Eliza. Industrial Research Associates, Buffalo NY, "Inventory of Historic Iron and Steel Sites," in *Rivers of Steel Management Action Plan* (Homestead, PA: Steel Industry Heritage Corporation, 1995), section E.

57. On patriarchy and the control of a feminine natural world, see Carolyn

Merchant, *The Death of Nature: Women, Ecology, and the Scientific Revolution* (San Francisco: Harper and Row, 1980); on the objectification of women and the mechanistic woman, see Jane Caputi, *The Age of Sex Crime* (Bowling Green University Popular Press, 1987), 173–88, *passim*.

58. Georgina Synge, *A Ride through Wonderland*, 62; Wingate, *Through the Yellowstone*, 114–15; and Cruikshank, "Notes," 28.

59. Lyon, "The Nation's Art Gallery," Watertown, South Dakota, 7 August 1891, in Scrapbook no. 1, 15, YNPARL.

60. Hardman, *Trip to America*, 161–64; and Cruikshank, "Notes," 28.

61. Arnold Hague, "Soaping Geysers," Transactions of the American Institute of Mining Engineers, February 1889, in *Scientific Papers On the Yellowstone Park*, 1–10, YNPARL; and *Livingston Enterprise*, 28 July 1888; quoted in Aubrey L. Haines, *The Yellowstone Story*, vol. 2, 18.

62. P. W. Norris, *The Calumet of the Coteau . . . Together with a Guidebook of the Yellowstone National Park* (Philadelphia: J. B. Lippincott, 1884), 250; Rudyard Kipling, *American Notes* (New York: F. F. Lovell Co., 1893), 155.

63. Owen Wister, "Old Yellowstone Days," in David Harmon, ed., *Mirror of America*, 29.

64. George Anderson, "Protection of the Yellowstone National Park," in Theodore Roosevelt and George Bird Grinnell, eds., *Hunting In Many Lands: Book of the Boone and Crockett Club*, vol. 2 (New York: Forest and Stream, 1895), 388; and "'Her' In the National Park," *Yellowstone Journal*, 1 April 1882; and George L. Henderson to Superintendent Conger, 28 June 1884, in Letter Box 9, Doc. no. 1453, YNPARL.

65. Gerrish, *Life In the World's Wonderland*, 186.

66. The term "people's park" was a common Yellowstone reference. See, for example, Lambart Price, *Summer On the Rockies*, 216.

67. Haines, *The Yellowstone Story*, vol. 1, 311–15.

68. *Livingston Enterprise*, 29 August 1885; and Haines, *The Yellowstone Story*, vol. 1, 322–23.

69. Haines, *The Yellowstone Story*, vol. 1, 323–25. The Cavalry's tenure at the park is generally highly regarded by Yellowstone historians. They established the paramilitary style and professional discipline of the National Park Service that succeeded them in 1916. For the full story, see Hampton, *How the U.S. Cavalry*.

70. Rollins, "The Three Tetons," 884; and Cole, "The Yellowstone," 129;

71. Dawes, "The Yellowstone Park," 18–19.

72. Kipling, *American Notes*, 135. For excellent synopses of the picturesque scenes visitors would have expected, see Schmitt, *Back to Nature;* and Huth, *Nature and the American*, esp. chapters 3 and 6.

73. Gerrish, *Life In the World's Wonderland*, 199–201; Thayer, *Marvels*, 72; and Guptill, *All About*, 71.

74. Olin D. Wheeler and the Northern Pacific Railroad, *6,000 Miles Through Wonderland* (Chicago: Rand McNally, 1893), 79.

75. Almon Gunnison, *Rambles Overland* (Boston: Universalist Publishing House, 1884), 70–71.

76. Olin Wheeler, *Sketches,* 45; Olin D. Wheeler, *Indianland and Wonderland* (Chicago: Rand McNally, 1894), 65; and Nathaniel Pitt Langford, *The Discovery,* introduction.

77. Guptill, *All About,* 74–75; Captain George Anderson, *Annual Report of the Superintendent of Yellowstone National Park for the Year 1890* (Washington, DC: Government Printing Office, 1891), 643–44; and Haines, *The Yellowstone Story,* vol. 2, 15–18, 126–27.

78. Emerson Hough, "The Wonderful Grand Canyon," n.d., n.p., in Scrapbook no. 1, 129, YNPARL; and "The Yellowstone National Park," *Harper's Weekly Magazine* 37 (1893): 723.

79. Cole, "The Yellowstone National Park," 443–44.

80. Wheeler, *Sketches,* 49.

81. Brockett, *Our Western Empire,* 1242; Hatfield, *Geyserland,* 79; and Gunnison, *Rambles,* 54.

82. Mattoon, "The National Yellowstone Park," 36; Wheeler, *Yellowstone National Park,* 93; and Wheeler, *Indianland and Wonderland,* 71.

83. Lears, *No Place of Grace,* 43–45.

84. Wheeler, *Yellowstone National Park,* 91; and Wingate, *Through the Yellowstone Park,* 128.

85. Mattoon, "The Yellowstone National Park," 33, 36.

86. Thayer, *Marvels,* 67.

87. Aubrey L. Haines, *The Yellowstone Story,* vol. 2, 6–9.

88. "A Trip Full of Peril," *Chicago Tribune,* 5 March 1887, Scrapbook no. 1, YNPARL.

89. G. L. Henderson, "Haynes' Winter Expedition," extracted from the *Helena Independent,* 6 February 1887, typed manuscript [photocopy], manuscript file, YNPARL.

90. Although Haynes made no deliberate attempt to counter the commercialization of the sublime in Yellowstone, it is interesting to note the mid-nineteenth-century efforts of a few members of the northeastern literati to recover the sublime qualities of what was by then an egregiously commercialized Niagara Falls. See McKinsey, *Niagara Falls,* chap. 4.

91. Wylie, *Great American Wonderland,* 59; Guptill, *All About,* 85; and Cruikshank, "Notes," 48. The archetype for the touristic consumption and conventionalization of the sublime was Niagara Falls. See McKinsey, *Niagara Falls,* esp. 38, 134–37, 157–62; and Sears, *Sacred Places,* 22.

92. F. Jay Haynes, *Catalog of Northern Pacific and National Park Views* (St. Paul: F. Jay Haynes, 1890), Haynes File, Montana Historical Society Archives, Helena.

Chapter Five

1. Nathaniel Pitt Langford, *The Discovery*, 96–97.

2. "The Yellowstone National Park," Letter to the Editors from Charles F. Driscoll, *The American Architect and Building News* 13 (17 March 1883): 130–31.

3. Wheeler, *6,000 Miles*, 75–76.

4. Alfred Runte, *Trains of Discovery: Western Railroads and the National Parks* (Flagstaff, AZ: Northland Press, 1984), 12.

5. *Livingston Enterprise*, 7 July 1888.

6. On the development of diverse western resources, see Patricia Nelson Limerick, *Legacy of Conquest: The Unbroken Past of the American West* (New York: W. W. Norton and Company, 1987), chap. 4; Trachtenberg, *The Incorporation*, 22; On the Northern Pacific's role, see William G. Robbins, "At the End of a Cracked Whip," *Montana: The Magazine of Western History*, Fall 1988, 2–11; and Hales, *Transformation of the American Landscape*, 48.

7. Nathaniel Pitt Langford, *Annual Report*, 4; Ferdinand Vandiveer Hayden, *Twelfth Report of the United States Geological and Geographical Survey of the Territories*, part 2 (Washington, DC: Government Printing Office, 1883), 488; and Lord Earl Dunraven, *The Great Divide* (London: Chatto and Windus, 1876), 194.

8. Haines, *The Yellowstone Story*, vol. 1, 196; and Bartlett, *A Wilderness Besieged*, 115–19.

9. Captain Moses Harris, 15 August 1888, *Report of the Superintendent of the Yellowstone National Park*, H. Ex. Doc. 1 (50–2) 2638, p. 636.

10. Bartlett, *A Wilderness Besieged*, 5–14. "Taking the waters"—from White Sulphur Springs to Saratoga—had been one of the most popular attractions of nineteenth-century American tourists. For travelers inhibited by a puritanical work ethic, the medicinal claim of hot springs served as a ploy to disguise a pleasure trip; countless others were drawn to the authentic and chimerical reports of their healing properties. Western railroads foresaw the dollarable promise of hot springs and erected luxurious hotels at places like Colorado Springs and Las Vegas, New Mexico. See Marta Weigle and Peter White, *The Lore of New Mexico*, 50.

11. General [Colonel] John Gibbon, quoted in "The Wonders of the Yellowstone," *Journal of the American Geographical Society of New York* 5 (1874): 118.

12. C. L. Heizmann, "The Therapeutical Value of the Springs In the National Park, Wyoming Territory," *Philadelphia Medical Times*, 27 May 1876, 409–14.

13. Edward Frankland, "A Great Winter Sanitarium For the American Continent," *The Popular Science Monthly*, July 1885, 295.

14. See McKinsey, *Niagara Falls*.

15. Strahorn, *Montana and Yellowstone Park,* 163.

16. Bartlett, *A Wilderness Besieged,* 117–18.

17. Mary Caldwell Ludwig, "The Yellowstone: Beauties of a Trip There In Autumn," n.p., 1896, in Scrapbook no. 3, YNPARL. Yancey was kin to the famed southern fire-eater, William Lowndes Yancey.

18. Carl E. Schmidt, *A Trip to the Yellowstone Park* (Detroit: Herald Press, 1902), 58–70.

19. W. Hallett Phillips, 12 September 1885, transmitted in a *Letter From the Acting Secretary of the Interior to the United States Senate,* 29 January 1886, 49th Cong., 1st sess., Ex. Doc. 51, 9–12, in Record Group 62, Department of the Interior, Patents and Miscellaneous Division, Letters Received, 1872–1886, microfilm, reel 3, National Archives, Washington, DC (hereafter Phillips Report, RG 62, P&M, LR, 1872–1886, microfilm, reel 3).

20. Charles Gibson to Interior Secretary, 24 August 1885, included in testimony of Chief Clerk of the Department, Edward M. Dawson, in Committee on Public Lands, *Inquiry Into the Management and Control of the Yellowstone National Park,* 52d Cong., 1st sess. (1892) (Serial no. 3051), 243, 246; Bartlett, *A Wilderness Besieged,* 151, notes that Gibson's philanthropy and abiding interest in the establishment of urban parks made him an appropriate choice to oversee the proper cultivation of the national pleasure ground.

21. "A Derelict Park Syndicate," *Forest and Stream,* 6 October 1887, 201–202. See also Haines, *The Yellowstone Story,* vol. 2, 42.

22. Haines, *The Yellowstone Story,* vol. 2, 42–53; Bartlett, *A Wilderness Beseiged,* 151–76; and "Yellowstone Park: Charles Gibson's Inside Scheme," *St. Louis Globe Democrat,* 13 April 1892, in Scrapbook no. 1, YNPARL. As Haines and Bartlett have chronicled, at the turn of the century the Northern Pacific Railroad became the target of President Theodore Roosevelt's successful attempt to enforce the Sherman Anti-trust Act. The Northern Securities Company of which they were a part was ordered to disband. That event, coupled with the renewed charges of preferential exclusion made by the remaining independent concessionaires in Yellowstone, raised the ugly specter of a Yellowstone Park monopoly once more. Although Yellowstone had finally become a source of great profit, the railroad feared an investigation and in 1907 finally sold its Park Association share to Harry Child. Heavily subsidized by the NPRR into the 1920s, Child's family dynasty continued to rule park concessions for the next six decades.

23. Bartlett, *A Wilderness Besieged,* 150–56.

24. *Cyclopedia of American Biography* vol. 22, 364; and *New York Times,* 17 February 1931, both quoted in Bartlett, *A Wilderness Besieged,* 131.

25. Haines, *The Yellowstone Story,* vol. 1, 272; Bartlett, *A Wilderness Beseiged,* 131; and Rudyard Kipling, *From Sea to Sea,* excerpt reprinted in Harmon, ed., *Mirror of America,* 55.

26. Haines, *The Yellowstone Story,* vol. 1, 272–74.

27. Alice Wellington Rollins, *The Three Tetons: A Story of the Yellowstone* (New York: Cassell and Co., 1887), 33.

28. *Livingston Enterprise,* 20 July 1883; and William Hardman, *Trip to America,* 143, 148.

29. Liberty Cap [probably G. L. Henderson], "The National Park: Three Days at Mammoth Hot Springs—the Terraces," 1885?, n.p., in Scrapbook no. 2, YNPARL.

30. See Martin V. Melosi, *Garbage In the Cities: Refuse, Reform, and Environment 1880–1980* (College Station: Texas A & M University Press, 1981).

31. Phillips Report in RG 62, P&M, LR, 1872–1886, microfilm, reel 3.

32. Captain Moses Harris, *Report of the Superintendent of the Yellowstone National Park to the Secretary of the Interior, 1887* (Washington, DC: Government Printing Office, 1887), 637.

33. Haines, *The Yellowstone Story,* vol. 1, 277.

34. "Derelict Park Syndicate," 202; and Charles Gibson to Superintendent Moses Harris, 28 January 1887, in Letter Box 1, Doc. 124, YNPARL.

35. Weimer to Superintendent Wear, 7 November 1885, pre-1916, Letter Box 9, Doc. No. 1580, YNPARL; and O. S. T. Drake, "A Lady's Trip to the Yellowstone Park," *Every Girl's Annual* (London: Hatchard's, 1887), 348, quoted in Haines, *The Yellowstone Story,* vol. 1, 116.

36. Price, *Summer On the Rockies,* 185; and Haines, *The Yellowstone Story,* vol. 2, 116–17.

37. Northern Pacific president C. S. Mellen to N.P. vice-president Colonel D. C. Lamont, 29 December 1899, quoted in Bartlett, *A Wilderness Besieged,* 188.

38. Haines, *The Yellowstone Story,* vol. 2, 134–38; and Bartlett, *A Wilderness Besieged,* 187–89.

39. In Yosemite at the turn of the century, tourists found "fire-falls"—a "celebrated evening cascade of glowing embers pushed over the cliff at Glacier Point"—an irresistable spectacle. The overwhelming public approval of that artificial marvel—despite condemnation by cultural aesthetes and park officials alike—was enough to secure its continuity for decades. See Alfred Runte, *Yosemite: The Embattled Wilderness* (Lincoln: University of Nebraska Press, 1990), 90–99.

40. Frazier A. Boutelle, *Report of the Superintendent of the Yellowstone National Park to the Secretary of the Interior, 1890,* (Washington, DC: Government Printing Office, 1890), 353.

41. Barbara H. Dittl and Joanne Mallmann, "Plain to Fancy: The Lake Hotel, 1889–1929," *Montana: The Magazine of Western History,* Spring 1984, 38.

42. Reau Campbell, *New Revised Complete Guide and Descriptive Book of the Yellowstone Park* (Chicago: H. E. Klamer, 1909), 158; on the Arcadian Myth in the East, see Schmitt, *Back to Nature.*

43. Weimer to Superintendent Wear, 18 July 1885, Pre-1916, Letter Box 9, Doc. No. 1584, YNPARL.

44. Wheeler, *Indianland and Wonderland,* 55.

45. "The Yellowstone National Park," *Harper's Weekly* 37 (1893): 722–23; and Susan C. Scofield and Jeremy C. Schmidt, *The Inn At Old Faithful* (Yellowstone National Park, Wyoming: Crownset Associates, 1979), 6.

46. Haines, *The Yellowstone Story,* vol. 2, 119; and Bartlett, *A Wilderness Besieged,* 173.

47. Anne Farrar Hyde, *An American Vision: Far Western Landscape and National Culture, 1820–1920* (New York University Press, 1990), 255. Reamer also designed the Lake Hotel and the park's second Canyon Hotel.

48. Ibid., 256; and Charles Francis Adams, *What Jim Bridger and I Saw in Yellowstone Park* (n.p., circa 1912–1914), 12–18.

49. Jack E. Haynes, *Haynes Official Guide to Yellowstone Park* (St. Paul: Haynes Publishing, 1915), 69, quoted in Anne Farrar Hyde, An American Vision, 257.

50. Scofield and Schmidt, *The Inn,* 19–21; and Rod Fensom, *America's Great Resort Hotels: Eighty Classic Resorts in the United States and Canada* (Charlotte, NC: East Woods Press, 1985), 195–96; and Bartlett, *A Wilderness Besieged,* 183.

51. Weigle and White, *The Lore of New Mexico,* 57–63; Pomeroy, *In Search of the Golden West,* 164; and "tepee-like," from Fensom, *America's Great Resort Hotels,* 196.

52. Bob Randolph O'Brien, "The Yellowstone National Park Road System: Past, Present and Future" (Ph.D. diss., University of Washington, 1965), 17–19, 43–44; and Wayne F. Replogle, *Yellowstone's Bannock Indian Trails,* Yellowstone Interpretive Series, no. 6 (Mammoth Hot Springs, Wyoming: Yellowstone Library and Museum Association, 1956), 5.

53. Bartlett, *A Wilderness Besieged,* 118; and Haines, *The Yellowstone Story,* vol. 1, 145–46. Partially dismantled and burned by the Nez Perce Indians in their 1877 flight through Yellowstone, Baronett's bridge was bought and rebuilt by the government and it continued to serve miners and tourists.

54. Wingate, *Through the Yellowstone Park,* 60–61; and Haines, *The Yellowstone Story,* vol. 1, 188–89, who notes that Henderson's road passed into the hands of "Yankee Jim" George who operated it for a toll until 1910.

55. O'Brien, "The Yellowstone Park Road System," 10; as O'Brien notes, despite the complaints of tourists, funding for Yellowstone roads came 15 years before the first state-funded road construction occurred in America, and 40 years before federal road building began in 1916.

56. Ibid., 57; and Haines, *The Yellowstone Story,* vol. 2, appendix C, table 2, 478.

57. Georgina A. Synge, *A Ride through Wonderland,* 120.

58. O'Brien, "Yellowstone Park Road System," 63.

59. "In Yellowstone Park," *Chicago Weekly News,* August 23, 1883. The writer was one of dozens of Associated Press journalists who enjoyed an all-

expenses-paid park junket following the AP convention in Chicago—yet another major Yellowstone touring party that summer. Not surprisingly, this one was compliments of Charles Fee and the Northern Pacific Railroad.

60. Hampton, *How the U.S. Cavalry,* 65.

61. Haines, *The Yellowstone Story,* vol. 2, 211; the figure eight was complete save for the segment from the Grand Canyon to Tower Falls, constructed in 1905. For discussions of the Grand Tour concept in Europe and America, see McCannell, *The Tourist,* 5, 60 (page references from reprint edition); and Sears, *Sacred Places,* 4. The conceptual design of Yellowstone's Grand Loop originates ultimately with the European "Grand Tour" of the seventeenth century and subsequent American versions in the East. It offered efficient cultural edification and a mark of social status.

62. George Thomas, "My Recollections of Yellowstone National Park, 1883," 5, in manuscript file, YNPARL; G. L. Henderson, "A Wonderland," in an unidentified West Union, Iowa newspaper, 30 January 1884, Ash Scrapbook, YNPARL.

63. Frances Lynn Turpin, "A Trip through Yellowstone Park," assembled by Florence Ballinger, 13, in manuscript file, YNPARL.

64. "Affairs in the Yellowstone Park," *Forest and Stream,* 5 November 1885.

65. Phillips Report, 8; and *Report of the Superintendent of the Yellowstone National Park, Supplemental Report of Captain Moses Harris,* First Cavalry, Acting Superintendent, 4 October 1886 (Washington, DC: Government Printing Office, 1886) H. Ex. Doc. 49–2 (Serial No. 2468), 1077.

66. For a particularly germane analysis of the efficiency impulse of Americans, see Samuel P. Hays, *Conservation and the Gospel of Efficiency: The Progressive Conservation Movement, 1880–1920* (Cambridge: Harvard University Press, 1959).

67. Kenneth H. Baldwin, ed., *Enchanted Enclosure: The Army Engineers and Yellowstone National Park: A Documentary History* (Washington, DC: Government Printing Office, 1976), 93.

68. Guptill, *All About,* 34, 71.

69. Sessions, "The Yellowstone Park," 444.

70. Charles J. Gillis, *Another Summer: The Yellowstone Park and Alaska* (New York: J. J. Little and Co., 1893), 25.

71. Rollins, "The Three Tetons," 872.

72. Charles W. Eliot to the editor of *Garden and Forest,* 13 February 1889; quoted in Peter J. Schmitt, *Back to Nature,* 61; on page 163, Schmitt states that the national park roads were shaped as "garden pathways" of a "Romantic garden."

73. James B. Irwin, *Report of the Acting Superintendent of Yellowstone National Park* (Washington, DC: Government Printing Office, 1898) H. Ex. Doc. 5 (54–2) (Serial No. 3758), 13; quoted in O'Brien, "The Yellowstone Park Road System," 92–93.

74. Olin D. Wheeler, *Yellowstone National Park,* 85.

75. Theodore Gerrish, *Life In the World's Wonderland* (n.p., 1887), 229–36.

76. "The Yellowstone National Park," *Harper's Weekly* 37 (1893): 729.

77. Henderson, "Dear Herald and Readers of the Herald," letter, 22 September 1890, 5, in Ash Collection, YNPARL.

78. Ibid., 5.

79. Ibid., 5.

80. "A Railroad through the Park," *Livingston Enterprise,* 15 July 1883.

81. Cruikshank, "Notes"; and Pierrepont, *From Fifth Avenue,* 246–48. Alice Welington Rollins and Edward Dawes are among the other Yellowstone literateurs who longed for a Wonderland railroad.

82. Haines, *The Yellowstone Story,* vol. 2, 31–32.

83. "A Problem for Engineers," *Pioneer Press,* 25 March 1882, in the Northern Pacific Railway Company Records (St. Paul: Minnesota Historical Society), clippings scrapbooks, microfilm, reel 6.

84. "Speech of Hon. Henry A. Coffeen, of Wyoming, U.S. House of Representatives, 17 December 1894," in Scrapbook no. 1, YNPARL; on the railroads as undemocratic, see Marx, *The Machine In the Garden,* 210–11.

85. Hoyt letter, "Our National Park," *Cheyenne Daily Leader,* 17 February 1883.

86. Ibid.

87. For a broad and brilliant analysis, see Marx, *The Machine In the Garden.*

88. Ralph Glidden, *Exploring the High Country: A History of the Cooke City Area* (Cooke City Store, 1976), 81–88; and Virginia Hansen and Al Funderburk, *The Fabulous Past of Cooke City* (Billings: Billings Printings Company, 1962).

89. Glidden, *Exploring the High Country,* 91.

90. Haines, *The Yellowstone Story,* vol. 2, 34–41. Haines refers to the imbroglio, which also included debate over bison and wildlife preservation, as The Yellowstone Crusade.

91. Hague to Vest, 28 December 1883, reprinted in *Forest and Stream,* 13 March 1884.

92. W. H. Randall Jr. to Hon John D. White, 28 January 1883, RG 62, P&M, letters received, microfilm, reel 2.

93. Secretary Teller to George Vest, RG 62, letters sent, 29 February 1884.

94. "Railroad Routes to Cooke," *Forest and Stream,* 8 April 1886; and "Cooke and the Clark's Fork Mines," *Forest and Stream,* 20 May 1886. The value of Yellowstone Park to the Northern Pacific would have increased immeasurably with a tourist line through the reserve. Evidence supporting Grinnell's contention was overwhelming. For example, Northern Pacific operative Carroll T. Hobart spent the winter of 1883–1884 lobbying for the railroad bill.

95. Bartlett, *A Wilderness Besieged,* 315.

96. "The Yellowstone National Park," *Garden and Forest,* 4 April 1894, 131.

97. "Sacred Yellowstone Park," *New York World,* 1 June 1886.

98. *Congressional Record,* 49th Cong., 2d sess., 18, 11 December 1886, 94, and 14 December 1886, 150.

99. "The Railroads and the Park," *Forest and Stream,* 13 May 1886.

100. "No Railroad In Yellowstone Park," *Forest and Stream,* 18 February 1886.

101. *Harper's Weekly Magazine,* 12 March 1892, 158.

102. Chittenden, *The Yellowstone National Park,* 133–34. Electric rail received endorsements from previous rail opponents including engineer Chittenden, who believed such a modern system would have posed fewer dangers to forests and wildlife.

103. Haines, *The Yellowstone Story,* vol. 2, 34, 40–41.

104. Runte, *Trains of Discovery,* 10–15.

105. Colonel John Pitcher, *Report of the Acting Superintendent of the Yellowstone National Park* (Washington, DC: Government Printing Office, 1902) H. Ex. Doc. 5 (57–2) (Serial no. 4460), 456.

106. Colonel John Pitcher, *Report of the Acting Superintendent of the Yellowstone National Park to the Secretary of the Interior* (Washington, DC: Government Printing Office, 1903), H. Ex. Doc. 5 (58–2) (Serial no. 4647), 501.

107. Manning's Report, appendix A of Chittenden, "Annual Report Upon the Construction, Repair, and Maintenance of Roads and Bridges In the Yellowstone National Park," appendix GGG in *Annual Report of the Chief of Engineers for 1903* (Washington, DC: Government Printing Office, 1903), 1894–1898, quoted in Haines, *The Yellowstone Story,* vol. 2, 165; Schmitt, *Back to Nature,* 69–72; and Stilgoe, *Borderland,* 212–13.

108. *Gardiner Wonderland,* 20 August 1903; quoted in Haines, *The Yellowstone Story,* vol. 2, 165.

109. Thomas, "My Recollections," 4, YNPARL.

110. Haines, *The Yellowstone Story,* vol. 2, 162–69.

111. Stout was a millionaire from Iowa who visited the park in 1893. His comments were quoted by his state's Representative Henderson (brother of George L. Henderson), in *Congressional Record,* (26) 53d Cong., 2d sess., April 7, 1896, 4282.

Chapter Six

1. "The Buffalo Heads," *Livingston Enterprise,* 18 December 1883.

2. Wheeler, *Yellowstone National Park,* 23.

3. Pitcher, *Annual Report,* 1903, 503.

4. George Catlin, *North American Indians,* 294–95. Catlin first published these volumes in London in 1841, based on his experiences in the 1830s.

5. On the frontier myth, see Richard Slotkin, *Regeneration through Violence:*

The Myth of the Frontier in the Age of Industrialization, 1800–1890 (New York: Atheneum, 1985).

6. For contemporary examples of Yellowstone's virgin myth, see Yandell, *Guide*, 70; Crandall, *Yellowstone: The Story behind the Scenery*, 4; and Goldblatt, *Yellowstone*.

7. Richard A. Bartlett, *Great Surveys of the American West* (Norman: University of Oklahoma Press, 1962), 37–38.

8. Alston Chase, *Playing God in Yellowstone: The Destruction of America's First National Park* (New York: Atlantic Monthly Press, 1986), 106; and Haines, *The Yellowstone Story* vol. 1, 21–30; see also Janetski, *Indians*, 82–83.

9. For the claim of "superstitious awe," see Philetus Norris, *Annual Report, 1880*, 3, 35. Beal, *The Story of Man In Yellowstone*, 84–91, broke the native story for historians.

10. L. P. Brockett, *Our Western Empire*, 1263–1264; and Wheeler, *6,000 Miles*, 86.

11. "The Nation's Great Park," *New York World*, 8 March 1887, 3.

12. See Marta Weigle, "From Desert to Disney World: The Santa Fe Railway and the Fred Harvey Company Display the Indian Southwest," *Journal of Anthropological Research* 45 (1989): 115–37.

13. G. Edward White, *The Eastern Establishment*, 105, citing Frederic Remington, *Pony Tracks* (Norman: University of Oklahoma Press, 1961), 28–29; Brockett, *Our Western Empire*, 153; and Mohr, *Excursion through America*, 132.

14. Gustave Koerner, *Memoirs of Gustave Koerner, 1809–1896*, ed. Thomas J. McCormack, vol. 2 (Cedar Rapids, Iowa: The Torch Press, 1909), 687.

15. Charles S. Fee, *Northern Pacific Railroad: The Wonderland Route to the Pacific Coast* (St. Paul: Northern Pacific Railroad, 1885), 21.

16. Wheeler, *Indianland and Wonderland*, 24–27.

17. "The Yellowstone Valley," *The Yellowstone Journal*, 17 March 1883, 1; and Norris, *The Calumet of the Coteau*, 269.

18. Charles C. Howell, "My First Trip to Yellowstone Park–1883," handwritten script in manuscript file, YNPARL.

19. J. L. Hill, *The Passing of the Indian and Buffalo* (Long Beach, CA: George W. Moyle, n.d.), 12, in F. Jay Haynes Collection, Montana State University Library Special Collections, Bozeman.

20. Hill, *The Passing of the Indian*, 18.

21. Slotkin, *The Fatal Environment*, 531; Patricia Nelson Limerick, *Legacy of Conquest*, 25.

22. The best work on this subject is Lears, *No Place of Grace*.

23. "The Crow Indian Reservation," *The Northwest*, February 1883, 8.

24. Chase, *Playing God*, 112–15.

25. Captain Moses Harris to P. Gallagher, 2 October 1888; and Fort Hall Agency (unsigned) to Harris, 12 December 1888, in pre-1916 archives, Letter Box 2, Documents 317 and 318, YNPARL.

26. "Our Mountain Bison," *The Yellowstone Journal*, 28 April 1883; and Ira Dodge to Captain George Anderson, 27 September 1893, pre-1916 archives, Letter Box 4, YNPARL.

27. "Protect the National Park," *Frank Leslie's Illustrated Newspaper*, 27 April 1889, 182.

28. See, for example, Merchant, *Ecological Revolutions*, 47–50. As Merchant notes, other excellent works on the hunting practices and philosophies of American Indians include Jose Ortega y Gasset, *Meditations On Hunting* (New York: Scribner's, 1972), and Calvin Martin, *Keepers of the Game: Indian-Animal Relationships and the Fur Trade* (Berkeley: University of California Press, 1978).

29. "A Case for Prompt Action," *Forest and Stream*, 11 April 1889; for background on Grinnell's Indian ethnographic work, see Andrew Giarelli, "An Indian Understanding of Things," 18–22, unknown Yale Alumni publication in manuscript file, American Heritage Center, University of Wyoming Library, Laramie; and John F. Rieger, ed., *The Passing of the Great West: Selected Papers of George Bird Grinnell* (New York: Winchester Press, 1972).

30. "Their Right to Roam," *Forest and Stream*, 18 April 1889.

31. Letters to the Editor from "Montana," "H." of Yellowstone National Park, and Archibald Rogers of Hyde Park, *Forest and Stream*, 11 April 1889.

32. Jack Solomon, *The Signs of Our Time. Semiotics: The Hidden Messages of Environments, Objects, and Cultural Images* (Los Angeles: Jeremy Tarcher, Inc., 1988), 28, 32–37; Genesis 1: 26–31, wherein Adam is directed to "have dominion over . . . the whole earth . . . and subdue it. " The precise meaning of Adam's responsibility to the animal world remains, of course, a matter of interpretation.

33. "Wanton Destruction of Game," *Yellowstone Journal*, 6 May 1882; for excellent discussions of scientific issues and popular perceptions of animal ecology, see Schmitt, *Back to Nature*, 8–9, 35–40 (page references from reprint edition); and Donald Worster, *Nature's Economy: A History of Ecological Ideas* (Sierra Club Books, 1977; reprint, New York: Cambridge University Press, 1990), 158–71 (page references from reprint edition).

34. Lily-Marlene Russow, "Changing Perceptions of Animals: A Philosophical View," in *Perceptions of Animals in American Culture*, R. J. Hoage, ed. (Washington, DC: Smithsonian Institution Press, 1989), 35.

35. Ibid., 33–34.

36. Schmitt, *Back to Nature*, 45–55.

37. Dunlap, *Saving America's Wildlife*, 25–31.

38. Schmitt, *Back to Nature*, 45–55.

39. Thomas Dunlap, "Sport Hunting and Conservation," *Environmental Review*, 12, no. 1 (Spring 1988): 54, citing Theodore Roosevelt, *The Wilderness Hunter* (1893). See also Pomeroy, *In Search of the Golden West*, 102–103; and White, *The Eastern Establishment*, 104–107.

40. Dunlap, *Saving America's Wildlife*, 13–15; and Lisa Mighetto, ed., *Muir*

among the Animals: The Wildlife Writings of John Muir (San Francisco: Sierra Club Books, 1986), xi-xxv.

41. Wingate, *Through the Yellowstone Park,* 208.

42. "The Elk," *The Northwest,* July 1883, 5.

43. For example, see "Game In the Yellowstone Park," *Forest and Stream,* 18 February 1886, 62. Paul Schullery explains that market hunters killed thousands of park elk and bison before the military assumed administration of the Park in 1886. Sportsmen, as Schullery notes, were "more moderate but just as deadly." See Paul Schullery, *The Bears of Yellowstone,* rev. ed.(Boulder: Roberts Rinehart in cooperation with the National Park Foundation, 1986), 82.

44. Bartlett, *A Wilderness Besieged,* 316.

45. Wingate, *Through the Yellowstone Park,* 161–65.

46. Wheeler, *Sketches,* 27.

47. Douglas B. Houston, *The Northern Yellowstone Elk, Parts I and II: History and Demography* (Yellowstone National Park, WY, 1974), 24–25. Houston notes that, rather than a result of enlightened management, the present "overpopulation" of park elk is a remnant of a once-much-larger number that lived throughout the Yellowstone ecosystem.

48. Dan Beard, "In a Wild Animal Republic," *Recreation* 15, no. 6 (December 1901): 417–23.

49. Frances Lynn Turpin, "A Trip through Yellowstone Park, 1895," 16, manuscript file, YNPARL.

50. On the shooting of prairie dogs, see, for example, Herman Haupt, *The Yellowstone National Park* (New York: Stoddart, 1883), 22; and Wingate, *Through the Yellowstone National Park,* 54.

51. Sessions, "The Yellowstone Park," 443.

52. "Depredating Wolves," *The Northwest,* December 1884, 4.

53. "Wolves In Yellowstone Park," 1896, n.a., in Scrapbook no. 3, YNPARL.

54. Elwood Hofer, "Yellowstone Park Notes," 1897, n.p., Scrapbook no. 3, YNPARL; and Haines, *The Yellowstone Story,* vol. 2, 80–82.

55. "Wolves In Yellowstone Park," YNPARL.

56. Synge, *A Ride through Wonderland,* 77–79.

57. For a thoughtful analysis of the changing perceptions of bears in American culture, see Daniel Gelo, "The Bear," in Angus K. Gillespie and Jay Mechling, eds., *American Wildlife in Symbol and Story* (Knoxville: University of Tennessee Press, 1987), 133–62; for a good natural history of Yellowstone bears, see Schullery, *The Bears of Yellowstone.*

58. Wheeler, *Yellowstone National Park,* 22–23.

59. George Bird Grinnell and Theodore Roosevelt, eds., *Hunting in Many Lands: Book of the Boone and Crockett Club,* (New York: Forest and Stream Publishing Co., 1895), vol. 2, 418; Mattoon, "The Yellowstone National Park."

60. Arnold Hague to Captain Anderson, 25 June 1891, pre-1916 archives, Letter Box 5, YNPARL.

61. "Liked Meat Too Well," *The Evening Star,* n.d., Scrapbook no. 1, 88–92, YNPARL.

62. Captain George S. Anderson, *Annual Report of the Superintendent of the Yellowstone National Park* (Washington, DC: Government Printing Office, 1891) H. Ex. Doc. 1, Serial nos. 2935, 647; and Secretary of the Interior to Captain George Anderson, 13 June 1892, pre-1916 archives, Letter Box 2, Doc. No. 371, YNPARL.

63. S. P. Langley to Superintendent Anderson, 7 April 1893, pre-1916 archives, Letter Box 3, YNPARL.

64. Secretary of the Interior to S. P. Langley, Secretary of the Smithsonian Institution, 8 January 1891, pre-1916 archives, Letter Box 2, YNPARL.

65. Ernest Thompson Seton, "The National Zoo at Washington," *The Century Magazine,* 60, no. 1 (May 1900): 4.

66. For a general but insightful discussion of these issues of perception, imperialism, and animals, see John Berger, *About Looking* (New York: Pantheon, 1980), 19–24.

67. Robert M. Utley, *The Indian Frontier of the American West, 1846–1890* (Albuquerque: University of New Mexico Press, 1984), 227–29.

68. Cy Martin, *Saga of the Buffalo* (New York: Hart Publishing, 1973), 10; and Michael S. Sample, *Bison: Symbol of the American West* (Helena, MT: Falcon Press, 1987), 32–34.

69. David Dray, *The Buffalo Book: The Full Saga of the American Animal* (Ohio University: Swallow Press, 1989), 118–20; and Martin, *Saga of the Buffalo,* 138–40.

70. Fee, *Northern Pacific Railroad: The Wonderland Route,* 19.

71. Olaf T. Hagen and Ray H. Mattison, "Pyramid Park—Where Roosevelt Came to Hunt," *North Dakota History,* 19, no. 4 (October 1952): 229–39.

72. Martin, *Saga of the Buffalo,* 10. For further discussions of Roosevelt's first and last bison hunt, see R. L. Wilson, *Theodore Roosevelt: Outdoorsman* (New York, 1971), 33–39; Paul Cutright, *Theodore Roosevelt: The Naturalist* (New York, 1956), 38–42; and Herman Hagedorn, *Roosevelt in the Badlands* (Boston, 1921), 28–46.

73. Leroy Barnet, "Ghastly Harvest: Montana's Trade In Buffalo Bones," *Montana: The Magazine of Western History,* Summer 1975, 2–13.

74. J. L. Hill, *The Passing of the Indian,* 37.

75. "The American Buffalo," *The Northwest,* September 1884, 6; reprinted from *The Mandan Pioneer.*

76. Paul Russell Cutright, *Theodore Roosevelt: The Making of a Conservationist* (Chicago: University of Illinois Press, 1985), 158, quoting Theodore Roosevelt, *Hunting Trips of a Ranchman* (New York: G. P. Putnam's Sons, 1886), 312.

77. Cutright, *The Making of,* 168, quoting Theodore Roosevelt, *Works, Memorial Edition,* 24 vols., ed. Hermann Hagedorn (New York: Charles Scribner's Sons, 1923), xviii.

78. Grinnell and Roosevelt, *Hunting at,* 436–37; and Bartlett, *A Wilderness Besieged,* 142.

79. "A Memorial of the Great Plains," *Forest and Stream,* 18 August 1887.

80. Larry Barsness, *Heads, Hides and Horns: The Compleat Buffalo Book,* with a foreword by Ron Tyler (Fort Worth: Texas Christian University Press, 1985), 104; Synge, *A Ride through Wonderland,* 132–33.

81. Hampton, *How the U.S. Cavalry,* 72; and Captain George Anderson, *Report of the Superintendent of Yellowstone National Park, 1892* (Washington, DC: Government Printing Office, 1892) H. Ex. Doc. 1 (Serial no. 3089), 652.

82. Margaret Mary Meagher, *The Bison of Yellowstone Park* (Washington, DC: National Park Service, 1973), Science Monograph Series, no. 1, 120–26.

83. Captain George Anderson, *Report of the Acting Superintendent of the Yellowstone National Park to the Secretary of the Interior, 1894* (Washington, DC: Government Printing Office, 1894), 9–10.

84. The original account of the Howell capture is found in "'Forest and Stream's' Yellowstone Park Game Expedition," *Forest and Stream,* 5 May 1894.

85. Haines, *The Yellowstone Story,* vol. 2, 63–64; full text of the Lacey Act found on pp. 473–76 of vol. 2.

86. Hampton, *How the U.S. Cavalry,* chap. 7; and Grinnell, ed., *Hunting in High Altitudes,* 438.

87. Beard, "In a Wild Animal Republic," 422.

88. Phillips to Anderson, 15 May 1894, pre-1916 archives, Letter Box 6, Doc. No. 1217, YNPARL; Grinnell to Anderson, 3 April 1894, pre-1916 archives, Letter Box 5, Doc. no. 936, YNPARL; and E. S. Thompson to Anderson, 23 October 1894 and 22 December 1894, pre-1916 archives, Letter Box 7, YNPARL.

89. Haines, *The Yellowstone Story,* vol. 2, 71–72, 75–76; and William Timmons, *Twilight on the Range: Recollections of a Latterday Cowboy* (Austin: University of Texas Press, 1962), 69.

90. Sample, *Symbol of the West,* 45–46; and Barsness, *Heads, Hides, and Horns,* 155.

91. Sample, *Symbol of the West,* 47–48.

92. Edmund B. Rogers, comp., "Bills in Congress to Revise the Boundaries of Yellowstone National Park," Haynes Collection, Montana State University Library.

93. Haines, *The Yellowstone Story,* vol. 2, 94–99.

94. Hays, *Conservation;* and Nash, *Wilderness,* 133–36.

95. The argument was being tested at about the same time in the Adirondack Mountains of New York. Forest advocates won there as well, based on the fear that destruction of forest had caused long-term damage to down-state New York City. See Terrie, *Forever Wild;* Yellowstone defenders occasionally referred to the Adirondack case: see, for example, Arnold Hague to Secretary Henry M. Teller, 28 January 1884, Record Group 62, *Records of the Department of the Interior*

Relating to Yellowstone National Park, microfilm, reel 2, National Archives, Washington, DC (hereafter RG 62).

96. William Hallett Phillips to Interior Secretary Lamar, 4 October 1886, RG 62, reel 3, National Archives.

97. Mary Caldwell Ludwig, "The Yellowstone," n.d., n.p., Scrapbook no. 3, 21, YNPARL.

98. "The Corner Stone Was Laid," (Gardiner, MT) *Wonderland,* 30 April 1903, 1, Scrapbook no. 2, YNPARL.

99. Haines, *The Yellowstone Story,* vol. 2, 97.

100. "The Corner Stone Was Laid," 1. Interestingly, much of the publicity surrounding the President's 1903 trip (the first by a U.S. president since the Arthur expedition) focused on his decision not to hunt any game while in the West. See "President May Not Fire Gun on Hunt," *Washington Star,* 16 March 1903, Scrapbook no. 4, YNPARL.

101. Owen Wister, "Old Yellowstone Days," in Harmon, ed., *Mirror of America,* 25.

102. Pitcher, *Annual Report, 1903,* 503.

103. Theodore B. Comstock, "The Yellowstone National Park," *The American Naturalist,* 8 (1874): 163.

104. Schullery, *Bears of Yellowstone,* 85.

105. "The Corner Stone Was Laid," 1.

106. *Report of the Acting Superintendent of Yellowstone National Park* (Washington, DC: Government Printing Office, 1903), H. Ex. Doc. 5 (Serial no. 4647), 501; and Paul Schullery, *Road-Guide for the Four-Season Road from Gardiner to Cooke City Through Yellowstone National Park* (Yellowstone Library and Museum Association with the National Park Service, 1960), 7.

107. Gifford Pinchot, *The Fight for Conservation* (1910; reprint Seattle: University of Washington Press, 1973), 44–45.

Chapter Seven

1. *Glamour,* "Travel USA: Glamour's Top Ten Destinations," April 1995, 289.

2. Goldblatt, *Yellowstone.*

3. Ibid; and Finley, *Geysers of Yellowstone.*

4. *Our National Parks: A Seasonal Tour* (Washington, DC: Wolfgang Bayer Productions for National Geographic Society, 1989), 30 minutes, videocassette.

5. Todd Wilkinson, "Global Warning," *National Parks* 70 (March-April 1996): 34.

6. I am indebted to Michael Barton for pointing out to me this history's gray ambiguity long ago at Penn State University in Harrisburg.

7. Dennis Glick, Mary Carr and Bert Harting, eds., *An Environmental Profile of the Greater Yellowstone Ecosystem* (Bozeman: Greater Yellowstone Coalition,

1991), 10. The grizzly bear study was conducted by Frank and John Craighead. Also influential in the development of the ecosystem concept was Rick Reese's study, *Greater Yellowstone: The National Park and Its Adjacent Wildlands,* Montana Geographic Series no. 6 (Helena: Montana Magazine Inc., 1984).

8. Glick, Carr and Harting, *An Environmental Profile,* 10.

9. Ibid., 111.

10. Dan Whipple, "Speakers Clash Over Park 'Vision' Document," *Casper Star-Tribune,* 18 November 1990, A3, citing the introduction to the *Vision* document and a speech by Warren Morton, oilman and representative of the Wyoming Multiple Use Coalition at a public hearing.

11. "Yellowstone 'Vision' detractors not extremists," *Casper Star-Tribune,* 30 November 1990, n.p.; and Richard Stroup, Montana State University economist, quoted in "Ownership of Public Lands Defended," *Casper Star-Tribune,* 19 November 1990, n. p.

12. Kurt J. Repanshek, "Official Quits, Tried to Save Yellowstone," *Albuquerque Journal,* 16 April 1992, A3; and Angus M. Thuermer Jr., "Mintzmeyer Calls 'Vision' Paper a Political Fraud," *Jackson Hole News,* 25 September 1991, 1.

13. Interview with Micah Morrison, author of *Fire in Paradise* (New York: Harper Collins, 1993), quoted in Barry Noreen, "Yellowstone Park is at center of battle over protection of ecosystem far beyond its boundaries," *Colorado Springs Gazette Telegraph,* 29 October 1993.

14. Roger Koopman, "Lessons from the Yellowstone bison herd," *Bozeman Daily Chronicle,* 28 December 1991, presents the most extreme form of Yellowstone privatization; the idea has gotten varying degrees of support in other forms—see the national park ideas of James Watt, former Secretary of the Interior and select members of the 104th Congress. For a less radical approach to "wise use" economic ecology see J. Baden, ed., *A Yellowstone Primer: Policy Reform Via the New Resource Economics* (Bozeman: Political Economy Research Center, 1990).

15. Quoted in "Ownership of Public Lands defended," *Casper Star-Tribune,* 19 November 1990, n.p.

16. J. Carl Ganter, "Yellowstone In Flames," *Jackson Hole Guide,* 2 October 1991, E3; Ganter cites a number of outside fire ecologists who essentially agree with the philosophy of "let-burn," but who challenge its denial of human history. See also Alston Chase, *Playing God in Yellowstone,* for a broader and more critical discussion of National Park Service policies.

17. Ganter, "Yellowstone In Flames," E3-E4; Ganter cites the work of Thomas Bonnicksen, a fire ecologist at Texas A&M University.

18. Brokaw quote recounted to author by Paul Anderson, TW Services tour guide, 22 December 1991.

19. Paul A. Witteman, "Springtime In the Rockies," *Time,* 29 May 1989, 94; and Lawrence Zuckerman, "'We Could Have Stopped This,'" *Time,* 5 September 1988, 19.

20. Brandon Loomis, "Telling the Fire Story," *Jackson Hole Guide,* 2 October 1991, E15.

21. George Hackett with Michael Lerner and Mary Hager, "Fighting for Yellowstone," *Newsweek,* 19 September 1988, 18–20.

22. See, for example, "Yellowstone A Year Later," *Sunset: The Magazine of Western Living,* May 1989, 108–18.

23. Glick, Carr, and Harting, *An Environmental Profile,* 115.

24. Marv Hoyt, "Citizens Come Out Against Targhee Plan," *Greater Yellowstone Report: The Quarterly Journal of the Greater Yellowstone Coalition* (Bozeman, MT), 13, no. 3 (Summer 1996): 15 (hereafter *Greater Yellowstone Report*); the story quotes the Targhee National Forest Draft Fifteen-Year Management Plan.

25. "1872 Mining: A Law With No Brain," *Greater Yellowstone Report,* 6 (Autumn 1989): 1; and Todd Wilkinson, "A Clash Between Two Kinds of Wealth," *High Country News,* 4 June 1990, 11.

26. "1872 Mining," 17.

27. Wilkinson, "A Clash," 11; and "New World Mining Project," *Greater Yellowstone Coalition Fact Sheet* (Bozeman, MT, 1991).

28. Fen Montaigne, "Mining Plans Near Yellowstone Touch Off Furious Opposition," *Knight-Ridder/Tribune News Service,* 6 October 1995, p1006K8440 (Internet source).

29. Wilkinson, "A Clash," 11; and Montaigne, "Mining Plans."

30. *New York Times* editorial, 29 August 1994, quoted in "'Mine From Hell' Threatens Yellowstone," *Greater Yellowstone Coalition Fact Sheet,* 1994.

31. Quoted in Montaigne, "Mining Plans."

32. Ibid.

33. President Bill Clinton, "Yellowstone More Precious Than Gold," text of his speech delivered 12 August 1996 at the New World Mine Site, Cooke City, Montana, reprinted in *Greater Yellowstone Report,* 13, no. 3 (Summer 1996): 7.

34. Montaigne, "Mining Plans."

35. Michael Satchell, "To the Rescue at Yellowstone," *U.S. News and World Report,* 26 August 1996, 12.

36. "Bill's Trail of Tears," *The Nation,* 14 October 1996, 10.

37. Glick, Carr and Harting, *An Environmental Profile,* 103–106; "Golf and Housing Development Posed Next to Yellowstone Park," *Greater Yellowstone Report,* 13, no. 3 (Summer 1996): 14; and Dennis Glick, "Going Downhill Fast?" *Greater Yellowstone Report,* 13, no. 4 (Fall 1996): 1, 4–7.

38. Tom Kenworthy, "Lujan Omission Criticized," *Albuquerque Journal,* 20 October 1991, A3; and Louisa Wilcox, "Yellowstone's Geysers: Explosive, Mysterious—But Protected?" *Greater Yellowstone Today, A Publication of the Greater Yellowstone Coalition* 1 (Winter 1991): 4.

39. Michael Satchell, "There's Gold In Them Thar Pools: Tourists Like the Sights. Biotech companies are Mining Yellowstone's Attractions for Profit," *U.S. News and World Report,* 2 December 1996, 81.

40. Michael Milstein, "Bio-Prospecting In Yellowstone," *Greater Yellowstone Report*, 13, no. 4 (Fall 1996): 16, article originally appearing in the *Billings Gazette* and the *Boston Globe*.

41. Satchell, "There's Gold In Them Thar Pools," 81.

42. Milstein, "Bio-Prospecting In Yellowstone," 15.

43. Glick, Carr, and Harting, *An Environmental Profile*, 104.

44. *Sierra*, March-April 1998, 35.

45. Dennis Glick, "The Future of Ranching," *Greater Yellowstone Report*, 13, no. 1 (Winter 1996): 8–9; and "A How-To Manual for 'Ranchettes,'" *Greater Yellowstone Report*, 11, no. 4 (Fall 1994): 8–9.

46. "Own a Piece of Paradise—Montana Land!" advertising brochure, (Bozeman: Yellowstone Basin Properties, 1991).

47. Glick, Carr, and Harting, *An Environmental Profile*, 105–106.

48. Author's trip to Yellowstone, 20–27 December 1991.

49. TW Services, "Yellowstone, The World's First National Park," full page ad, *Old West Trail 1988 Vacation Guide*, 9.

50. Joel Connelly, "'Mother' Yellowstone Ails at 119," *Seattle Post-Intelligencer*, 7 July 1991, A3; and Chase, *Playing God in Yellowstone*, 371.

51. Stephen Budiansky, "Yellowstone's Unraveling: The Ecosystem is in Grave Peril and the Most Damage is Caused by Elk," *U.S. News and World Report*, 16 September 1996, 80.

52. Alan Kesselheim, "Horn Wars," *Backpacker*, September 1996, 17.

53. Budiansky, "Yellowstone's Unraveling," 80.

54. Aldo Leopold, *A Sand County Almanac and Sketches Here and There* (New York: Oxford University Press, 1949; 1989 commemorative edition), with an introduction by Robert Finch), 130.

55. Yandell, *Guide*, 73.

56. Glick, Carr and Harting, *An Environmental Profile*, 72; and "Yellowstone Wolf Reintroduction," *Greater Yellowstone Coalition Information Sheet*, 1991.

57. "Bringing Wolves Back is Stirring Howls of Protest," *Seattle Post-Intelligencer*, 1 September 1991, 11.

58. Renee Askins, "Releasing Wolves from Symbolism," *Harper's Magazine*, April 1995, 15.

59. Jon Scieszka, *The True Story of the Three Little Pigs by A. Wolf*, illustrated by Lane Smith (New York: Scholastic, Inc, 1989).

60. "Feeling the Pinch: Yellowstone Park's Budget Crisis Worsens," *Greater Yellowstone Report*, 13, no. 3 (Summer 1996): 16.

61. "Days of Garbage-Guzzling Grizzlies Long Gone," *Seattle Post-Intelligencer*, 7 July 1991, A9.

62. Bob Ekey, "Lake Trout Infestation Has Frightening Consequences," *Greater Yellowstone Report*, 13, no. 1 (Winter 1996): 13.

63. Michael Satchell, "Walking Stick? Don't Ask," *U.S. News and World Report*, 121, no. 13 (September 30, 1996): 61.

64. National Public Radio report, 18 January 1997.

65. "Help America's Buffalo Roam Free," *Greater Yellowstone Coalition Fact Sheet,* 1996.

66. Associated Press wire story, 11 March 1997.

67. Michael Satchell, "A Discouraging Word for Buffalo," *U.S. News and World Report,* 30 September 1996, 61.

68. "Help America's Buffalo Roam Free. "

69. The effects of gawking, wintertime tourists on bison were reported to the author by a park guide on a December 1991 visit.

70. Jeanne-Marie Souvigney, "Yellowstone Winter Use Climbing," *Greater Yellowstone Report,* 13, no. 4 (Fall 1996): 9.

71. Conversation with Tom Tankersley, park historian, 9 October 1992.

72. TW Services, "Yellowstone, The World's First National Park," Mammoth, WY, 1991, advertising brochure, 9.

73. "Yellowstone A Year Later," *Sunset,* 119.

74. Paul Schullery, *Bears of Yellowstone,* xiv.

75. "In the Park," *Livingston Enterprise,* 3 March 1900.

76. John E. Rosenow and Gerald L. Pulsipher, with editorial assistance by Kathryn Collura, *Tourism: The Good, the Bad and the Ugly* (Lincoln, NE: Media Productions and Marketing, 1979), 88.

77. *Yellowstone, Official Map and Guide,* (Yellowstone National Park, Wyoming: National Park Service), 1991.

78. With apologies to M. Scott Peck.

79. Angus M. Thuermer Jr., "Fair Concession," *Jackson Hole News,* 24 July 1991, 8A; Thuermer, "Money in Wonderland, *Jackson Hole News,* 11 September 1991, 1A; and "Park Service Receives One Bid for Yellowstone Concessions," *The Casper* Star Tribune, 29 July 1991.

80. Jeanne-Marie Souvigney, "Feeling the Pinch," *Greater Yellowstone Report,* 13, no. 3 (Summer 1996): 16–17.

81. Jeanne-Marie Souvigney, "Corporate Sponsorship is Not the Answer," *Greater Yellowstone Report,* 13, no. 3 (Summer 1996): 17.

82. "Noise from Snowmobile Emissions Can Shatter the Peaceful Silence of a Yellowstone Winter," *Greater Yellowstone Report,* 13, no. 1 (Winter 1996): 6.

83. Tom Tankersley, Yellowstone Park historian, conversation with the author, 9 October 1992. Tankersley noted that although suggested by a member of Wyoming's congressional delegation, the proposal would not likely receive serious consideration. He was right.

84. Colgate Hoyt, "Roughing It Up the Yellowstone," ed. Carroll Van West, *Montana: The Magazine of Western History,* Spring 1986, 35.

85. Michael Scott, "Yellowstone to the Yukon," *Greater Yellowstone Report,* 13, no. 2 (Spring 1996): 5.

Works Cited

Secondary Sources:
Books, Articles and Dissertations

Albers, Patricia C., and William R. James. "Tourism and the Changing Photographic Image of the Great Lakes Indians." *Annals of Tourism Research* 10 (1983): 123–148.

Athearn, Robert G. *The Mythic West in Twentieth Century America*. With a foreword by Elliott West. Kansas City: University of Kansas Press, 1986.

Baden, J., ed. *A Yellowstone Primer: Policy Reform Via the New Resource Economics*. Bozeman, MT: Political Economy Research Center, 1990.

Baldwin, Kenneth H., ed. *Enchanted Enclosure: The Army Engineers and Yellowstone National Park, A Documentary History*. Washington, DC: Government Printing Office, 1976.

Barber, John F. *Old Yellowstone Views*. Missoula: Montana Press Publishing Company, 1987.

Barsness, Larry. *Heads, Hides and Horns: The Compleat Buffalo Book*. With a foreword by Ron Tyler. Fort Worth: Texas Christian University Press, 1985.

Barnet, Leroy. "Ghastly Harvest: Montana's Trade In Buffalo Bones." *Montana: The Magazine of Western History* 25 (Summer 1975): 2–13.

Bartlett, Richard A. *Great Surveys of the American West*. Norman: University of Oklahoma Press, 1962.

———. *Nature's Yellowstone*. Albuquerque: University of New Mexico Press, 1974.

———. "The Senator Who Saved Yellowstone Park." *The Westerners Brand Book*. New York 16 (1969): 49–52.

———. "Those Infernal Machines in Yellowstone." *Montana: The Magazine of Western History* 20 (July 1970): 16–29.

———. *Yellowstone: A Wilderness Beseiged*. Tucson: University of Arizona Press, 1985.

Beal, Merrill D. *The Story of Man in Yellowstone*. Caldwell, ID: Caxton Printers, 1949.

Berger, John. *About Looking*. New York: Pantheon Press, 1980.

———. *Ways of Seeing*. Middlesex, England: Pelican Press, 1972.

Bernstein, Richard. "Unsettling the Old West." *New York Times*, March 18, 1990, Sec. 6, 57.

Bright, Deborah. "Of Mother Nature and Marlboro Men: An Inquiry into the Cultural Meanings of Landscape Photography." In *The Contest of Meaning*, edited by R. Bolton, 161–69. Cambridge, MA: MIT Press, 1989.

"Bringing Wolves Back Is Stirring Howls of Protest." *Seattle Post-Intelligencer*, September 1, 1991, 11.

Brooks, Chester L., and Ray H. Mattison. *Theodore Roosevelt and the Dakota Badlands*. Washington, DC: Government Printing Office, National Park Service, 1958.

Brown, Mark H. *The Plainsmen of the Yellowstone: A History of the Yellowstone Basin*. Lincoln: University of Nebraska Press, 1961.

Bryans, William S. "A History of Transcontinental Railroads and Coal Mining on the Northern Plains to 1920." Ph.D. diss., University of Wyoming, 1987.

Buss, Dietrich G. *Henry Villard: A Study of Transatlantic Investments and Interests, 1870–1895*. Dissertations in American Economic History Series, advisory ed. Stuart Brichey. New York: Arno Press, 1978.

Chase, Alston. *Playing God in Yellowstone: The Destruction of America's First National Park*. New York: Atlantic Monthly Press, 1986.

Chittenden, Hiram Martin. *The Yellowstone National Park: Historical and Descriptive*. Edited and with an introduction by Richard A. Bartlett. Norman: University of Oklahoma Press, 1964.

Clark, Clifford Edward, Jr. *The American Family Home, 1800–1860*. Chapel Hill: University of North Carolina Press, 1986.

Clinch, Thomas A. "The Northern Pacific Railroad and Montana's Mineral Lands." *Pacific Historical Review* 34 (1965): 323–35.

Connelly, Joel. "'Mother' Yellowstone Ails at 119." *Seattle Post-Intelligencer*, July 7, 1991, A3.

Cramton, Louis C. *Early History of Yellowstone National Park and its Relation to National Park Policies*. Washington, DC: Government Printing Office, 1932.

Cutright, Paul Russell. *Theodore Roosevelt: The Making of a Conservationist*. Chicago: University of Illinois Press, 1985.

Dray, David. *The Buffalo Book: The Full Saga of the American Animal*. Athens: Ohio University Press, 1974.

"Days of Garbage-Guzzling Grizzlies Long Gone." *Seattle Post-Intelligencer*, July 7, 1991, A9.

D'Emilio, Sandra, and Suzan Campbell. *Visions and Visionaries: The Art and Artists of the Santa Fe Railway*. Salt Lake City: Gibbs-Smith Publishers, 1991.

DeVoto, Bernard. "The West: A Plundered Province." *Harper's Magazine* (August 1934): 356–64.

Deloria, Vine, Jr., ed. *American Indian Policy in the Twentieth Century.* Norman: University of Oklahoma Press, 1985.

Dimock, George. *Exploiting the View: Photographs of Yosemite and Mariposa by Carleton Watkins.* North Bennington, VT: Park-McCullough House, July 8, 1984. Published transcript of lecture, in University of New Mexico Fine Arts Library, Albuquerque.

Dippie, Brian W. *The Vanishing American: White Attitudes and U.S. Indian Policy.* Middletown, CT: Wesleyan University Press, 1982.

Dittl, Barbara H., and Joanne Mallmann. "Plain to Fancy: The Lake Hotel, 1889–1929." *Montana: The Magazine of Western History* 34 (Spring 1984): 32–45.

Douglas, Ann. *The Feminization of American Culture.* New York: Alfred A. Knopf, 1977.

Dunlap, Thomas. *Saving America's Wildlife.* Trenton, NJ: Princeton University Press, 1988.

———. "Sport Hunting and Conservation, 1880–1920." *Environmental Review* 12 (Spring 1988): 51–60.

Early, Katherine E. *"For the Benefit and Enjoyment of the People": Cultural Attitudes and the Establishment of Yellowstone National Park.* Georgetown Monograph in American Studies Series. Washington, DC: Georgetown University Press, 1984.

"1872 Mining: A Law with No Brain." *Greater Yellowstone Report* 6 (Autumn 1989). Bozeman, MT: Greater Yellowstone Coalition.

Ellis, Elmer. *Henry Moore Teller: Defender of the West.* Caldwell, ID: n.p., 1941.

Fensom, Rod. *America's Great Resort Hotels: Eighty Classic Resorts in the United States and Canada.* Charlotte, NC: East Woods Press, 1985.

Fine, Harry L. "Gold Creek, Montana." *Western Express: Research Journal of Early Western Mails* 16 (July 1966): 11.

Fitzsimmons, A. K. "National Parks: The Dilemma of Development." *Science* 191 (1976): 440–43.

Frantz, Joe B. "Yellowstone National Park: Genesis of an Urban Solution." In *Aspects of the American West: Three Essays,* with a foreword by Eugene Hollon, 21–44. College Station, TX: Texas A&M University Press, 1976.

Ganter, J. Carl. "Yellowstone In Flames." *Jackson Hole Guide,* October 2, 1991, E3.

Giarelli, Andrew. "An Indian Understanding of the Nature of Things" Typed manuscript (photocopy). Manuscript File. American Heritage Center. University of Wyoming, Laramie.

Ginger, Ray. *The Age of Excess: The United States from 1877 to 1914.* New York: Macmillan Co., 1965.

Glick, Dennis, Mary Carr and Bert Harting, eds. *An Environmental Profile of the Greater Yellowstone Ecosystem.* Bozeman, MT: Greater Yellowstone Coalition, 1991.

Goetzmann, William H. *Exploration and Empire: The Explorer and the Scientist in the Winning of the West.* New York: Alfred A. Knopf, 1966.

Graburn, Nelson H. H. "Tourism: The Sacred Journey." In *Hosts and Guests: The Anthropology of Tourism,* edited by Valene L. Smith, 17–31. Philadelphia: University of Pennsylvania Press, 1977.

Grana, Cesar. *Fact and Symbol.* New York: Oxford University Press, 1971.

Grinnell, George Bird. *The Selected Papers of George Bird Grinnell.* Edited by John F. Reiger. New York: Winchester Press, 1972.

Hagen, Olaf T., and Ray H. Mattison. "Pyramid Park—Where Roosevelt Came to Hunt." *North Dakota History* 19 (1952): 215–41.

Haines, Aubrey L. *The Yellowstone Story: A History of Our First National Park.* 2 vols. Mammoth Hot Springs, Wyoming: Yellowstone Library and Museum Association, in cooperation with Colorado Associated University Press, 1977.

Hales, Peter B. *William Henry Jackson and the Transformation of the American Landscape.* Philadelphia: Temple University Press, 1988.

Hamilton, James McClellan. *History of Montana: From Wilderness to Statehood.* Edited by Merrill G. Burlingame. Portland: Binfords and Mort, 1957.

Hampton, H. Duane. *How the U.S. Cavalry Saved Our National Parks.* Bloomington: Indiana University Press, 1971.

Harnsberger, John L. "Land Speculation, Promotion and Failure: The Northern Pacific Railroad, 1870–1873." *Journal of the West* 9 (January 1970): 33–45.

Hart, E. J. *The Selling of Canada: The Canadian Pacific Railway and the Beginnings of Canadian Tourism.* Banff, Canada: Altitude Publishing, Ltd., 1983.

Hays, Samuel P. *Conservation and the Gospel of Efficiency: The Progressive Conservation Movement, 1890–1920.* Cambridge: Harvard University Press, 1959.

Hedges, James B. *Henry Villard and the Railways of the Northwest.* New York: Russell and Russell, 1930.

———. "The Colonization Work of the Northern Pacific Railroad." *Mississippi Valley Historical Review* 13 (December 1926): 311–42.

Houston, Douglas B. *The Northern Yellowstone Elk, Parts I and II: History and Demography.* Yellowstone National Park, WY: National Park Service, 1974.

Howe, George Frederick. *Chester A. Arthur: A Quarter-Century of Machine Politics.* New York: Frederick Ungar Publishing Co., 1935; reprint 1957.

Hudson, John C. "Main Streets of the Yellowstone Valley." *Montana: The Magazine of Western History* 35 (Autumn 1985): 63–64.

Huth, Hans. *Nature and the American: Three Centuries of Changing Attitudes.* Berkeley: University of California Press, 1957. New edition, Lincoln: University of Nebraska Press, 1990, with an introduction by Douglas H. Strong.

Hutton, Paul A. "Phil Sheridan's Crusade for Yellowstone." *American History Illustrated* 19 (February 1985): 10–16.

Hyde, Anne Farrar. *An American Vision: Far Western Landscape and National Culture.* New York: New York University Press, 1990.

Irwin, Leonard Bertram. "Pacific Railways and Nationalism in the Canadian-American Northwest, 1845–1873." Ph.D. diss., University of Pennsylvania, 1939.

Ise, John. *Our National Park Policy: A Critical History.* Baltimore: Johns Hopkins University Press, 1961; reprint 1967.

———. *The United States Forest Policy.* New Haven: Yale University Press, 1920.

Jackson, John B. *American Space—The Centennial Years: 1865–1876.* New York: W. W. Norton and Co., 1972.

Jakle, John A. *The Tourist: Travel in Twentieth-Century North America.* Lincoln: University of Nebraska Press, 1985.

Janetski, Joel. *Indians of Yellowstone Park.* Salt Lake City: University of Utah Press, 1987.

Jones, Howard Mumford. *The Age of Energy: Varieties of American Experience, 1865–1915.* New York: Viking Press, 1971.

Josephson, Matthew. *The Robber Barons: The Great American Capitalists, 1861–1901.* New York: Harcourt, Brace and Co., 1936.

Kasson, John F. *Civilizing the Machine: Technology and Republican Values, 1776–1900.* New York: Penguin Books, 1977, 1988; originally published, 1976.

Kenworthy, Tom. "Lujan Omission Criticized." *Albuquerque Journal,* October 20, 1991, A3.

Kirkland, Edward Chase. *Dream and Thought in the Business Community, 1860–1950.* Ithaca: Cornell University Press, 1956.

———. *Industry Comes of Age: Business, Labor and Public Policy, 1860–1897.* New York: Holt Rinehart, 1961.

Kolodny, Annette. *The Land before Her: Fantasy and Experience of the American Frontier, 1630–1860.* Chapel Hill: University of North Carolina Press, 1984.

———. *The Lay of the Land: Metaphor as Experience and History in American Life and Letters.* Chapel Hill: University of North Carolina Press, 1975.

Koopman, Roger. "Lessons from the Yellowstone Bison Herd." *Bozeman Daily Chronicle,* December 28, 1991, 12A.

Krauss, Rosalind. "Photography's Discursive Spaces: Landscape/View." *Art Journal* 42 (Winter 1982): 312–17.

Limerick, Patricia. *Legacy of Conquest: The Unbroken Past of the American West.* New York: W.W. Norton and Co., 1987.

"Livingston: Railroad Town On the Yellowstone." *Montana: The Magazine of Western History* 35 (Autumn 1985): 84–86.

Loomis, Brandon. "Telling the Fire Story." *Jackson Hole Guide,* October 2, 1991, E15.

Lowenthal, David. *The Past is a Foreign Country.* New York: Cambridge University Press, 1985.

Lyon, Thomas J., ed. *This Incomparable Lande: A Book of American Nature Writing.* Boston: Houghton Mifflin, 1989.

MacCannell, Dean. "Staged Authenticity: Arrangements of Social Space in Tourist Settings." *The American Journal of Sociology* 19 (1973): 589–603.

———. *The Tourist: A New Theory of the Leisure Class.* New York: Schocken Books Inc., 1976; reprint 1989, with a new introduction by the author.

MacFarlane, Robert S. *Henry Villard and the Northern Pacific: The Spectacular Career of a German Immigrant Who Completed America's First Northern Transcontinental Railroad.* New York: Newcomen Society, 1954.

Martin, Cy. *Saga of the Buffalo.* New York: Hart Publishing, 1973.

Marx, Leo. *The Machine in the Garden: Technology and the Pastoral Ideal in America.* New York: Oxford University Press, 1964.

McKinsey, Elizabeth. *Niagara Falls: Icon of the American Sublime.* New York: Cambridge University Press, 1985.

Meagher, Mary Margaret. *The Bison of Yellowstone Park.* Science Monograph Series, no. 1. Washington, DC: National Park Service, 1973.

Melosi, Martin V. *Garbage in the Cities: Refuse, Reform, and Environment, 1880–1980.* College Station: Texas A&M University Press, 1981.

Merchant, Carolyn. *Ecological Revolutions: Nature, Gender and Science in New England.* Chapel Hill: University of North Carolina Press, 1989.

———. *The Death of Nature: Women, Ecology, and the Scientific Revolution.* San Francisco: Harper and Row, 1980.

Miller, Perry. *Errand into the Wilderness.* New York: Harper and Row, 1956.

Montana Historical Society. *F. Jay Haynes, Photographer.* Helena: Montana Historical Society Press, 1981.

Morris, Edmund. *The Rise of Theodore Roosevelt.* New York: Ballantine Books, 1979.

Nash, Roderick. *Wilderness and the American Mind.* 3d. ed. New Haven: Yale University Press, 1982.

———. *The American Environment: Readings in the History of Conservation.* Reading, MA: Addison-Wesley, 1968.

National Cyclopedia of American Biography. New York: James T. White and Company, 1921.

National Park Service. "Yellowstone, Official Map and Guide." Mammoth Hot Springs, Wyoming, 1991.

Nelson, Steve. "Walt Disney's EPCOT and the World's Fair Performance Tradition." *The Drama Review* 30 (Winter 1986): 106–46.

"New World Mining Project." *Greater Yellowstone Coalition Fact Sheet.* Bozeman, MT: Greater Yellowstone Coalition, 1991.

Nolan, Edward W., and John C. Smart. "A Portfolio of F. Jay Haynes Photographs." *Montana: The Magazine of Western History* 33 (Summer 1983): 24–33.

Nolan, Edward W. "'Not Without Labor and Expense': The Villard-Northern Pacific Last Spike Excursion, 1883." *Montana: The Magazine of Western History* 33 (Summer 1983): 2–11.

———. *Northern Pacific Views: The Railroad Photography of F. Jay Haynes, 1876–1905.* Helena: Montana Historical Society Press, 1983.

Novak, Barbara. *Nature and Culture: American Landscape and Painting, 1825–1875.* New York: Oxford University Press, 1980.

O'Brien, Bob Randolph. "The Yellowstone National Park Road System: Past, Present and Future." Ph.D. diss., University of Washington, 1965.

Percy, Walker. *The Message in the Bottle: How Queer Man Is, How Queer Language Is, and What One Has to Do with the Other.* New York: Farrar, Straus and Giroux, 1975.

Plummer, Norman B. *Crow Indians.* New York: Garland, 1974.

Pomeroy, Earl. *In Search of the Golden West: The Tourist in Western America.* New York: Knopf, 1957.

Reiger, John F. *American Sportsmen and the Origins of Conservation.* New York: Winchester Press, 1975.

———. "George Bird Grinnell and the Development of American Conservation, 1870–1901." Ph.D. diss., Northwestern University, 1970.

———., ed. *The Passing of the Great West: Selected Papers of George Bird Grinnell.* New York: Winchester Press, 1972.

Reese, Rick. "Greater Yellowstone: The National Park and Adjacent Wildlands." Montana Geographic Series, no. 6. Helena: Montana Historical Society Press, April 1984.

Reeves, Thomas C. *Gentleman Boss: The Life of Chester Alan Arthur.* New York: Alfred Knopf, 1975.

———. "President Arthur in Yellowstone." *Montana: The Magazine of Western History* 19 (Summer 1969): 18–29.

Repanshek, Kurt J. "Official Quits Who Tried to Save Yellowstone." *Albuquerque Journal,* April 16, 1992, A3.

Roosevelt, Theodore. *The Autobiography of Theodore Roosevelt.* Edited and with an introduction by Wayne Andrews. New York: Charles Scribner's Sons, 1958.

Robbins, William G. "'At the End of a Cracked Whip': The Northern West, 1880–1920." *Montana: The Magazine of Western History* 38 (Autumn 1988): 2–10.

Rodman, Paul W. *The Far West and the Great Plains in Transition, 1859–1900.* The New American Nation Series, ed. Henry Steele Commager and Richard B. Morris. New York: Harper and Row, 1988.

Rohe, Randall E. "Hydraulicking in the American West: The Development and

Diffusion of a Mining Technique." *Montana: The Magazine of Western History* 35 (Spring 1985): 18–35.

Rosenow, John E., and Gerald L. Pulsipher, with editorial assistance by Kathryn Collura. *Tourism: The Good, the Bad and the Ugly.* Lincoln, NE: Media Productions and Marketing, 1979.

Runte, Alfred. *National Parks: The American Experience.* Lincoln: University of Nebraska Press, 1979; revised edition, 1987.

————. "The National Parks in Idealism and Reality." *Montana: The Magazine of Western History* 38 (Summer 1988): 75–76.

————. "The West: Wealth, Wonderland and Wilderness." In *The American Environment: Perceptions and Policies,* ed. J. Wreford Watson and Timothy O'Riordan, 47–63. New York: John Wiley and Sons, 1976.

————. *Trains of Discovery: Western Railroads and the National Parks.* Flagstaff, AZ: Northland Press, 1984.

————. *Yosemite: The Embattled Wilderness.* Lincoln: University of Nebraska Press, 1990.

Russow, Lilly-Marlene. "Changing Perceptions of Animals: A Philosophical View." In *Perceptions of Animals in American Culture,* ed. R. J. Hoage, 25–39. Washington, DC: Smithsonian Press, 1989.

Sabo, Lewis. "When Wagon Trails were Dim." *Pacific Northwesterner* 28 (Spring 1984): 23–24.

Sample, Michael S. *Bison: Symbol of the American West.* Billings, MT: Falcon Press, 1987.

Schivelbusch, Wolfgang. *The Railway Journey: Trains and Travel In the Nineteenth Century.* New York: n.p., 1979.

Schmitt, Peter J. *Back to Nature: The Arcadian Myth In Urban America.* New York: Oxford University Press, 1969; reprint, Baltimore: Johns Hopkins University Press, 1990, with a foreword by John R. Stilgoe.

Schullery, Paul. *The Bears of Yellowstone.* Boulder: Roberts Rinehart, in cooperation with the National Park Foundation, 1986.

————. *Road-Guide for the Four-Season Road from Gardiner to Cooke City Through Yellowstone Park.* Mammoth Hot Springs, WY: Yellowstone Library and Museum Association, with the National Park Service, 1960.

Scofield, Susan C., and Jeremy C. Schmidt. *The Inn at Old Faithful.* Yellowstone National Park, WY: Crownset Associates, 1979.

Sears, John F. *Sacred Places: American Tourist Attractions in the Nineteenth Century.* New York: Oxford University Press, 1989.

Seckinger, Katherine Villard, ed. "The Great Railroad Celebration, 1883: Narrative by Francis Jackson Garrison." *Montana: The Magazine of Western History* 33 (Summer 1983): 12–23.

Shepard, Paul. *Man in the Landscape: A Historic View of the Esthetics of Nature.* New York: Alfred Knopf, 1967.

Slotkin, Richard. *The Fatal Environment: The Myth of the Frontier in the Age of Industrialization, 1800–1890.* New York: Atheneum, 1985.

Smith, Burton M. "Politics and the Crow Indian Land Cessions." *Montana: The Magazine of Western History* 36 (Autumn 1986): 24–37.

Smith, Henry Nash. *Virgin Land: The American West as Symbol and Myth.* Cambridge: Harvard University Press, 1958; reissued with a new preface by the author, 1970.

Solomon, Jack. *The Signs of Our Time. Semiotics: The Hidden Messages of Environments, Objects, and Cultural Images.* Los Angeles: Jeremy P. Tarcher, Inc., 1988.

Sontag, Susan. *On Photography.* New York: Farrar, Straus and Giroux, 1973.

Stilgoe, John R. *Borderland: Origins of the American Suburb, 1820–1839.* New Haven: Yale University Press, 1988.

Strauss, David. "Toward a Consumer Culture: 'Adirondack Murray' and the Wilderness Vacation." *American Quarterly* 36 (Summer 1984): 270–86.

Szarkowski, John, ed. *American Landscapes: Photographs from the Collection of the Museum of Modern Art.* Boston: Museum of Modern Art of New York, 1981.

Terrie, Philip. *Forever Wild: Environmental Aesthetics and the Adirondack Forest Preserve.* Philadelphia: Temple University Press, 1985.

Thuermer, Angus M., Jr. "Fair Concession." *Jackson Hole News,* July 24, 1991, 8A.

———. "Mintzmeyer Calls 'Vision' Paper a Political Fraud." *Jackson Hole News,* September 25, 1991, 1.

———. "Money in Wonderland." *Jackson Hole News,* September 11, 1991, 1A.

———. "Park Service Receives One Bid for Yellowstone Concessions." *Casper Star Tribune,* July 29, 1991, 8A.

Tilden, Freeman. *Following the Frontier with Frank Jay Haynes: Pioneer Photographer of the Old West.* New York: Alfred Knopf, 1964.

Trachtenberg, Alan. *Brooklyn Bridge: Fact and Symbol.* Chicago: University of Chicago Press, 1965; reprint, 1979.

———. *The Incorporation of America: Culture and Society In the Gilded Age.* New York: Hill and Wang, 1982.

Turner, Victor, and Edith Turner. *Image and Pilgrimage in Christian Culture.* New York: Columbia University Press, 1978.

Utley, Robert M. *The Indian Frontier of the American West, 1846–1890.* Albuquerque: University Of New Mexico Press, 1984.

Van Orman, Richard. *The Explorers: Nineteenth Century Expeditions in Africa and the American West.* Albuquerque: University of New Mexico Press, 1984.

Weigle, Marta. "From Desert to Disney World: The Santa Fe Railway and the Fred Harvey Company Display the Indian Southwest." *Journal of Anthropological Research* 45 (1989): 115–37.

Weigle, Marta, and Peter White. *The Lore of New Mexico.* Albuquerque: University of New Mexico Press, 1988.

White, G. Edward. *The Eastern Establishment and the Western Experience: The*

West of Frederic Remington, Theodore Roosevelt, and Owen Wister. New Haven: Yale University Press, 1968.

Whittlesey, Lee. *Yellowstone Place Names.* Helena, MT: Montana Historical Society Press, 1988.

Wiebe, Robert H. *The Search for Order: 1877–1920.* New York: Hill and Wang, 1967.

Wilcox, Louisa. "Yellowstone's Geysers: Explosive, Mysterious—But Protected?" *Greater Yellowstone Today* 1 (Winter 1991). Bozeman, MT: Greater Yellowstone Coalition.

Wild, Peter. *Pioneer Conservationists of Eastern America.* Missoula, MT: Mountain Press Publishing Co., 1986.

Wilkinson, Todd. "A Clash Between Two Kinds of Wealth." *High Country News,* June 4, 1990.

Witteman, Paul A. "Springtime in the Rockies." *Time,* May 29, 1989, 94.

Worster, Donald. *Nature's Economy: A History of Ecological Ideas.* New York: Cambridge University Press, 1977.

"Yellowstone A Year Later." *Sunset: The Magazine of Western Living* (May 1989): 108–22.

"Yellowstone Wolf Reintroduction." *Greater Yellowstone Coalition Information Sheet.* Bozeman, MT: Greater Yellowstone Coalition, 1991.0

Primary Sources: Guidebooks, Travel Books, Articles, and Railroad Advertising

"Address of President Villard." *The Northwest,* September 1883, 14–15.

"Affairs in the Yellowstone Park." *Forest and Stream,* November 5, 1885.

"The American Buffalo." *The Northwest,* September 1884.

"Among the Terraces." *New York Herald,* April 26, 1888. Ash Scrapbook: Miscellaneous Newspaper Clippings Collected by George L. Henderson from 1882 through 1905. Yellowstone National Park Archives and Research Library. Mammoth Hot Springs, WY.

Anderson, George. "The Protection of Yellowstone National Park." In *Hunting In Many Lands: Book of the Boone and Crockett Club,* ed. George Bird Grinnell and Theodore Roosevelt, 392–421. New York: Forest and Stream Publishing, 1895.

"Attacks Upon the Northern Pacific." *The Daily Statesman,* January 26, 1882.

Austin, H., et al., to the U.S. Department of the Interior, 1881. "Haynes, F. Jay—Letters Concerning Appointment as Photographer." Typed manuscript (photocopy). Manuscript File, Yellowstone National Park Archives and Research Library, Mammoth Hot Springs, WY.

Ayer, I. Winslow. *Life in the Wilds of America, and Wonders of the West in and beyond the Bounds of Civilization.* Grand Rapids, MI: Central Publishing, 1880.

Baker, Ray Stannard. "A Place of Marvels." *Century* 66 (August 1903): 481–91.

Beard, Dan. "In a Wild Animal Republic." *Recreation* 15 (December 1901): 417–23.

"Boiling: The Geysers In the Yellowstone National Park." *Brooklyn Daily Eagle,* August 15, 1883.Scrapbook no. 2. Yellowstone National Park Archives and Research Library. Mammoth Hot Springs, WY.

Brockett, L. P. *Our Western Empire: or the New West Beyond the Mississippi.* Philadelphia: Bradley, Garretson and Company, 1881.

"The Buffalo Heads." *Livingston Enterprise,* December 18, 1883.

Bunker, Miriam C. "Northern Pacific Officials Visit Montana, 1880." In Haynes File, F. J. Haynes Collection of the Burlingame Special Collections at Montana State University, Bozeman.

C., W. K. "Hand of God Alone." Scrapbook no. 2, n.p., n.d. Yellowstone National Park Archives and Research Library. Mammoth Hot Springs, WY.

Campbell, Reau. *New Revised Complete Guide and Descriptive Book of the Yellowstone National Park.* Chicago: H. E. Klamer, 1909.

"A Case for Prompt Action." *Forest and Stream,* April 11, 1889.

Catlin, George. *North American Indians: Being Letters and Notes on their Manners, Customs, and Conditions, Written During Eight Years' Travel Amongst the Wildest Tribes in North America, 1832–1839.* Minneapolis: Ross and Haines, 1965 reprint; first printed in London, 1841.

"The Clark's Fork Country." *The Yellowstone Journal,* March 10, 1883.

Cole, Ashley. "The Yellowstone National Park." *The Manhattan* 4 (August 1884): 129–44.

Comstock, Theodore B. "The Yellowstone National Park." *The American Naturalist* 8 (1874): 155–66.

Cook, Charles W., David E. Folsom, and William Peterson. *The Valley of the Upper Yellowstone.* Edited and with an introduction by Aubrey L. Haines. Norman: University of Oklahoma Press, 1965.

Cook, John R. *The Border and the Buffalo.* Topeka: n.p., 1907.

Cope, E. D. "The Condition of Yellowstone National Park." *The American Naturalist* 19 (1885): 1037–1040.

"The Cornerstone Was Laid." *(Gardiner, MT) Wonderland,* April 30, 1903. F. Jay Haynes Collection, Montana State University, Burlingame Special Collections, Bozeman.

Crandall, Hugh. *Yellowstone: The Story behind the Scenery.* Las Vegas, NV: KC Publications, 1977.

Crosby, J. Schuyler, Governor, Montana Territory to N. G. Ordway, Governor, Dakota Territory. Letter, February 7, 1883, typed manuscript (photocopy). Manuscript File. Yellowstone National Park Archives and Research Library.

"The Crow Indian Reservation." *The Northwest,* February, 1883.

Cruikshank, Margaret A. "Notes On the Yellowstone Park, August 1883" Typed manuscript (photocopy). Manuscript File, Yellowstone National Park Archives and Research Library. Mammoth Hot Springs, WY.

"Dance of the Crow Indians." *Harper's Weekly,* December 15, 1883, 798–800.

Danger to Montana Mineral Lands: Proceedings Relating to the Northern Pacific Railroad's Claim to the Mineral Lands of Montana. Helena: Helena Daily Herald Printers and Publishers, 1888. Microfilm, University of Wyoming, Laramie.

Dawes, J. H. "The Yellowstone Park; A Paper Read March 16th, 1891, before the Buffalo Historical Society." In F. Jay Haynes Collection, Burlingame Special Collections. Montana State University, Bozeman.

"Decorations at the Depot." *Livingston Enterprise,* September 7, 1883.

"Depredating Wolves." *The Northwest,* December 1884.

Downing, Andrew Jackson. *A Treatise On the Theory and Practise of Landscape Gardening Adapted to North America; with a View to the Improvement of Country Residences.* New York, 1841, 63. Quoted in Hans Huth, *Nature and the American: Three Centuries of Changing Attitudes.* New edition with an introduction by Douglas Strong. Lincoln: University of Nebraska Press, 1990, 67.

Drake, O.S.T. "A Lady's Trip to the Yellowstone National Park." *Every Girl's Annual.* London: Hatchard's, 1887.

"The Elk." *The Northwest,* July 1883.

Emmons, Myra. "From New York to Heaven." *Recreation* 15 (December 1901): 431–34.

Everts, Truman C. *Thirty-Seven Days of Peril: A Narrative of the Early Days of the Yellowstone.* With a preface by James McDonald. San Francisco: E. and R. Grabhorn and James McDonald, 1923.

Fee, Charles S., and the Northern Pacific Railroad. "A Romance of Wonderland." St. Paul: Northern Pacific Railroad, 1889. Tourist brochure, in Haynes Collection at Burlingame Special Collections, Montana State University, Bozeman.

———. "Alice's Adventures in the New Wonderland." St. Paul: Northern Pacific Railroad, 1884. Tourist brochure, in Yellowstone National Park Archives and Research Library. Mammoth Hot Springs, WY.

———. *The Northern Pacific Railroad. The Wonderland Route to the Pacific Coast.* St. Paul: Northern Pacific Railroad, 1885.

Ferris, George T., ed. *Our Native Land: Or, Glances at American Scenery and Places with Sketches of Life and Character.* New York: D. Appleton and Co., 1891.

Field, Henry M. *Our Western Archipelago.* New York: Charles Scribner's Sons, 1895.

Frankland, Edward. "A Great Winter Sanitarium for the American Continent."
    Popular Science Monthly 27 (July 1885): 189–195.
"Game In the Yellowstone Park." *Forest and Stream,* February 18, 1886.
Gerrish, Theodore. *Life In the World's Wonderland . . . A Graphic Description
    of the Great Northwest.* n.p., 1887.
Gibson, Francis. "Pocket Diary Kept on a Trip through Yellowstone, August
    7–27, 1882." Manuscript File. Yellowstone National Park Archives and
    Research Library. Mammoth Hot Springs, WY.
Gillis, Charles J. *Another Summer: The Yellowstone Park and Alaska.* New
    York: J.J. Little and Co., 1893.
"The Great Northwest." *Philadelphia Press,* December 23, 1882.
Grinnell, George Bird to Jack Ellis Haynes. Letter, April 3, 1922. In F. Jay Haynes
    Photographic Studio Collection, Montana Historical Society Archives,
    Helena.
Grinnell, George Bird, and Theodore Roosevelt, eds. *Hunting in Many Lands:
    Book of the Boone and Crockett Club.* New York: Forest and Stream Pub-
    lishing, 1895.
Gunnison, Almon. *Rambles Overland.* Boston: Universalist Publishing House,
    1884.
Guptill, A. B. *All About Yellowstone Park: A Practical Guide.* St. Paul: F. Jay
    Haynes Publishing, 1894.
———. "Yellowstone Park." *Outing* 16 (July 1885): 256–63.
Hague, Arnold. "Soaping Geysers." Transactions of the American Institute of
    Mining Engineers, February 1889. In *Scientific Papers On the Yellowstone
    National Park.* Yellowstone National Park Archives and Research Library.
    Mammoth Hot Springs, WY.
Hardman, William. *Trip to America.* London: T.V. Wood, 1884.
Hatfield, W. F. *Geyserland and Wonderland: A View and Guidebook of the
    Yellowstone National Park.* San Francisco: Hicks-Judd Co., 1901. Yellow-
    stone National Park Archives and Research Library.
Haupt, Herman. *The Yellowstone National Park.* New York: Stoddart, 1883.
Hayden, Ferdinand V. "The Yellowstone Park." In *The Pacific Tourist.* Edited
    by Frederick E. Shearer, 140–46. New York: Adams and Bishop, 1885.
———. *Twelfth Report of the United States Geological and Geographical Sur-
    vey of the Territories.* Part 2. Washington, DC: Government Printing
    Office, 1883.
Haynes, F. Jay, and Lily (Snyder) Haynes, Personal and Business Correspon-
    dence, 1876–1905. In Haynes File, Haynes Collection, Burlingame Special
    Collections, Montana State University, Bozeman.
Haynes, F. Jay. *Catalogue of Northern Pacific and National Park Views.* St. Paul:
    F. Jay Haynes Publishing, 1883, 1884, 1890, 1908. In F. Jay Haynes' Pho-
    tographic Studio Collection, Montana Historical Society Archives, Helena.

Heigmann, C. L. "The Therapeutical Value of the Springs in the National Park, Wyoming Territory." *Philadelphia Medical Times,* May 27, 1876, 409–14.

Helena Daily Herald, March 1, 1872, September 13, 1883.

Helmuth, William Ted. "The Yellowstone National Park and How It was Named." Ash Scrapbook: Miscellaneous Newspaper Clippings Collected by George L. Henderson from 1882–1905, August 7, 1892. Yellowstone National Park Archives and Research Library. Mammoth Hot Springs, WY.

Henderson, George L. "A Wonderland." In an unnamed West Union, Iowa publication, January 30, 1884. Ash Scrapbook. Yellowstone National Park Archives and Research Library.

———. "Haynes' Winter Expedition." Extract from the *Helena Independent,* February 6, 1887. Manuscript File. Yellowstone National Park Archives and Research Library. Mammoth Hot Springs, WY.

———. "National Park Manual: Wonderland Condensed." Scrapbook no. 1. Yellowstone National Park Archives and Research Library. Mammoth Hot Springs, WY.

———. *Yellowstone Park Guide and Manual.* Mammoth Hot Springs, WY: privately printed, 1885.

———. Letter to Secretary of the Interior John Noble. March 9, 1891. Ash Collection. Yellowstone National Park Archives and Research Library.

Hill, Alexander Staveley. *From Home to Home: Autumn Wanderings in the Northwest.* New York: Judd Company, 1885), 58. Quoted in Earl Pomeroy, *In Search of the Golden West: The Tourist In Western America.* New York: Alfred Knopf, 1957.

Hill, J. L. *The Passing of the Indian and the Buffalo.* Long Beach, CA: George W. Moyle, n.d. F. Jay Haynes Collection, Special Collections. Montana State University, Bozeman.

Hillman, George N. *Driving the Golden Spike,* n.p., 1932. In F. Jay Haynes Collection, Burlingame Special Collections, Montana State University, Bozeman.

Hofer, Elwood. "Yellowstone Park Notes, 1897." Scrapbook no. 3. Yellowstone National Park Archives and Research Library.

Hough, Emerson. "Forest and Stream's Yellowstone Park Game Expedition." *Forest and Stream,* May 5, 1894.

———. "The Wonderful Grand Canyon." N.d., n.p. Scrapbook no. 1. Yellowstone National Park Archives and Research Library.

Howell, Charles C. "My First Trip to Yellowstone Park–1883." Handwritten manuscript. Manuscript File. Yellowstone National Park Archives and Research Library.

Hoyt, Colgate. "Roughing it up the Yellowstone." Edited by Carroll Van West. *Montana: The Magazine of Western History* 36 (Spring 1986): 31–39.

Hyde, John. *Official Guide to the Yellowstone National Park: A Manual for Tourists.* St. Paul: Northern News Co., 1888.

"In the Park." *Livingston Enterprise,* March 3, 1900.

"In Yellowstone Park." *Chicago Weekly News,* August 23, 30, 1883.

"The Indian War Dance at Gray Cliff." *Bozeman Avant-Courier,* September 9, 1883.

Irvin, George W. "When General Grant Drove Northern Pacific's Last Spike." *Denver Times,* February 2, 1902.

Journey through the Yellowstone National Park and Northwestern Wyoming, 1883. Photographs of Party and Scenery Along the Route Traveled, and Copies of the Associated Press Dispatches Sent Whilst En Route. In *Western Americana, 1550–1900: Frontier History of the Trans-Mississippi West.* Reel 292, no. 2926. New Haven: Research Publications, 1975. Microform.

Kipling, Rudyard. *American Notes.* New York: F. F. Lovell Co., 1893.

———. "On Tour through the Yellowstone." In *From Sea to Sea: Letters of Travel.* 2 vols. New York: Doubleday and McClure, 1899. In *Mirror of America: Literary Encounters with the National Parks,* ed. David Harmon, 52–69. Boulder: Roberts Rinehart and the National Park Foundation, 1989.

Kirk, [n.n.]. Typescript for lecture and slideshow. Manuscript File. Yellowstone National Park Archives and Research Library. Mammoth Hot Springs, WY.

Koch, Peter. "Discovery of the Yellowstone National Park. A Chapter of Early Exploration in the Rocky Mountains." *Magazine of American History* 11 (June 1884): 497–512.

Koerner, Gustave. *Memoirs of Gustave Koerner.* Edited by Thomas J. McCormick. Cedar Rapids, IA: The Torch Press, 1909.

Langford, Nathaniel Pitt. *The Discovery of Yellowstone National Park.* With a foreword by Aubrey L. Haines. Lincoln: University of Nebraska Press, 1972.

"The Last Spike." *Livingston Enterprise,* September 10, 1883.

"Letters to the Editor" from "Montana," "H." of Yellowstone National Park, and Archibald Rogers of Hyde Park, New York. *Forest and Stream,* April 11, 1889.

"Liked Meat Too Well." *The Evening Star,* n.d. Scrapbook no. 1. Yellowstone National Park Archives and Research Library.

Linton, Edwin. "Overhead Sounds in the Vicinity of Yellowstone Lake." *Science* 22 (November 3, 1893), 244–46.

Livingston Enterprise, June 6, 1883; June 29, 1883; July 15, 1883; July 21, 1883; July 31, 1883; August 4, 1883; August 7, 1883; August 19, 1883; August 22, 1883; August 24, 1883; August 27, 1883; August 30, 1883; September 17, 1883; September 20, 1883; December 14, 1883; January 10, 1884; January 29, 1884; February 4, 1884; March 28, 1884; September 5, 1885; September 19, 1885; July 7, 1888.

Ludwig, Mary Caldwell. "The Yellowstone: Beauties of a Trip There in Autumn." Publication unknown, 1896. Scrapbook no. 3. Yellowstone National Park Archives and Research Library.

Lyon, [n.n.]. "The Nation's Art Gallery." Watertown, South Dakota, unnamed
    publication, August 7, 1891. Scrapbook no. 1. Yellowstone National Park
    Archives and Research Library.

Maguire, H. N. "The Black Hills and American Wonderland." *The Lakeside
    Library*. Chicago: Donnelly, Loyd and Co, 1877. In *Western Americana,
    Frontier History of the Trans-Mississippi West, 1550–1900*. New Haven,
    CT: Research Publications, 1975, no. 3444. Microform, Denver Public
    Library.

Manning, Warren. Plans for the Improvement of Mammoth Hot Springs. Appen-
    dix A, Hiram Martin Chittenden, "Annual Report Upon the Construction,
    Repair, and Maintenance of Roads and Bridges In the Yellowstone
    National Park. Appendix GGG in *Annual Report of the Chief of Engineers
    for 1903*. Washington, DC: Government Printing Office, 1903, 2894–98.

Mattoon, A. M. "The Yellowstone National Park, Summer of 1889" Typed
    manuscript (photocopy). Manuscript File. Yellowstone National Park
    Archives and Research Library.

McElrath, Thomas P. *The Yellowstone Valley: What It Is, and How to Get
    There. A Handbook for Tourists and Settlers*. St. Paul: Pioneer Press, 1880.

"A Memorial of the Great Plains." *Forest and Stream*, August 18, 1887.

Mitchell, S. Weir. "Through the Yellowstone Park to Fort Custer." *Lippincott's
    Magazine of Popular Literature and Science* 26 (1880): 29–41.

Mohr, Nicolaus. *Excursion through America*. Edited by Ray Allen Billington;
    translated by LaVern J. Rippley. The Lakeside Classics Series. Chicago:
    R. R. Donnelly and Sons Co., 1973.

Muir, John. "The Yellowstone National Park." *Atlantic Monthly* 81 (April
    1898): 509–22.

"Naming a Geyser." *Norristown Herald*, January 19, 1889. Ash Scrapbook:
    Miscellaneous Newspaper Clippings Collected by George L. Henderson
    from 1882 through 1905. Yellowstone National Park Archives and
    Research Library.

"The Nation's Great Park." *New York World*, March 8, 1887.

"The National Park." *The Northwest*, September 1883, 4–5.

New York Journal, August 17, 1883.

New York Times, April 21, 1883; September 5, 1883; November 19, 1886;
    February 24, 1893.

New York Tribune, August 2, 1883.

Norris, Philetus W. *The Calumet of the Coteau, and other Poetical Legends of
    the Border Together with a Guide-book of the Yellowstone National Park*.
    Philadelphia: Lippincott, 1884.

"The North Pacific Job." *New York World*, January 28, 1881.

Northern Pacific Railroad. *Records of the Northern Pacific Railway Company*.
    St. Paul: Minnesota Historical Society.

"The Northern Pacific Country." *The Pioneer Press*, October 11, 1883.

Omaha Daily Bee, June 19, 1883.

"Our Mountain Bison." *The Yellowstone Journal,* April 28, 1883.

"The Park Grab." *Forest and Stream,* January 4, 1883.

"The Passing of Arthur." *Chicago Inter-Ocean,* September 5, 1883.

Pierrepont, Edward. *From Fifth Avenue to Alaska.* New York: G. P. Putnam's Sons, 1885.

"The Preservation of the Yellowstone Park." *Yellowstone Journal,* May 6, 1882.

"The President." *Chicago Tribune,* August 2, 1883; August 9, 1883; August 13, 1883; August 14, 1883; August 27, 1883.

"President Arthur Will Spend His Vacation Entirely in the West." *Chicago Tribune,* July 16, 1883.

"President May Not Fire Gun On Hunt." *Washington Star,* March 16, 1903. Scrapbook no. 3. Yellowstone National Park Archives and Research Library.

"President Villard's Guests." *New York Times,* August 28, 29, 1883.

Price, Sir Major Rose Lambart. *A Summer On the Rockies.* London: Sampson Low, Marston and Co., 1898.

"Protect the National Park." *Frank Leslie's Illustrated Newspaper,* April 27, 1889.

Replogle, Wayne F. *Yellowstone's Bannock Indian Trails.* Yellowstone Interpretive Series, no. 6. Mammoth Hot Springs, WY: Yellowstone Library and Museum Association, 1956.

Riley, William C. *Grand Tour Guide to the Yellowstone National Park—A Manual for Tourists.* St. Paul: privately printed, 1889.

Rogers, Edmund B., comp. "Bills In Congress to Revise the Boundaries of Yellowstone National Park, n.d." F. Jay Haynes Collection. Montana State University, Bozeman.

Rollins, Alice Wellington. *The Three Tetons: A Story of the Yellowstone.* New York: Cassell and Company, 1887.

———. "The Three Tetons." *Harper's New Monthly Magazine* 74 (1887): 869–90.

Roosevelt, Theodore. *The Autobiography of Theodore Roosevelt.* Edited and with an introduction by Wayne Andrews. New York: Charles Scribner's Sons, 1958.

Russell, Lord Charles. *Diary of a Visit to the United States.* New York: U.S. Catholic Historical Society, 1910.

Rutgers, Lispenard. *On and Off the Saddle.* New York: G.P. Putnam's Sons, 1894.

Schmidt, Carl E. *A Trip to the Yellowstone National Park.* Detroit: Free Press, 1902.

Schwatka, Frederick, and John Hyde. *Through Wonderland with Lieutenant Schwatka.* St. Paul: Northern Pacific Railroad, 1886.

Selmes, Patty M. F. No title, no date. Scrapbook no. 2, 146. Yellowstone National Park Archives and Research Library.

"Senator Conkling at Mammoth, 1883." *New York Herald,* April 24, 1888. Ash

Scrapbook: Miscellaneous Newspaper Clippings Collected by George L. Henderson from 1882 through 1905. Yellowstone National Park Archives and Research Library.

Sessions, Francis C. "Yellowstone National Park." *Magazine of Western History* 6 (1890): 433–45.

Shearer, Frederick E., ed. *The Pacific Tourist*. New York: Adams and Bishop, 1885.

Sheridan, Philip H. *Personal Memoirs of Philip Henry Sheridan, General, United States Army: New and Enlarged Edition, with an Account of His Life from 1871 to His Death, in 1888*. Edited by Michael V. Sheridan. 2 vols. New York: D. Appleton and Company, 1904.

———. *Report of an Exploration of Parts of Wyoming, Idaho, and Montana in August and September 1882, Made by Lieutenant Gen. P. H. Sheridan*. Washington, DC: Government Printing Office, 1882.

Smalley, Eugene V. *History of the Northern Pacific Railroad*. New York: G.P. Putnam's Sons, 1883.

———. "The Yellowstone National Park." *The Northwest* 5 (May 1887): 1, 3; and 2 (July 1884): 4.

Stoddard, John L. *John L. Stoddard's Lectures*. Boston: Balch Brothers, 1902.

Strahorn, Robert. *Montana and Yellowstone Park*. Kansas City: Millett and Hudson, 1881.

Synge, Georgina A. *A Ride through Wonderland*. London: Sampson, Low and Marston, 1892.

Thayer, William M. *Marvels of the New West*. Norwich, CT: Henry Bill Publishing, 1891.

Thomas, George. "Recollections of the Yellowstone National Park, 1883." Typed manuscript (photocopy). Manuscript File. Yellowstone National Park Archives and Research Library.

Thompson-Seton, Ernest. "The National Zoo at Washington." *The Century Magazine* 60 (May 1900): 1–10.

Timmons, William. *Twilight On the Range: Recollections of a Latterday Cowboy*. Austin: University of Texas Press, 1962.

Topping, E. S. *The Chronicles of the Yellowstone*. St. Paul: Pioneer Press, 1888.

"A Trip Full of Peril." *Chicago Tribune*, March 5, 1887. Scrapbook no. 1. Yellowstone National Park Archives and Research Library.

"Trout Fishing." *Chicago Weekly News*, September 1, 1883.

Turpin, Frances Lynn. "A Trip Through Yellowstone Park, 1895." Typed manuscript (photocopy). Manuscript File. Yellowstone National Park Archives and Research Library.

"Uncle Rufus Interviewed—He Makes Some Startling Revelations." *Chicago Tribune*, August 27, 1883.

Vest, George Graham. "Notes on the Yellowstone Trip." *Forest and Stream*, November 3, 1883.

"Views In the Yellowstone." *Frank Leslie's Illustrated Newspaper,* August 11, 1883, 402.

"Villard's Guests." *Livingston Enterprise,* August 28, 1883.

"Villard's Voyagers." *Chicago Tribune,* August 29, 1883.

"Wanton Destruction of Game." *Yellowstone Journal,* May 6, 1882.

Wells, Henry P. "Winter in Yellowstone Park." *Harper's Weekly,* April 9, 1887, 259.

Wheeler, Olin D. "A Soliloquy of Liberty Cap, the Terrace Sentinel," ca. 1895. F. Jay Haynes Collection. Montana State University, Bozeman.

Wheeler, Olin D., and the Northern Pacific Railroad. *Indianland and Wonderland.* Chicago: Rand McNally, 1894.

———. *6,000 Miles through Wonderland.* Chicago: Rand McNally, 1893.

———. *Sketches of Wonderland.* Chicago: Rand McNally, 1895.

———. *Wonderland '96.* Chicago: Rand McNally, 1896.

———. *Wonderland '99.* Chicago: Rand McNally, 1899.

———. *Yellowstone National Park: Descriptive of the Beauties and Wonders of the World's Wonderland.* St. Paul: W.C. Riley, 1901.

"Wickes, Montana." *The Northwest.* (August 1886): 17.

Wingate, George. *Through the Yellowstone Park on Horseback.* New York: O. Judd Co., 1886.

Wister, Owen. "Old Yellowstone Days." In *Mirror of America: Literary Encounters with the National Parks.* Boulder: Roberts Rinehart with the National Park Foundation, 1989, 20–32.

"Wolves In Yellowstone Park, 1896." No publisher, no author. Scrapbook no. 3. Yellowstone National Park Archives and Research Library.

Wylie, W. W. *Yellowstone National Park; or the Great American Wonderland.* Kansas City, MO: Ramsey, Millett and Hudson, 1882.

Yandell, Michael D., ed. *A Photographic and Comprehensive Guide to Yellowstone National Park.* National Parkways Series. Casper, WY: World-Wide Research and Publishing Co., 1976.

Yellowstone Park. Written, Produced and Directed by Dan Goldblatt. 60 minutes. America's Playground Series, 1990. Videocassette.

"Yellowstone Park: Charles Gibson' Inside Scheme." *St. Louis Globe Democrat,* April 13, 1892. Scrapbook no. 1. Yellowstone National Park Archives and Research Library. Mammoth Hot Springs, Wyoming.

"Yellowstone Park In Winter." n.p., 1891. Scrapbook no. 1, Yellowstone National Park Archives and Research Library.

"Yellowstone, The World's First National Park." TW Services Advertisement in *Old West 1988 Vacation Guide,* n.p.

"The Yellowstone National Park." *The American Architect and Building News* 13 (March 17, 1883): 130–31.

"The Yellowstone National Park." *Harper's Weekly* 37 (1893): 719–23.

"The Yellowstone National Park." *Livingston Enterprise,* May 22, 1884.

"The Yellowstone Park." *Forest and Stream,* December 20, 1883, 401–402.

"The Yellowstone Park." No author, no publisher, November 6, 1902. In Eaton Ranch Collection. Accession no. 296 [N213p-Yel]. American Heritage Center. University of Wyoming, Laramie.

"The Yellowstone Scientific Expedition." *Helena Daily Herald,* July 11, 1871.

"The Yellowstone Valley." *The Yellowstone Journal,* March 17, 1883.

Government Documents

Annual Reports of the Superintendents and Acting Superintendents of the Yellowstone National Park to the Secretary of the Interior. Washington, DC: Government Printing Office, 1880–1903. [Serial Set nos. 2191, 2379, 2468, 2542, 2638, 2726, 2842, 2935, 3089, 3211, 3307, 3383, 3490, 3642, 3758, 3917, 4103, 4292, 4460 and 4647]. House Executive Documents 46–2 through 58–2.

Congressional Globe. Senate Debate, 42d Congress. Washington, DC: Government Printing Office, 1872.

Congressional Record. 47th Cong., 2d sess., XIV, part 4.

National Archives. Washington, DC: Government Printing Office. Record Group 62, *Records Relating to the Yellowstone National Park.* Patents and Miscellaneous Division, Department of the Interior, Letters Received, 1872–1886.

"Report of the Secretary of the Interior on the Administration of Yellowstone National Park." Senate Executive Document 47, part 3, 48th Cong., 1st sess. [SN 2162], 3.

Senate Executive Document 10, 47th Cong., 2d sess. [SN 2073].

Senate Report 911, 47th Cong., 2d sess. [SN2087], 1–11.

United States Department of the Interior. William Hallett Phillips Report, September 12, 1885. *Letter from the Acting Secretary of the Interior to the U.S. Senate.* January 29, 1886. 49th Cong., 1st sess. Executive Document 51, 9–12.

United States Geological Survey. *Hayden Survey 1872 Report.* House Miscellaneous Document No. 112. Washington, DC: Government Printing Office, 1972.

Yellowstone National Park. Administrative Records, pre-1916 archives. Letter Box 1–9. Yellowstone National Park Archives and Research Library. Mammoth Hot Springs, WY.

Yellowstone Park Organic Act. *U.S. Statutes at Large,* vol. 17, chap. 24, 32–33.

Index

Accommodations, 44, 109, 115, 117, 118, 186; monopoly privilege on, 108; placement of, 137

Adams, Charles Francis: on Old Faithful Inn, 118

Adirondack Mountains, 130, 228n95

Agribusiness, wolf reintroduction and, 185

Agricultural system, negative impacts of, 181–82

Alexis of Russia, Grand Duke: hunting by, 67

Allen's Taxidermy Store (Haynes), 34, 34 (fig.)

American Bison Society, 161

American Forestry Association, bison and, 163

American myth, xiii, 116, 124, 139

Anaconda Mine, 36

Anderson, George S., 153; on bison poaching, 159; on park vandalism, 96–97

Anderson, Ole, 133

Antelope, 155, 156 (fig.)

Arapahoes, 4, 141

Arapooish, 36, 37, 202n48

Army Corps of Engineers, road building by, 121, 123

Arthur, Chester Alan, 44, 96, 209n70; Excelsior geyser and, 93; Sheridan expedition and, 69–74; Yellowstone Park Improvement Company and, 74

Artists' Paintpots, 90–91

Askins, Renee: wolf reintroduction and, 183–84

Atchison, Topeka & Santa Fe Railway, traffic on, 54

Audubon, Grandma, 67, 208n63

Audubon, John James, 13, 67

Automobiles: impact of, 187–88. See also Road building

Ayer, I. Winslow: Arapooish and, 37

Babbitt, Bruce, 179

Baker, Ray Stannard, 81, 84

Bannocks, 5, 141; hunting by, 146, 148; trails of, 120

Baronett, "Yellowstone Jack," 4, 8, 70, 120, 220n53

Barrett, Jim, 178

Bartlett, Richard A., xii, 218n22

Bath Pools, 88, 89 (fig.)

Bears: capture/shipment of, 153–54; feeding by, 153. See also Grizzly bears

Bicyclists at Minerva Terrace (Haynes), 45, 47 (fig.)

Bighorn sheep, infection for, 181

Biodiversity, 171, 180, 182

Biotechnology industry, 180

Bismarck Bridge, illustration of, 59 (fig.)

Bison: cattle and, 181; controversy over, 185; decline of, 139, 152, 155–57, 158, 160–61, 167; hunting, 150; migration of, 185; poaching of, 158; preservation of, 131, 140, 162; slaughter of, 54, 67, 68, 139, 158, 185, 186; tourism and, 186

Blackburn, W. H.: at Zoological Garden, 154

Black Hills: military expedition to, 28; Sioux and, 27

Blaine, James G., 15

Bonanza Farming, 23–24, 35, 42; Haynes's views of, 26

Boone and Crockett Club, 157, 159, 163

Boosters, 2, 79

Bottler Ranch, 120

Bridger, Jim, 5

Brockett, L. P., 142; on geysers, 89–90; on hydraulic mining, 42

Brokaw, Tom: Yellowstone fire and, 174

Brooklyn Daily Eagle, on geysers, 90

Brown, Arthur: watercolor sketches by, 76

Brucellosis, animals carrying, 185

Bryant, William Cullen, 13

Buffalo. *See* Bison

Buffalo houses, construction of, 154–55

Buffalo Hunting, Montana (Haynes), 33–34, 33 (fig.)

Buffalo In Enclosure, Nearly As Tame As Domestic Animals (Haynes), 161, 162 (fig.)

Buffalo Jam, 187 (fig.)

Buffington, Leroy S., 112

Bunsen Theory, 93

Burgess, Felix, 159

Burroughs, John, 149

Bush, George: on Yellowstone, 171

Butcher's Work, The (Haynes), 159, 160 (fig.)

Camp Arthur, Sheridan at, 71–72

Carpenter, Robert Emmett, 75

Catlin, George, 13, 221n4; on nation's park, 139

Cattle: bison and, 181; brucellosis and, 185

Chenoweth, Helen: wolf reintroduction and, 183

Chicago Tribune, 56; on Arthur/Yellowstone, 72; on vandalism, 98

Chicago Weekly News, on Rufus Hatch Department, 65, 74

Child, Harry, 118, 218n22

Chittenden, Hiram Martin, 133, 164, 223n102; on reserves, 164

Civilization: nature and, 167; sprawl of, 178–79, 182; wildlife/natives and, 139

Clagett, William H., 17

Clark's Fork, 32; degradation of, 178; gold on, 120; mining camp at, 36

Clear-cutting, xii, 175

Clinton, Bill: on Yellowstone, 179

Clouph, Ernest, 95

Cody, William F. "Buffalo Bill," 67, 157

Coffeen, Henry A., 133; park railroads and, 127–28

Cole, Ashley, 78; on Grand Canyon, 100–102; on Yellowstone, 98

Cole, Cornelius: on Yellowstone, 18

Cole, Thomas, 7, 13

Colter, John: in Yellowstone region, 5

Concessionaires, 108, 125; income for, 188–89; virgin myth and, 182

Conger, Omar D., 44, 62, 74–75

Conservationists, 67, 68, 77, 140, 167, 169, 181; forest reserves and, 163

Cooke, Jay, Jr., 9, 17, 23, 129

Cooke City, Montana, 36, 37, 176; mining at, 129, 130, 132, 170; NPRR at, 129, 132, 157

Cooke City Mining District, 128

Cooke City Railroad, conservationists and, 181

Cooper, James Fennimore, 13

Coors Brewing Company, 204n80

Cowan party, Nez Perce and, 194n10

Coxe, Tench, 39

Crabb, Patricia, 178

Craighead, Frank and John: grizzly bear study by, 230n7

Crosby, J. Schuyler, 68, 71

Crow country, 36, 37

Crow Indian Council at Last Spike (Haynes), 32 (fig.)

Crow Reservation, 141; reduction of, 32, 37

Crows, 10, 32, 59; dog soup by, 58; tribal dances by, 57; Yellowstone and, 142, 146

Cruikshank, Margaret, 95, 96, 110, 126; on geysers, 95; on Marshall's Hotel, 66–67; on Old Faithful, 93

Cultural history, 140, 175, 197n54
Cultural imperialism, 42; Yellowstone
    fire and, 174
Curbin, Barbara: wolf reintroduction
    and, 183
Custer, George Armstrong, 28, 40, 68,
    68
Cutthroat trout, saving, 184–85

Daisy Geyser, 115
Dalrymple Farm, 23–24, 27 (fig.)
Davis, H. C.: Gold Spike ceremony
    and, 59
Dawes, Henry M., 15
Dawes, J. H.: on Gibbon Paint Pots,
    90–91; on Yellowstone, 98–99
Dawes Act (1887), 148, 209n76
Department of Agriculture, forests and,
    164
Department of Compromise, Noranda
    and, 179
Department of the Interior, 171; forests
    and, 164; lease requests and, 43, 44;
    park concessions and, 61; subsurface
    development and, 180; wildlife speci-
    mens and, 154–55; YPA and, 112
Desecration of Our National Parks
    (Rogers), 66 (fig.)
Devil's Den, 80, 211n6
Diana Spring, 87
Doane, Gustavus Cheyney: exploration
    by, 2
Dodge, Ira: on Native Americans/
    Yellowstone, 146
Dodgson, Charles Lutwidge, 194n5
Dot Island, 99, 161
Douglas, Henry F., 61
Downing, Andrew Jackson: on land-
    scape architecture, 14
Driscoll, Charles F., 107; on accommo-
    dations, 109; Yellowstone and, 108
Dunraven, Lord: Mammoth Hot
    Springs and, 109

E. and H. T. Anthony, 26
Eaton, George O., 129
Eaton, Howard, 155

Economic development, xii, 35, 60;
    biologically sustainable, 171
Economic Geyser, 94
Ecosystem management, 174, 181, 190;
    debate over, 173; timber-
    cutting/road-building and, 175
Ecosystems, 170–71; managing, 171,
    173; notion of, 191
Edmunds, George: on Yellowstone,
    17–18
Eliot, Charles W., 123
Elk, 148, 155, 165, 167; brucellosis
    and, 185; in Gardiner, 182; hunting,
    150; migration of, 185; species
    diversity and, 182
Emerson, Ralph Waldo, 39
Emmons, Myra, 84
End, The (Garretson), 156 (fig.)
Endicott, William, Jr., 75
Environmental history, cultural/envi-
    ronmental forces shaping, 169
Environmentalism, 4, 77, 169, 170,
    191
Environmentalists, 179; bison and,
    185–86; New World Mining and,
    178
Environmental Protection Agency
    (EPA), cleanup by, 176
Evangeline Geyser, 95, 212n54
Evans, Estwick, 7
Evarts, William: Gold Spike ceremony
    and, 58
Everts, Truman C., 1, 2, 6, 11, 19, 70,
    90; article by, 4; Baronett and, 10,
    128; Grand Canyon and, 104; on
    Yellowstone, 8–9, 20, 190–91; on
    Yellowstone Lake, 7
Excelsior Geyser, 91–92, 93

Fargo Argus, Haynes and, 34–35
Fee, Charles S., 30, 34, 202n33,
    221n59
Field, Eugene: on Arthur expedition, 73
Field, Henry M.: on geysers, 93
Finley, Mike, 179, 180; on
    ecosystem/visitation, 189
Firehole Hotel, 114

Firehole River, 1, 12, 66, 107, 110, 115; road along, 124
Fire policy, 191; debate over, 173–74
Folsom, David E.: on Yellowstone Lake, 6
Forest and Stream, 150, 159; bison and, 163; on Grand Loop, 122; Grinnell and, 68; on park railroad, 131; Yellowstone and, 147
Forest Reserve Act (1891), 163
Forest reserves, 163, 164
Forest Service, 169; multiple-use policy and, 175
Formation, The, 87 (fig.)
Fort Hall, 147; Native Americans at, 146
Fort Lemhi, 147
Fort Washakie; reservation at, 141; Sheridan expedition at, 71, 209n76
Fort Yellowstone, 134–35, 136 (fig.), 161
Forwood, W. H., 71, 72
Fountain Geyser, 114–15
Fountain Hotel, 49, 115; bears at, 153
Frankland, Edward: on development, 110
Frank Leslie's Illustrated, on Native American problems, 147
Frontier myth, 165, 170

Ganter, J. Carl: fire ecologists and, 230n16
Garbage dumps, 113, 153; grizzly bears and, 184
Garden and Forest magazine, conservationists and, 130
Gardiner, Montana, 64; elk in, 182; railroad at, 126–27
Gardiner River, 120, 123
Gardiner Wonderland, on Mammoth Hot Springs, 135
Garfield, James, 44
Garland, Hamlin: on yeoman farmers, 42
George, "Yankee Jim": Henderson's road and, 220n54
Geothermal networks, threats to, 180

Gerrish, Theodore, 39–40; on Mammoth/vandalism, 97; on Old Faithful, 93–94; on roads, 124
Geysers, 1, 5, 10, 16, 17, 48, 53, 83, 180, 187; appeal of, 89, 92–93; described, 89–98; naming, 81, 95; soaping, 96; timetables for, 93; vandalism of, 66, 68, 72–73, 96–97
Giant Geyser, The (Haynes), 46 (fig.), 48
Gibbon, John: on bath stalls, 109
Gibbon Falls, 36, 99
Gibbon Falls, 1882 (Haynes), 46, 48 (fig.), 49 (fig.)
Gibbon Paint Pots, 90–91
Gibbon River, 12, 123
Gibson, Charles, 114, 116, 218n20; on Indian problem, 141–42; NPRR and, 111
Gibson, Francis M., 83
Gilded Age, 42; railroad and, 39
Gillis, Charles J., 123
Glamour, quote from, 168
Gold Creek, Montana, 206n23; Villard and, 58
Golden Gate Canyon, road in, 122
Gold Spike ceremony (NPRR), 32, 54, 55, 113, 206–7n27; social impact of, 60
Graham, John, 178
Grand Canyon, 7, 10, 16, 36, 49, 62, 83, 84, 113–14, 126, 152, 186; described, 100–103, 106, 107; fire at, xi; Haynes's views of, 34; road to, 122; sublimity of, 19; tourist culture and, 98–99; wintertime trek to, 103–4
Grand Loop Road, 76, 84, 124, 137, 221n61; construction of, 120, 121, 133
Grand Prismatic Spring, 91
Grant, Ulysses S.: Gold Spike ceremony and, 55, 59; park act and, 19
Gray Cliff, spectacle at, 57, 206n22
Grazing, legacies of, 181
Greater Yellowstone Coalition (GYC), 171, 189

Greater Yellowstone Ecosystem,
    170–71, 175, 191; agricultural
    around, 181–82; environmental
    problems facing, 189–90; grazing in,
    181; map of, 172 (fig.); mining in,
    176, 179; road building in, 184;
    wolf reintroduction in, 183
Great Falls, 105 (fig.)
Grinnell, George Bird, 76, 129, 130,
    148, 150, 153, 157, 222n94;
    Audubon Society and, 208n63; on
    park railroad, 131; poaching investi-
    gation and, 159; protection move-
    ment and, 67; public management
    and, 54; wildlife protection and,
    160, 161; Yellowstone and, 68, 69,
    147
Grizzly bears: garbage dumps and, 184;
    habitat for, 170–71, 178; survival
    of, 184. See also Bears
Guidebooks, 84, 104; help from, 82–84;
    Yellowstone aesthetic and, 81
Gunnison, Almon: on Mount Wash-
    burn, 99
Guptill, A. B., 123; on Yellowstone lit-
    erateurs, 81
Guptill-Haynes guide, 104
GYC. See Greater Yellowstone Coalition

Hague, Arnold, 80, 129–30, 153,
    157–58; on geyser-soaping, 96
Haines, Aubrey L., xii, 197n51
Hales, Peter B.: on survey, 198n65
Hall, Justice, 98
Hardman, William, 65, 113; commen-
    tary by, 65; on Monarch Geyser, 96;
    on Norris Basin, 90, 92
Harper's Weekly, 65–66, 86, 117; on
    Grand Canyon, 100; Haynes in, 50,
    104; on railroad, 131–32; on roads,
    124–25
Harris, Moses, 114, 123, 146
Harrison, Benjamin: forest reserves
    and, 163; Lacey Act and, 160
Hart Lake, 80
Harvesting, 27 (fig.)
Hatch, Rufus, 56, 61, 62, 73, 74, 76,

208n55; excursion by, 64–65, 67;
    Hobart and, 75; hotel and, 112; Vest
    and, 69; Yellowstone Park Improve-
    ment Company and, 54
Haupt, Herman: manual by, 104
Hauser, Samuel Thomas: Washburn
    expedition and, 12
Hawthorne, Nathaniel: on American
    wilderness, 7
Hayden, Ferdinand Vandiveer: on gey-
    sers/hot springs, 1; Mammoth Hot
    Springs and, 109; NPRR and, 15; on
    park bill, 19; report by, 18, 24; West
    and, 15, 24; Yellowstone and, 2, 4,
    14–15, 16–17, 20
Hayden Survey, 16, 45
Hayden Valley, 99, 161
Haynes, Frank Jay, 21, 52, 76, 104,
    117–18, 133, 190; Bonanza Farms
    views by, 26; changing landscapes
    and, 200–202n32; commercializa-
    tion and, 216n90; Grand Canyon
    views by, 34; Interior and, 44;
    NPRR and, 29–30, 31, 38, 39;
    poaching investigation by, 159; self-
    promotion by, 26, 202n33; winter-
    time trek by, 104; work of, 26–34;
    Yellowstone and, 22, 35
Haynes, Jack, 35, 202n41
Haynes, Lily V. Snyder, 26, 27, 34,
    202n32; work of, 201n31
Haynes studio, 45 (fig.), 202n41
Hedges, Cornelius, 12
Helena Daily Herald: on nature's inex-
    haustibility, 60; Washburn in, 10; on
    Yellowstone Park Act, 35
Hell-Broth Springs, 79–80
"Hell Gate" Canyon, 122
Hell's Half Acre, 80, 91, 213n39
Helmuth, William Tod: poem by, 80
Henderson, A. Bart, 6, 120
Henderson, George L., 80, 85, 122,
    170; on Evangeline Geyser, 95; on
    Mammoth Hot Springs, 87–88; on
    roads, 125; on vandalism, 96–97; on
    visitors, 126
Hennepin, Father, 56

Hetch-Hetchy Valley, conservationists and, 132–33

Hill, J. L.: on bison decline, 156; on Native Americans, 143

Hobart, Carroll T., 61, 62, 63, 65; Hatch and, 75; lobbying by, 222n94

Hofer, T. E. "Billy": poaching investigation by, 159

Holistic Resource Management, 181

Homestead Act (1862), 200n9

Hornaday, William T., 157, 161

Horr, Harry: accommodations by, 109

Hotels. See Accommodations

Hot Spring Cone, 99, 100 (fig.)

Hot springs, 1, 5, 16, 48, 180; curative power of, 109–10, 217n10; railroads and, 217n10

Hough, Emerson: on Grand Canyon, 100; poaching investigation by, 159

Houston, Douglas B.: on park elk, 226n47

Howell, Charles C.: on Native Americans, 143–44

Howell, Edgar, 175; on bison, 159, 161

Hoyt, Colgate, 23, 189, 190; on railroads/Yellowstone, 21

Hoyt, John W.: park access and, 128; on Yellowstone protection/improvement, 128–29

Hunney, Hart, 80

Hunting, 149–51, 165; Native American, 146; tourism and, 185; in Yellowstone, 140

Hunting Trips of a Ranchman (Roosevelt), 157

Hyde, John, 37; on geysers, 92; guidebook by, 83; on Liberty Cap, 86

Hydrological network, threats to, 180

Hymen Terrace, 87

Indianland and Wonderland (NPRR), 142–43

Indians. See Native Americans

Industrialism, 24, 68–69, 84, 92, 131, 132

Ingalls, John J., 78, 106, 173; on Yellowstone Park survey, 62

Inness, George: painting by, 39, 40 (fig.)

Inspiration Point, 101 (fig.), 190; view from, 100–101

In Yellowstone Park (Haynes), 49, 51 (fig.)

Iron Bull, Gold Spike ceremony and, 58–59

Irwin, James B.: roads and, 123–24

Jackson, Andrew, 204n65

Jackson, Helen Hunt: assimilation and, 148

Jackson, William Henry, 15, 19, 31, 44, 45

Jefferson, Thomas, 39

Johnson, Andrew: Cooke and, 9

Jones, Charles J. "Buffalo," 161

Joslyn, Merritt: Park Grab and, 60

Jupiter Terrace, 87

Kay, Charles, 182, 183

Keeney, Joe: vandalism and, 98

Kelly, Judge, 17, 18

Kepler Cascades, 99

Kingman, Daniel C.: Grand Loop and, 76, 122; roads by, 123–24

Kipling, Rudyard, 90, 112; on Old Faithful vandalism, 96; on Yellowstone, 99

Kirkwood, Samuel, 44

Koch, Peter, 5, 6

Koerner, Gustave, 142

Lacey, John F.: wildlife protection and, 160

Lacey Act (1894), 160, 165

Lackawanna Railroad Company, 39

Lackawanna Valley (Inness), 39, 40 (fig.)

Lake Hotel, 116, 117 (fig.), 220n47

Lakeside Library, The, 28

Langford, Nathaniel Pitt, 2, 5, 11, 12, 13, 23, 43, 44, 108, 116; article by, 10; Cooke and, 9; Grand Loop and, 120–21; infernal motif and, 80; on park bill, 19; promotions by, 15; on protectionism, 199n79; Yellowstone and, 18, 20; on Yellowstone Lake, 1, 99, 107

Laramie Treaty (1868), 28

Last Spike Pavilion, 60 (fig.)

Leopold, Aldo: Mexican wolf and, 183

Let-burn policy, 173–74, 230n16

Liberty Cap, 85 (fig.), 85–86, 88

Life in the World's Wonderland (Gerrish), 39–40; title page of, 41 (fig.)

Lincoln, Abraham: NPRR and, 23

Lincoln, Robert, 70

Little Big Horn, 28, 68, 141

Livingston, Montana: NPRR and, 56–57

Livingston Enterprise, 139; on autos/Yellowstone, 187–88; on Gardiner, 64–65; on Gold Spike ceremony, 206–7n27; on gratuitous advertising, 76; on Hatch's "big bugs," 64; on Mammoth Hotel, 112; on NPRR, 56; on railroad/park affairs, 108, 126; on taxidermy, 34

Lockwood, William H., 26

London Daily Telegraph, on Mammoth Hot Springs, 76

Long, William J.: on Wood Folk, 149

Lower Falls, 6, 10, 16, 102, 103 (fig.), 107

Lower Geyser Basin, 107; hotel at, 110, 112, 114

McCartney, James C., 109, 111

McElrath, Thomson P., 41; on tourism, 40

McGuirk, Matthews: accommodations by, 109

MacCannell, Dean: on tourist culture, 206n22

Madison, James, 204n65

Magazine of Western History, Sessions in, 85, 152

Maguire, H. N., 28

Mammoth Hot Springs, 76, 83, 89 (fig.), 107, 109, 113, 114 (fig.), 125; accommodations at, 44, 61; acculturation of, 88–89, 133–34; Arthur at, 73; described, 84–89, 111–12; Haynes and, 44; map of, 134 (fig.); Niagra Falls and, 89; road to, 121, 122, 123; subsurface development near, 180; vandalism at, 97

Mammoth Hot Springs Hotel, 119, 121; construction of, 75; criticism of, 66–67; described, 64–65, 112–14

Management, 140, 170, 171, 173, 191; framework for, 77; public, 54

Man and Nature (Marsh), 14, 130

Manifest Destiny, xiii, 15

Manning, Warren: Mammoth and, 135

Marent Gulch Tressle, 1883 (Haynes), 30–31, 30 (fig.)

Market hunters, 155, 226n43

Marsh, George Perkins, 14, 130

Marshall, George, 61, 111, 112; accommodations by, 66–67, 110

Marshall, William, 12

Marshall House, 114

Mattoon, A. M., 91–92, 95, 153; on Grand Canyon, 102–3

Meagher, Thomas F., 197n52

Medill, Joseph, 98; Gold Spike ceremony and, 55; vandalism and, 98

Melville, Herman, 45

Microorganisms, mining, 180

Midway Geyser, 91, 92, 213n39

Minerva Terrace, 49, 87, 88

Mining, 179; environmental hazards of, 176–77; hydraulic, 42; of microorganisms, 180; tourism and, 178

Mining Law (1872), 177, 179, 200n9

Mintzmeyer, Lorraine, 173

Mohr, Nicholas: Gold Spike ceremony and, 58; on Native Americans, 142; on Yellowstone, 60–61

Monarch Geyser, 96

Monorail transport system, 189, 223n102

Moose, 156 (fig.)

Moran, Thomas, 15, 19

Morrison, Micah: ecosystem management debate and, 173

Mountain sheep, 156 (fig.)

Mount Stephens, 80

Mount Washburn, 99, 107; Haynes at, 104

Muir, John, 83, 149, 170; national forests and, 163; preservation and, 163; on Yellowstone, 80

Multiple-use policy, 163, 164, 169, 175

Murkowski, Frank, 189

National Forest Service, 165
National Hotel, 64, 73, 113 (fig.), 122, 134
National Park Protective Act (1894), 160, 165
National Park Service, 63, 175, 215n69; challenge of, 170; fire policy of, 173; subsurface development and, 180; *Vision for the Future* and, 171, 173; wolf reintroduction and, 183–84
Native Americans: assimilation of, 148; decline of, 139, 145, 167, 174; hunting by, 148; management of, 139, 167; myth of, 143, 145; problems with, 145–46, 147; Yellowstone experience of, 4–5, 141, 142–43
Nature, 140; as commodity, 14; civilization and, 167
Nettleton, A. B., 17
Nevada Territorial Enterprise, on Yellowstone, 19
Newsweek, on Yellowstone fire, 174, 175
New World Mine, 178, 189–90
New World Mining District, 176, 177 (fig.); redevelopment of, 177–78
New York Times, 56; on mining/Yellowstone, 178
New York Tribune, Cook-Folsom expedition and, 6
New York World, 104, 130–31; Gibson in, 141–42; on Hatch expedition, 63–64
Nez Perce, 5; flight of, 141, 220n53; harassment by, 194n10
Niagra Falls, 6, 110, 186; commercialization of, 19, 43, 115, 216n90; Mammoth Hot Springs and, 85, 89; sublimity of, 13, 216n91
Noranda, Inc., 178, 179
Norris, Philetus, 141; Fort Yellowstone and, 135; geysers and, 81, 91, 96; Liberty Cap and, 85; on Native Americans/Yellowstone, 5; Obsidian

Cliffs and, 120–21; roads and, 44, 120; on Soda Butte, 143
Norris Geyser Basin, 65, 90, 91 (fig.), 92, 107; road to, 122
Northern Pacific Railroad (NPRR), xiii, 11, 15, 17, 43; accommodations and, 118; advertisement by, 11 (fig.), 22, 25 (fig.), 142; Black Hills military expedition and, 28; Cooke City and, 9, 23, 132; Crow Reservation and, 142; Gold Spike ceremony of, 32, 54, 112; Haynes and, 29–30, 31, 38, 39; impact of, 23, 55, 56, 77; park branch of, 12, 57, 59, 127, 128, 129, 130; travel literature on, 141; wildlife and, 151, 152, 153, 155; Yellowstone and, xii, 2, 14, 24, 30, 37, 54, 73, 74, 127; Yellowstone Park Act and, 12; Yellowstone Park Improvement Company and, 75; YPA and, 112, 116–17, 218n22
"Northern Pacific Stereoscopic Views" (Haynes), 27; Black Hills views in, 39; described, 37–38; park views in, 105; title page of, 38 (fig.)
Northern Securities Company, 218n22
NPRR. *See* Northern Pacific Railroad

O'Brien, Bob Randolph: roads and, 220n55
Obsidian Cliffs, 83–84; road past, 120–21; tourists at, 143
Old Faithful, xii, 9–10, 36, 49, 62, 79, 92, 94 (fig.), 136, 169, 180, 186, 187, 190; described, 93–94; freeway interchange for, 188; hotel at, 118; vandalism of, 96; Yellowstone fire and, 173
Old Faithful Inn, 117 (fig.), 121, 119 (fig.), 187; construction of, 116; Haynes's portraits in, 118; rusticity of, 118–20; staying at, 137; Yellowstone fire and, 173
Old Faithful Lodge, 187
Olmsted, Frederick Law, 13, 123
Oregon Trail, bison and, 155
Otherness, 149, 167

Our Western Empire (Brockett), 42

Paint Pots, 49
Panic of 1873, 11
Paradise Valley, 37, 170
Park Grab, 60–61, 63
Park railroad, 127–28; debate over, 131–32; defeat of, 132–33; support for, 130
Passing of the Indian and the Buffalo, The (Hill), 145
Payson, Lewis, 98; protectionism and, 131; on vandalism, 97
Peale, Albert C., 15
Perham, Josiah: death of, 199–200n3
Phillips, William Hallett, 122, 124, 157, 163, 164; on Mammoth Hot Springs, 111; wildlife protection and, 161
Pierrepont, Edward, 65, 86; on railroads, 126
Pinchot, Gifford, 163, 167; conservation/development and, 164; multiple-use policy and, 169
Pitcher, John, 138; proposal by, 165, 175; on waterworks system, 135
Pleasant Valley, log hotel in, 110–11
Poaching, 158, 159, 163, 183; guarding against, 97
Pomeroy, Samuel Clarke, 17
Pot-hunting, 149
Preservation, 18, 43, 54–55, 97–98, 132, 163, 206n19, 222n90; development and, 52; environmental, 169; nature, 77, 133; selective, 139–40; wilderness, 22; wildlife, 160, 161, 162
President Arthur's Yellowstone Expedition, 54
Presidential Party at the Upper Geyser Basin (Haynes), 79 (fig.)
Pritchett, George, 4
Progressives, multiple-use policy and, 163
Prospect Peak, 80
Protection, 67, 77, 128–29, 131; selective, 139–40; wildlife, 140, 160, 161

Pulitzer, Joseph: Gold Spike ceremony and, 55
Pulpit Terrace, 88
Pyramid Park, Roosevelt at, 155

Railroads: Gilded Age and, 39; hot springs and, 217n10; improvement companies and, 201n28; indemnity areas for, 24; promotion by, 26; regional development and, 126–27; Yellowstone and, 21, 108–9, 125. *See also* Park railroad
Reamer, Robert, 116, 220n47; Old Faithful Inn and, 118–20
Recreation magazine: on bison demand, 161; Emmons in, 84; wildlife and, 152
Red River Valley, 23; large-scale efficiency in, 27
Remington, Frederic, 304n2; on Sioux, 142
Reservations, 32, 37, 141, 142, 146
Road building, 120–21, 184, 187–88; conditions of, 120; criticism of, 125; described, 123–25; ecosystem management and, 175; nature improvements and, 124
Rocky Mountain News, Washburn in, 10
Rollins, Alice Wellington, 83–84, 113, 222n81; on Paint Pots, 91; on roads, 123
Rollins, Daniel G., 71
Roosevelt, Theodore, 182, 205n2, 218n22; book by, 157; forest reserves and, 164; multiple-use policy and, 163; at Pyramid Park, 155; Roosevelt Arch and, 140, 165, 166; wildlife preservation and, 149
Rufus Hatch Department, 64, 74
Runte, Alfred: preservation and, 132
Russell, Lord Charles, 55, 56; Gold Spike ceremony and, 58
Russell, Osborne: on Lamar Valley, 6

St. Paul *Pioneer Press,* on Yellowstone railroad, 127

Sawtell (park guide), 84
Schmidt, Carl E., 110, 111
Schmitt, Peter J.: on roads, 221n72
Schullery, Paul: on market hunters, 224n43
Schurz, Carl, 44; Gold Spike ceremony and, 55
Schwatka, Frederick: expedition of, 104
Scribner's, 7, 8, 17; Cook-Folsom Yellowstone Expedition and, 6; Everts in, 4; Langford in, 10, 12
Sessions, Francis, 123, 152; on Excelsior Geyser, 93; on Mammoth Hot Springs, 86
Seton, Ernest Thompson, 154; on Wood Folk, 149
Sheep, 181; wolf predation on, 185
Sheepeaters, 4, 141
Sheridan, Michael V., 71
Sheridan, Philip, 74; Alexis and, 67; anti-monopoly movement and, 157; Arthur and, 54, 71–73; bison slaughter and, 139; expedition of, 69–74; forest reserves and, 163; Grinnell and, 68; Hatch excursion and, 67; park enlargement and, 128; protectionism and, 62, 63; Vest and, 70; wildlife and, 67; on Yellowstone, 5, 66, 72; Yellowstone Park Improvement Company and, 69
Sherman Anti-Trust Act, 218n22
Shoshone, 141; hunting by, 146, 148
Signal Hill near Central City, Dakota Territory (Haynes), 28, 29 (fig.)
Sioux, 56, 141; Black Hills and, 27; images of, 142
Smalley, Eugene V., 94–95, 152, 190, 214n54; on bison decline, 157; on Crows/Yellowstone, 146; on elk, 150; on Evangeline Geyser, 95; hunting and, 150; on park vandalism, 97
Smith, Scott, 75
Smith, Sydney, 13
Smithsonian Institution: bison breeding by, 161; wildlife for, 154; Zoological Garden of, 153

Soda Butte Creek, 36, 129, 130; polluting of, 176
Sportsman's code, 72, 140, 150
Sportsmen-conservationists, 165; Native Americans and, 147; selective preservation and, 139–40
Sprawl, rural, 178–79, 182
Stager, Anson, 70
Stanley, Edwin: on geysers, 92
Stoddard, John L.: on Yellowstone exploration, 20
Stout, Henry L., 136
Strahorn, Robert, 110
Sullivan, Louis, 118
Sundry Civil Appropriations bill (1884), 62
Synge, Georgina, 95; on bison, 158; on predator population, 153

Targhee National Forest, clear-cutting of, 175, 176 (fig.)
Taxidermy, 34, 57, 112
Teller, Henry M., 44, 57, 71, 74, 130; park concessions and, 61; park improvements and, 108; regulations by, 63
Terrace Mountain Road, 122
Teton Reserve, 163
Thayer, William, 39
Theodore Roosevelt Arch, 140, 165, 166 (fig.), 182, 183; described, 166–67
"Thirty-Seven Days of Peril" (Everts), 4
Thomas, George, 122; on North Geyser Basin, 90; on Paint Pots, 91
Thoreau, Henry David, 13, 39
Timber-cutting, 165; ecosystem management and, 175
Tourism, 6, 33, 40, 112, 116, 139, 141; bison and, 186; dependence on, 178; elite nature of, 56; hunting and, 185; mining and, 178; naming and, 211n5
Tourist culture, 9, 50, 58, 142–43
Tourist landscapes, 28, 81
Tourists: Native Americans and, 146; vandalism by, 96–97; wildlife and, 152

Tower Falls, 107, 221n61
Trout, Yellowstone Lake (Haynes), 45, 47 (fig.)
Trumbull, Lyman: on Yellowstone, 18
Trumbull, Walter: lobbying by, 19–20; Yellowstone Park Act and, 128
Turner, Frederick Jackson, 145
Turpin, Frances Lynn, 152; on Golden Gate road, 122
TW Recreational Services, 188

Union Pacific Railroad, 126; bison and, 155; bridge by, 158
U.S. Cavalry: bison breeding by, 161; park management by, 63, 98, 215n69
U.S. Electric Light Company, 112
U.S. Fish and Wildlife Service, 173
U.S. Land Office, Haynes and, 35
United States National Museum, wildlife for, 154
Upper Geyser Basin, 48, 61, 66, 73, 107, 112, 187; accommodations at, 44, 115, 117; described, 92; Haynes and, 44; map of, 82 (fig.); road to, 122
Upper Geyser Basin (Haynes montage), 50 (fig.)

Vandalism, 67, 69, 73; guarding against, 96–97
Varley, John: on bison slaughter, 185
Vest, George Graham, 70, 74, 76, 114, 129, 157, 188; Arthur expedition and, 54; Charles and, 138; congressional investigation by, 75; fishing by, 72; government swindles and, 62; Hatch excursion and, 66; park enlargement and, 128; protectionism and, 62; Yellowstone cause and, 69
Villard, Henry, 56, 205n5; Gold Spike ceremony and, 54, 55, 58, 206–7n27; Livingston and, 57; on Native Americans, 142; NPRR and, 55; recruiting agents and, 24; at Yellowstone, 60
Virginia Cascade, 80

Vision for the Future, 171, 173

Wakefield and Hoffman, 74; Yellowstone Park Improvement Company and, 65
Wallop, Malcolm: Yellowstone fire and, 174
Washburn, Henry Dana, 2, 8, 9–10, 12, 23, 66
Washburn-Doane Expedition, 2, 9–10, 12, 23, 66; Everts on, 4; Grand Canyon and, 196n41
Waters, E. C., 99, 161
Watt, James, 230n14
Weber, Max: Gold Spike ceremony and, 55
Weimer, D. W.: on Upper Geyser Basin hotel, 114
West: development of, 54; myth of, 186
Wheeler, Olin D., 99, 107, 138, 190; on Firehole River/road, 124; on Grand Canyon, 102; hunting and, 150–51; on Upper Geyser Basin, 92; on YPA investment, 116
White House Council on Environmental Quality, Noranda and, 179
Whitman, Walt, 39
Whitney, Asa, 199n3
Whittlesley, Lee H., xii, 211n5, 214n54
Wickes, Montana (Haynes), 31, 31 (fig.)
Wilderness, 139, 179; commodification of, xii; myth of, 133, 145
Wildlife, 152, 165; assault on, 147, 182, 184–85; capture/shipment of, 154; forest reserves and, 163; management of, 139, 148–49, 151, 167; Native Americans and, 148–49; protecting, 67, 159–60; selective preservation of, 139–40
Wingate, George, 90, 95; elk and, 150, 151; on Grand Canyon, 102; on Middle Falls, 83
Wister, Owen: forests and, 165; on geyser vandalism, 96
Wolves, 153; agribusiness and, 185; poisoning, 152; reintroduction of, 183–84, 185

Wonderland, xii, xiii, 2, 16, 20, 22, 23, 41, 53, 100, 105, 188; commodification of, 137; definition/density of, 4; futuristic view of, 189–90; myth of, 169; nature/civilization and, 54; nature consumption and, 106; NPRR and, 30, 56; preservation of, 77, 132–33; promoting, 25–26, 42, 51–52, 149, 186; tourist resources of, 24, 58, 187; wording of, 81–82

Wonderland Condensed (Henderson), 84, 87–88

Wonderland series (NPRR), 35–36, 37, 43, 83, 141; on bear feeding, 153; frontispiece of, 144 (fig.); on Grand Canyon, 102; Native American images in, 142, 143

"Wonders of the Yellowstone, The" (Langford), 10

World Heritage Committee, Yellowstone and, 169

Wright, Frank Lloyd, 118

Wylie, W. W., 92; on Hayden, 104; on tourist accommodations, 115

Wyman, John C., 64

Wyoming Multiple Use Coalition, 171

Yancey, John, 104; hotel of, 110–11

Yancey, William Lowndes, 216n17

Yancey's in Winter, 111 (fig.)

Yellowstone Crusade, 55, 220n90

Yellowstone fire (1988), 170; debate over, 173–74, 183; media coverage of, xi

Yellowstone Journal, The, 53; on Native Americans/Yellowstone, 147; on Obsidian Cliffs, 143; on regional development, 43; on Yellowstone, 36

Yellowstone Lake, 61, 84, 99, 126; described, 1, 7, 107; Dot Island and, 161; ecological disaster in, 184–85; exploration of, 4; fire at, 116; fishing at, 72; road to, 122

Yellowstone Park: acculturation of, 20, 133–35; biophysical health of, 171; commodification/consumption of,

77, 137; cultural enshrinement for, xiii, 8–9; democracy and, 166; economic motivation for, 14–15; environmental paradigm of, xiii, 191; establishment of, xii, xiii, 14, 19, 20; as imperial symbol, 22; improvement of, 108; map of, 3; mechanistic/natural in, 178–79; myth of, 4, 12–13, 140–41, 142, 186, 191; naming/marking of, 79–82, 83; as national icon, 22; railroads and, 21, 24, 37, 54, 108–9, 222n94; surveying, 62

"Yellowstone National Park and How It was Named" (Helmuth), 80

Yellowstone Park Act (1872), 2, 4, 35, 128, 166, 179; NPRR and, 12; passage of, 19

Yellowstone Park Association (YPA), 75, 113, 115, 116; accommodations and, 117; Dot Island and, 161; NPRR and, 116–17, 218n22

Yellowstone Park Branch (NPRR), 12, 57, 127–28, 129, 130–31; completion of, 59

Yellowstone Park Improvement Company, 44, 60, 74, 112, 127, 133, 188; criticism of, 66, 68–69, 108; Grinnell editorials on, 68–69; Hatch and, 54; investigation of, 62; leasehold property and, 64; NPRR and, 38, 75

Yellowstone Park Timberland Reserve, 163

Yellowstone River, 6; exploration of, 2

Yellowstone: The First National Park (video), quote from, 168

Yellowstone Valley, The (McElrath), 40

Yellowstone Valley and Crazy Mountains, 143 (fig.)

Yosemite National Park, 132

Yosemite Valley, 13, 18

Yount, Harry: on bison, 158

YPA. *See* Yellowstone Park Association

Zillah (steamboat), 99, 161

Zoological Garden (Smithsonian), 153, 154–55